門 文 大 話 巳
輪 ろ 馬 ハ か
武 龍 風
猫 ム
口
水 海 山 ん
陽
戦 頭 三 国 鷹

門 立 目 話
巳
門 大 馬
輪 ろ ハ か
猫 武 龍 風
口
水 海 山 ム
陽 ん
戦 頭 鷹
三 国

CRAZY FOR KANJI

CRAZY FOR KANJI

A Student's Guide to the Wonderful
World of Japanese Characters

Eve Kushner

Stone Bridge Press • **Berkeley, California**

PUBLISHED BY

Stone Bridge Press
P.O. Box 8208
Berkeley, CA 94707
www.stonebridge.com • sbp@stonebridge.com

PHOTOGRAPH AND ILLUSTRATION CREDITS The author and publisher would like to thank the many artists and photographers who contributed to this book. Image credits are presented in the forms stipulated by the rightsholders and are referenced by text page number. All other images were provided by the author. P. 18: Mikako Shindo; p. 23: Toru Uyama; p. 27: Sammy Engramer, private collection; p. 30: Masaaki Miyara (argyle street tea room); p. 34: Tsuji Keiko; p. 47: Mike Oliveri, www.mikeoliveri.com; p. 56: Michael Rowley, www.papernapkin.com; p. 58: Jenni Sophia Fuchs; p. 73: Steven Elliott James; p. 83: Jenni Sophia Fuchs; p. 85: Jenni Sophia Fuchs; p. 91: photograph by Sakamoto, Takeshi, a.k.a takeratta(tm)*; p. 102: Pierangelo Rosati; p. 105: Matthew Tyndale-Tozer; p. 106: Timothy Takemoto; p. 113: ©Walnut Creek CDROM, photograph by David Leong; p. 115: Paul Osborne, www.flickr.com/photos/paopix; p. 126: Edward Poet; p. 129: Ciro Cattuto; p. 132: Jenni Sophia Fuchs; p. 137: Neil Gray; p. 138: calligraphic scripts by H. E. Davey, from *The Japanese Way of the Artist*, www.senninfoundation.com; p. 139: Ed Jacob, www.quirkyjapan.or.tv; p. 143: Kanko*, www.flickr.com/photos/kankan; p. 146: Eden Politte; p. 147: Kanko*, www.flickr.com/photos/kankan; p. 154: George Bourdaniotis; p. 161: Sergio Quinonez / Custom Tattoo & Multi-Medium Artist; p. 167: ©iStockphoto.com / Andrew Cribb; p. 169: ©iStockphoto.com / Dan Brandenburg; p. 172: Kensuke Tsuruma; p. 174: ©iStockphoto.com / Frank Leung; p. 184: Matt Smith; p. 195: Ayumi Matsuzaki; p. 199: Forestry Commission of Wales; p. 211: Sébastien Bertrand.

Cover design by Linda Ronan.

Text © 2009 Eve Kushner.

2nd printing 2011.

Printed in the United States of America.

LIBRARY OF CONGRESS CATALOGING-IN-PUBLICATION DATA
Kushner, Eve.
 Crazy for kanji : a student's guide to the wonderful world of Japanese characters / Eve Kushner.
   p. cm.
 ISBN 978-1-933330-20-4 (pbk.)
 1. Japanese language—Study and teaching (Secondary)—English speakers. 2. Chinese characters—Study and teaching. I. Title.

PL519.K793 2007
495.6'11—dc22

                    2007032429

CONTENTS

CONTENTS

CONTENTS

CONTENTS

FALLING IN LOVE WITH KANJI

PREFACE

As my husband and I walked through Berkeley one summer day, I stopped to examine a tattered box of sesame seaweed crackers. I spotted Chinese writing and some English translations, and though Chinese characters can differ from Japanese ones, I felt drawn to the multilingual label, eager to see if I could work out any meanings. Mostly I couldn't, but I relished the momentary challenge.

My husband smiled, saying, "It's a sign of obsession if you stop to read trash in the road." I laughed, realizing how absurd I must have seemed. But then I'm so obsessed with kanji that these little moments of self-awareness don't shift my focus in the slightest.

For six years I've been hung up on kanji, one of three scripts used in Japanese writing. This interest makes virtually no sense in my life, as I don't intend to live in Japan and have few fantasies of even traveling there again. I don't read manga or play Japanese video games, so I rarely profit in a practical way from my kanji knowledge (though it helps me determine how long to boil soba noodles). I'm far from fluent by any measure. And yet I've allowed kanji to consume hours and hours of my life, my addiction even interfering with work at times.

I've had dreams about kanji, about the formation of certain characters. Once when I awoke, I realized I'd been wrong, but close! And being close afforded the strangest joy.

I know I'm in the minority on this, but Japanese conversation feels far removed from what I love about studying the language. Instead, my passion has everything to do with cracking the code of kanji. At times I become so immersed in it that I feel it's my own private code, and I'm surprised when I remember that millions of other people think along similar lines.

Creating Order out of Chaos

But not everyone has discovered the joy of kanji. As a Japanese-language teacher told me, "Kanji is one of the hardest things to interest students in. I've seen a lot of students stop learning Japanese because of kanji, and every time, I feel sorry that I can't interest them in it." I think many students feel shut out, as if they can't find the proper map to orient them in the vast and often chaotic world of kanji.

I certainly know that feeling. I haven't always experienced bliss and rapture at the mere sight of these complicated characters. When we began learning them in my third Japanese class, I felt as if I were flailing around in the ocean without a life preserver or any view of terra firma. As many grammar and conversation books do, our textbook introduced a few kanji per chapter, drawing them from dialogues that incorporated useful phrases. The kanji bore no relation to each other, which made for a scattershot approach, as if we were memorizing the phone book a few names at a time in no particular order.

The teacher may have briefly explained why characters tend to have two readings, but I probably felt overloaded and blocked out this information. After that, I never heard more about it. We focused on drawing strokes in the right order, in the proper proportions, and knowing what the characters said.

But it came to bother me more and more—why were there two radically different pronunciations for each character? Why do the Japanese interweave three scripts? They have two serviceable phonetic scripts and could write every word with these. Why, then, do they use kanji?

In my confusion, I turned to Michael Rowley's *Kanji Pict-o-Graphix,* which breaks kanji down to meaningful, smaller components, revealing the ingredients in each kanji concoction. Working with Rowley's fun, light-hearted book, I began to compile information about characters. That gave me some sense of control and ownership, though still not nearly enough.

Things took a turn for the better when I started making connections between words. Ah—社会 (*shakai:* society) and 会話 (*kaiwa:* conversation) share a kanji,

会, which means "to meet." So maybe we would keep encountering the same characters, which would allow us to build on our knowledge, rather than continually starting from scratch. Perhaps patterns would emerge from the randomness, all the dots turning into a lovely pointillist painting. That didn't happen right away. But when I took a kanji-centric course that used a terrific textbook (*Basic Kanji Book* by Chieko Kano, Yuri Shimizu, Hiroko Takenaka, and Eriko Ishii), I began to gain a sense of an underlying order.

By the time I took two more kanji courses, the obsession took over my life, motivating me to spend hours upon hours with the characters. I scored well on tests, and I could recognize and reproduce hundreds of kanji. When I moved back into grammar and conversation classes, my classmates seemed to think I knew a great deal about kanji. I thought I did, too.

Only when I researched the information in this book did I realize how much I'd been working in the dark. I'd had no idea what goes on inside a character, giving it sound and meaning. I'd known that when kanji look alike, they often have similar pronunciations, but I didn't know why. I couldn't make sense of why certain kanji become irregular at times, dropping their usual readings or meanings in favor of unrelated ones. I knew only a handful of prefixes and suffixes, nowhere near the range available.

Now I know so much more, including the role kanji can play in Japanese arts, in religious rituals, in advertising, and even in historic fireworks displays! Much to my surprise, I investigated Japanese metallurgy and Chinese sericulture (breeding silkworms to produce silk) because, believe it or not, these have shaped kanji! I also learned how these characters function in modern-day China and Korea (and in one tiny part of Wales!). With all this new information (which you'll find in the pages to come), I'm all the more enamored of kanji.

I bring to this book a passion not only for kanji but also for organizing things. With this book, I aim to create order out of apparent kanji chaos by providing background information and context. I believe that the key to kanji success is being able to think clearly when you confront nearly identical characters and a plethora of possible readings. I hope the information in this book provides you with a map to the world of kanji, helping you keep things straight so you can relax, look around, and enjoy the sights.

How Kanji Benefits Language Learners

Kanji reveals the deeper meaning of words, the ingredients in an object. Consider, for example, the word for "volcano" (火山, *kazan*), which is "fire" (火) + "mountain" (山). This kind of equation is simple, poetic, and fun, but it's also informative. Only when I encountered the kanji for "iceberg" and "glacier" did I even ponder the difference between the two concepts:

iceberg　　氷山 *(hyōzan)* = ice + mountain
glacier　　氷河 *(hyōga)* = ice + river

"Iceberg" refers to a floating, icy mass. Meanwhile, a glacier, as I've learned, is a body of ice moving down a slope or valley, possibly spreading outward on land in a riverlike way. So the characters nail it perfectly! See Exhibit 5, "Thematic Explorations: Words of Import," for more ways in which kanji illuminates English.

Often, until you've understood the kanji for a word, you don't truly know that word. Take the word *genkan,* the entrance hall in a Japanese house. If you asked me several years ago whether I knew the word, I would have shrugged and said yes. Then I learned the kanji 玄関, which breaks down as "occult" + "barrier" or "connection." What's occult about an entrance hall? Well, if you think about it, a *genkan* is hidden behind the front door, revealed only to the select few who enter. But how can the second character, 関, mean both "barrier" and "connection"? Aren't those opposites? Yes, but an entrance hall (and by extension a front door) both locks people out and allows them to enter. The kanji captures this paradox! And yet people think these characters get in the way of understanding Japanese!

Quite the contrary. Kanji lends clarity to a language so riddled with homonyms that *kami* means "god," "hair," and "paper" (all with different characters). "Insect" and "selflessness" are both *mushi.* And the word for "awarding a prize" sounds exactly like that for "receiving a prize," both *jushō.* Kanji makes clear what the ear misses. If you've ever wished a Japanese speaker would slow down so you could sort through homonyms, kanji provides a nice change of pace.

If you go to Japan, you'll definitely want to know kanji. Many students figure they'll only need to speak Japanese there, not read or write. They're shocked when they arrive in Japan and feel defeated by the signs.

It was my turn to be shocked when I learned that knowing kanji can add prestige to your spoken Japanese! When English speakers use words derived from Latin or Greek versus from Old English, we may not consciously register it, but that impresses us. Consider

the impact of "solar" versus "sun" or of "filial" versus "son." Knowing kanji gives you access to a set of vocabulary that will similarly wow people. It will also help you understand formal speech, such as that on TV news reports.

Including more kanji in your writing will definitely impress the Japanese. However, that's only true if you use the right kanji for homonyms! Exhibit 7, "Thematic Explorations: Bloopers," alerts you to the sorts of funny mistakes you might make if you're not careful with your kanji.

Oh, What a Feeling!

Clearly, kanji is practical to know. More surprisingly, it can also touch you emotionally. Consider the following spiritual benefits.

Understanding kanji affords a wonderful feeling of being in the know, as when you can decipher kanji on restaurant signs, tattoos, and T-shirts. The child in us longs to decode. That's why kids spend hours solving puzzles. And that's why you'll enjoy unlocking the door to a hitherto sealed-off area.

Teasing out the tangles in kanji provides endless entertainment, as well as thrilling epiphanies. For instance, 花火 *(hanabi:* fireworks) breaks down as "flower" + "fire"—a perfect way of describing fireworks! Kanji affords one "aha!" after another, putting a bounce in your step and drawing you back for more.

When I'm feeling low, kanji is my antidepressant. It's hard to know why this "drug" works so effectively, but I think it gives my overactive mind something to chew on, so it won't devour itself. Kanji presents a compelling challenge: I need to figure out what a character means and why. Kanji requires me to concentrate fully and has, in fact, become a form of meditation for me. By "meditation," I don't mean sitting with closed eyes, chasing away thoughts. Rather, I mean that kanji brings on a focused, accepting state in which I'm happy to be doing what I'm doing and there's nowhere else I'd rather be.

I should note that kanji can also bring one close to insanity! After studying kanji for four hours one Sunday, I told my husband, "I feel like I've been in some other world." "Japan?" he said. "No," I replied, "it was more like that windowless room in *A Beautiful Mind* where numbers fly by Russell Crowe's head while he tries to find patterns." As unstable as this "insanity" feels, it's also as invigorating as a caffeine high.

Studying kanji brings you into contact with Old

Japan—with a pure form of the culture and the Japanese mind. Dating back about fifteen hundred years in Japan (and much longer in China), kanji provides a time capsule, giving us insight into the way people once made sense of the world. As timeless human symbols, kanji characters can evoke the deepest feelings, above all joy.

Preview of Coming Attractions

This book is about a complicated topic, so there's a lot going on in these pages. But it shouldn't be hard to find just what you need. Here's how the chapters break down:

- The Preface will ideally whet your appetite for kanji.
- The Introduction and Chapters 1 and 2 look at how single kanji behave.
- Chapter 3 examines their behavior in groups of two or more.
- Chapter 4 explores what kanji say about Japan.
- Chapter 5 conversely looks at what the Japanese say about kanji.
- Chapter 6 compares Chinese and Japanese kanji, with a section on the use of these characters in Korean.
- Chapter 7 provides tips on studying kanji in enjoyable, effective ways.

Each chapter starts with "main text" that gives an overview of a topic. As one thinks about kanji, one's thoughts tend to shoot off in several directions. The structure of this book accommodates those trains of thought; a host of exhibits follow the main text. Cross-references within the main text let you know when it might be a good time to visit an exhibit. The Table of Contents (which you've already passed) provides a comprehensive list of exhibits.

If you want to read main text and exhibits in the order presented, you should have a smooth ride. And if you zigzag between the main text and exhibits, that'll work, too.

The book has something to offer all levels of learners, from those who don't know a word of Japanese (or who think they don't!) to experts in the language and in kanji. Those who want a solid explanation of the workings of kanji would do well to read the first half in order, from the Introduction through Chapter 3.

In the second half, Chapters 4 through 6 investigate cultural themes, from kanji-shaped bonfires to animal signs in the Chinese zodiac. In those chapters, the information doesn't build on itself, and you won't miss a thing if you read at random.

Chapter 7 presents tips on studying kanji. The main text should speak to students. But even casual kanji-tourists might enjoy some of the exhibits, including one on kanji in a Welsh national park.

The Answer Key comes next, providing solutions to the games scattered throughout the book. These puzzles and brain teasers vary in difficulty, and you'll find the level of difficulty rated on a scale from 1 (easiest) to 3 (most challenging). Making an easy game takes considerable skill and experience, and I probably came up short in that arena. I apologize for any frustration this may cause.

Some of the games require no prior knowledge of kanji or even of Japanese. In those cases, I've noted "Kanji Level: 0." Many games favor those who know a lot about kanji. The most extreme cases will say "Kanji Level: 3."

For certain games you'll need to know hiragana and katakana (two phonetic scripts that are collectively known as kana). Those will be marked with "Kana Needed: Y." The others will say "Kana Needed: N."

At the very end, just before Works Cited, you'll find a Glossary. If you forget the meaning of a term you saw earlier in the book, the Glossary should prove helpful.

Some kanji books present characters in a predetermined order, matching the simple-to-complex sequence in which Japanese kids learn them. This book is nothing like that. You'll find rare and complicated characters in the Preface, and you'll find an exploration of the simple gate (門) shape halfway through the book.

Students who are hellbent on memorizing kanji will want to know how many characters they'll acquire by reading this book. Not an easy question to answer! Exhibit 13, "Just the Facts: How Many Kanji Does It Take?" addresses the difficulty of counting the kanji in one's repertoire. Same goes for counting the kanji presented in this book. I hope this book invites you to stop counting the trees and instead to lose yourself happily in the vast forest of kanji. Intuition tells me that that has to be more rewarding in the end.

Acknowledgments

Spending a year scrutinizing characters as complex as 響, 撃, 魔, and 雄鶏, one could easily go off the deep end. To the extent that I didn't, I have several people to thank:

- My husband, Haroon Chaudhri, who seems to believe I can do anything except drive a stick shift. (We're both clear about that.)
- Laura Peticolas, who expressed boundless excitement about every stage of this project. She understands how I think, what I need, and all the ways in which kanji and writing feed me.
- Tom Immel, for his indispensable technical support. After my computer went belly-up in the middle of the project, he brought me a spare entirely of his own initiative, loaded it with software, helped me through rough patches with that machine, and later set up my new computer.
- Karen North Wells, who gave me the idea to write about kanji. With her trademark positive thinking, she cheered me on every step of the way.
- Saori Shiraishi, the first person to encourage my love of kanji. Oh, how patient she was, never acting as though I were a hopeless case!
- Peter Goodman, the Stone Bridge Press publisher who saw potential in my original, amorphous ideas and steered me in a more effective direction. When he asked me to write about Chinese, Korean, and several other topics well beyond my reach, I was stunned and more than a little nervous. But as answers began to come my way, I marveled at his keen editorial intuition. How lucky for me that he could see where to take this project. Thanks to the rest of the Stone Bridge staff, as well.

I'm also grateful for the Internet (especially Wikipedia, which supplied loads of useful information). As I exchanged emails with Chinese people in the States, an American expert in Korean based in the United Arab Emirates, and a Japanese woman in Italy, I marveled at how the Internet has shrunk distances and national differences.

But technology is only part of the story. I wouldn't have made progress without the extraordinary goodwill of strangers who said, "Sure, I'd love to explain my extremely complicated language to you. Ask me anything." For this I owe a huge amount to several people who speak Chinese: Tian Tang, Yaling Zhu, George Fang, Bei Li, Eva Shu, and Shawn Wang. I'm also quite grateful to a brigade of native Japanese speakers, all of whom cheerfully hunted down answers for me: Mayumi Sumiyoshi, Hitomi Iida, Yūta Yamada, Kenji Nagafuchi, Satoshi Watanabe, Kensuke Tsuruma, and Tomohiro Matsuzaki.

Additional thanks go to Rodney Tyson, an expert in Korean, and Tim Harland, who shared his knowledge of Afan Forest Park in Wales. I'm also grateful to Kanji Haitani for allowing me to quote from his website.

The editing process brought me many more reasons to be appreciative. Editors Laurence Wiig and Hiroshi Mori impressed me to no end with their insightful observations and sharp eyes for mistakes. I'm incredibly lucky that they brought enthusiasm, intelligence, and vast knowledge to the job.

I'm indebted most of all to a Japanese man so modest that he would prefer not to be named here. Back when he was my teacher, he made me feel that Japanese needn't be an impenetrable mystery. And as we worked on this book, he conveyed that all the more. It was quite a privilege to have access to his mind with its overarching, organized view of the language and everything that has shaped it. His generosity of spirit also amazed me. Though strapped for time, he worked with me week after week, patiently answering questions, searching for information that I couldn't find, offering the gentlest of corrections, and treating my ideas as if they were of utmost importance. He gave me all the room I needed to present material in quirky, personal ways. Reading English isn't his favorite activity, but he pored over hundreds of pages. And with Libra flexibility, he considered the text from multiple points of view: as a native speaker, as a teacher, and as a hypothetical non-native reader. Above all, he continually shared my excitement about kanji and about this project. For this and so much more, I am deeply grateful to him.

Words You've Heard

Even if you've never studied Japanese, you know more words than you might realize. Here's how they look in kanji, which tells you what they really mean.

Kimono

着物 *(kimono)* = to wear + thing
That's simple enough—a kimono is a thing to wear. But *kimono* is no longer a generic word for "clothes" in Japanese. Now it refers specifically to traditional Japanese garments.

Sushi

寿司 *(sushi)* = congratulations + to preside over
Japanese has had many writings for *sushi*. This odd combination is one of the most recent, the kanji chosen for their sound rather than their meaning. An alternate writing is 鮨, a single character that breaks down as "fish" + "delicious."

Tofu

豆腐 *(tōfu)* = bean + rotten
Rotten beans?! Surely something's wrong! No, 腐 breaks down as "meat rotting in a storehouse." Besides *tō*, the first kanji, 豆, can be read as *mame*, from which we get *edamame*.

Origami

折り紙 *(origami)* = to fold + paper
The character 紙 (paper) is normally read as *kami*. But it seems that *origami* flows off the tongue more smoothly than *orikami*, so the *k* changed to a *g* in a process known as "voicing." We'll learn more about this later.

Akita

秋田 *(akita)* = autumn + rice field
How does this add up to a big, furry dog? Akita is also the capital of Akita Prefecture in northern Honshu, Japan's main island. This fighting dog comes from that beautiful region. Also of note: There is or was a Japanese boxer called Kanji Akita. A light-middleweight boxer, that is—not the dog breed!

Karate

空手 *(karate)* = empty + hand
The hand is "empty" of weapons. According to Wikipedia, "The name can be interpreted literally or as a philosophical reference to the concept of the Void (Tao)."

Geisha

芸者 *(geisha)* = art + person, or "person of the arts"
As geisha perform dance, music, and poetry, these kanji suit them perfectly.

Zen

禅 *(zen)*
This character originally meant "clearing land in order to build an altar." Now some see the character as standing for "simple religion."

Kamikaze

神風 *(kamikaze)* = divine + wind
Though you may be tempted to fit this word into Japanese conversation, don't try, because native speakers probably won't hear it as a reference to suicide attacks. Instead, they associate the word with a typhoon that supposedly saved Japan from a Mongol invasion in 1281 (hence, a divine wind). Rather than referring directly to that typhoon, though, the Japanese tend to use *kamikaze* to speak metaphorically of something good that has miraculously happened. Also note that whereas we pronounce the word as "comma-kahzee," in Japanese it's "kah-mee-kah-zay."

Harakiri

腹切り *(harakiri)* = abdomen + to cut
Committing *harakiri* means fatally plunging a sword into one's abdomen *(hara)*, so this kanji combination makes perfect sense. As with our word "guts," *hara* indicates courage or resolve. By the way, the word *harakiri* tends to make Japanese people gasp. Many people instead refer to this form of suicide as *seppuku*.

Place Names of Note

It's helpful to know kanji for place names, especially at train stations. But the names also have interesting breakdowns, prompting one to puzzle over the etymology.

The Country

Nihon (Japan): 日本 (sun + origin). This name means "origin of the sun."

Main Islands (North to South)

Hokkaidō: 北海道 (north + sea + way)
Honshū: 本州 (origin + province)
Shikoku: 四国 (4 + country)
Kyūshū: 九州 (9 + province)
Okinawa: 沖縄 (open sea + rope)

Most Populous Cities

Fukuoka: 福岡 (fortune, happiness + hill)
Hiroshima: 広島 (wide + island). Hiroshima isn't on an island. Well, everything in Japan is on an island. But the kanji might make you think that this city is on an island in the nearby Inland Sea, when in fact it's on Honshu, the main island in Japan. Go figure.
Kawasaki: 川崎 (river + land jutting out into water)
Kitakyūshū: 北九州 (north + 9 + province)
Kōbe: 神戸 (god + door). An auspicious address, I would say!
Kyōto: 京都 (capital + capital)
Nagoya: 名古屋 (name + old + shop)
Ōsaka: 大阪 (big + slope)
Sapporo: 札幌 (paper money + awning)
Sendai: 仙台 (wizard, hermit + platform)
Tōkyō: 東京 (east + capital)
Yokohama: 横浜 (side + beach)

Busy Bodies

Some kanji are laughably complicated:

驚 *odoro•ku:* to be surprised

露 *tsuyu:* dew

熱 *atsu•i:* hot

KI: machinery, chance 機

議 *GI:* discussion

hana•reru: to separate 離

Real Lookers

A great-aunt of mine sometimes says in a thick New York accent, "Oh, I was a real looker (look-ah) back then!" I consider these kanji to be real lookers:

KA, sugi•ru: to exceed 過

歌 *KA, uta:* song

HI, to•bu: to fly 飛

I: intention 意

歯 *SHI, ha:* tooth

刻 *KOKU, kiza•mu:* to engrave

風 *FŪ, kaze:* wind, style

巡 *JUN, megu•ru:* to go around

Kana Needed: N / Kanji Level: 0 / Difficulty Level: 3

What Do You Get?

Even if you don't know what any kanji mean, you can still take this quiz. Here's an example: What do you get when you add water and silver?

a. Oil spill
b. Titanium
c. Mercury
d. Wet, grey hair

ANSWER:
c. *Mercury:* 水銀, *suigin,* is 水 (water) + 銀 (silver).

In some cases, two answers are correct. Answers appear in the Answer Key. *Ganbatte kudasai.* (Good luck!)

1. What do you get when you invert a big sheep?
   a. Beautiful
   b. Dog
   c. Road
   d. Arrive

2. What do you get when you combine piety with violence?
   a. Religion
   b. War
   c. Politics
   d. Teaching

3. What do you get when you look at a needle?
   a. Sewing
   b. Laser eye surgery
   c. Intimacy
   d. Parents

4. What do you call it when a cow goes to temple?
   a. Sweet
   b. Devout
   c. Special
   d. Bizarre

5. What do you get when you talk about dying and the heart?
   a. A fatal heart attack
   b. Heartbreak
   c. Busyness
   d. Forgetting

6. What do you become if you split yourself open?
   a. Bloody
   b. Public
   c. Embarrassed
   d. Famous

7. What is rain that you can hold in your hand?
   a. Snow
   b. Ice
   c. Teardrops
   d. Dew

8. What do you get when you put a pig in the river?
   a. Feast
   b. Famine
   c. Drowning
   d. Blowfish

9. If I said, "My, that's a capital fish!" what would I have seen?
   a. Goldfish
   b. Dolphin
   c. Whale
   d. Piranha

10. What do you get from a pleasure garden?
    a. Blooming roses
    b. Opium
    c. Prostitutes
    d. Paradise

Words of Import

Kanji continually opens my eyes to the meaning of English words. Take 空港 (*kūkō*: airport). As 空 means "air" and 港 means "port," this word breaks down as "air" + "port." The second character, 港, contains the water radical 氵, and when I first noticed this, it struck me as strange. There's little connection between airports and water. Then I realized that in English, we also create "ports" for airplanes, the ships of the sky.

On a trip to Los Angeles, I connected the English word "port" with kanji in another way. In a Japanese restaurant I scrutinized the kanji on the menu, especially stumped by 入荷. I knew 入 as "to enter" (read as *NYŪ* or *hai•ru*), and I recognized 荷 as "load" (as in 荷物, *nimotsu*: luggage). But I couldn't figure out what word they formed. *Nyūka,* or "import," said the server, explaining that the wine had been imported and that

荷 can be read as *KA,* not just *ni.* So "to enter" + "load" = "import." Well, that makes sense. An imported load of goods enters the country. But it's so different from the way English speakers think. Or is it? I realized with a rush of excitement that our word "import" breaks down the same way: "im" is a form of "in," and "port" = "to carry" (as in "portable")!

A further thought occurs to me now: maybe "important" has the same root and meaning as "import." I consult my dictionary, and sure enough that's correct! "Important" is abstract, so it's harder to see the connection. But if an object is important, you carry it with you. Or if you consider an idea important, you want to bring it into existence. Look how imported wine in L.A. has made me see my language with fresh eyes!

Tongue Twister

The following sentences come from a terrific grammar book (*Japanese Verbs at a Glance* by Naoko Chino) that neglects to mention how confusing this tongue twister would be to the ear (my ear, at any rate):

乗るなら飲むな。飲んだら乗るな。
Noru nara nomu na. Nondara noru na.
If you drive, don't drink. If you've been drinking, don't drive.

Kanji proves elucidating here. When you see the romanized version of the Japanese, you may grasp little. But kanji reveals the meaning of these similar sounds. Through the kanji, you can see that the *no-* of 乗 means "to board a vehicle," making it very different from the *no-* of 飲, which means "to drink."

Warning! Kanji Essential to Health!

Knowing kanji may be essential to your health! Imagine working near dangerous chemicals in Japan and being unable to read the kanji on warning labels. According to Sunstar, a Japan-based corporation that addresses health issues, Filipino migrants take dirty, dangerous, and difficult ("3D") jobs that Japanese typically avoid. Such work is also called "3K" for *kiken*

(危険: dangerous), *kitsui* (きつい: difficult), and *kitanai* (汚い: dirty). Legally hired workers are required to study Japanese, but illegal laborers don't want to invest the necessary time, and their employers don't enforce the rules. When foreign workers can't read kanji on signs, instructions, and labels, accidents sometimes result.

What's in That Udon?!

Udon are thick, white wheat noodles, often served in soup. The kanji for three types of udon will make you wonder, *what's* in that udon?!

狐うどん

kitsune udon: fox udon

To make: Add fried tofu.

Kanji: 狐 *(kitsune)* is a single kanji made of two parts: "dog," 犭, on the left and "rounded" or "melon" on the right. So a fox is a rounded dog?! Actually, the part that means "rounded" gives the kanji its sound.

Background: According to Japanese folktales, foxes have supernatural powers and love fried tofu! Some people say the udon acquired its name because fried tofu is as bright as fox fur.

狸うどん

tanuki udon: raccoon-dog udon

To make: Add the fried bits of flour that remain after one has made tempura (though this udon varies regionally).

Kanji: 狸 *(tanuki)* breaks down as "dog" + "village," for some reason.

Background: In folklore, the mischievous tanuki keeps getting into trouble. That lends the additional meaning of "cunning" to this kanji, as in 狸親父, *tanuki oyaji* (cunning old man, made from "cunning" + "relative" + "father") and 狸寝入り, *tanuki ne-iri* (feigning sleep, made from "cunning" + "to sleep" + "to enter").

月見うどん

tsukimi udon: moon-viewing udon

To make: Add an egg without breaking the yolk, which represents the moon.

Kanji: 月見 *(tsukimi)* is "moon" + "to see." For once it's simple!

Background: The Japanese hold *otsukimi* (moon-viewing) festivals in October, enjoying the full moon after harvesting crops. In the word *otsukimi*, the initial letter is an "honorific o," usually indicating that the Japanese hold something in high regard.

The largest characters, 阪急 (Hankyū), denote the name of a chain department store. This branch is in Shijō Kawaramachi (四条河原町), a Kyoto shopping district. If you're hungry in Japan—whether you're looking for udon or other typical lunch items—you'll always find a reasonable restaurant in a big department store like this one.

Bloopers

If you type in *kagaku*, the computer will ask whether you want to replace this homonym with 化学 (chemistry) or 科学 (general science). This technology is magical ... unless you're not so clear on kanji. Then sentences can go horribly awry. Mistakes during kanji conversion have become the basis for an annual typo award in Japan. Recent candidates included the sentence that turned a "sweeping victory after five seasons" (五季ぶり快勝) into "cockroach extermination" (ゴキブリ解消). One would read both phrases as *gokiburi kaishō*. With this potential for errors in mind, here are kanji bloopers—sentences that one would pronounce in identical ways but that contain different kanji and therefore mean different things.

1. *Tsukenasai!*

   点けなさい！
   Turn it on!

   漬けなさい！
   Marinate it!

2. *Aa, itai desuyo.*

   ああ、痛いですよ。
   Oh, it's painful!

   ああ、遺体ですよ。
   Oh, it's a dead body!

3. *Ano kuni dewa, shiki wa atsui desu.*

   あの国では、四季は暑いです。
   In that country, the four seasons are hot.

   あの国では、式は熱いです。
   In that country, ceremonies are passionate.

4. *Rekishi to wa hidoi mono desu.*

   歴史とはひどいものです。
   History is terrible.

   轢死とはひどいものです。
   It's terrible to be run over and killed.

5. *Tesuto o shita toki, jishin ga arimashita.*

   テストをした時、自信がありました。
   When I was taking the test, I felt confident.

   テストをした時、地震がありました。
   When I was taking the test, there was an earthquake.

6. *Kono gakki wa nagai desune.*

   この学期は長いですね。
   This school term is long, isn't it?

   この楽器は長いですね。
   This musical instrument is long, isn't it?

7. *Kono kikai o riyō shiyō!*

   この機会を利用しよう！
   Let's take this chance!

   この機械を利用しよう！
   Let's use this machine!

8. *Seikō suru chansu o fuyasu tame ni, mijikai sukāto o haita hō ga ii.*

   性交するチャンスを増やすために、短いスカートを履いたほうがいい。
   To increase your opportunities for sex, wear short skirts.

   成功するチャンスを増やすために、短いスカートを履いたほうがいい。
   To increase your opportunities for success, wear short skirts.

Atari and Other Brand Names

Atari
当たり *(Atari)*

Atari means "success," and its kanji (当) means "to hit" or "to win the lottery." But the company name derives from the game Go, in which *atari* resembles the concept of "check" in chess.

Nintendo
任天堂 *(Nintendō)*

In 1889, Fusajiro Yamauchi founded Nintendo as a playing-card company. The kanji breaks down as "to leave it to" + "heaven" + "hall." But taken together, the last two (天堂) mean "heaven." Some interpret this combination as "leave luck to heaven," but other translations abound, including, "Heaven blesses hard work" and "Work hard, but in the end it's in heaven's hands."

Seiko
精工 *(Seikō)*

The company used to be called 精工舎 (Seikōsha), "House of Precision Engineering." At one point the company dropped the 舎 *(sha),* which means "house." Thus, the official name now means "precision engineering." However, the company name is now written without any kanji (instead represented phonetically as セイコー).This ambiguity must help business, because people automatically associate the name with several *seikō* homonyms, all of which have positive connotations: 成功 (success), 精巧 (exquisite or delicate), and 性交 (sexual intercourse).

Toyota
豊田 *(Toyota)*

Kiichiro Toyoda founded this company in 1937. But he changed the *da* of his name to *ta* because it takes a lucky eight strokes to write *Toyota* phonetically in *katakana* (トヨタ), as opposed to ten for *Toyoda* (トヨダ). The kanji are fortuitous, too, breaking down as "excellent" or "rich" + "rice field."

Honda
本田 *(Honda)*

In 1948, Soichiro Honda established this company. The characters mean "origin" + "rice field."

Subaru
昴 *(Subaru)*

Subaru means "Pleiades star cluster," as depicted in the company logo.

Suzuki
鈴木 *(Suzuki)*

Michio Suzuki founded Suzuki Loom Works in 1909. Not until 1954 did it become Suzuki Motor Co. The kanji breaks down as "bell" + "tree."

Mitsubishi
三菱 *(Mitsubishi)*

The first kanji (三) means "three," and 菱 means both "water chestnut" and "rhombus" (a diamond shape). The company logo features three rhombuses.

Kawasaki
川崎 *(Kawasaki)*

Shozo Kawasaki founded this company in 1896. The name has nothing to do with the city of Kawasaki, though they have the same kanji: "river" + "land jutting out into water."

Nissan
日産 *(Nissan)*

Nissan is a contraction of **Ni**hon **San**gyō (日本産業), which means "Japan industry."

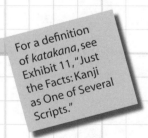

For a definition of *katakana*, see Exhibit 11, "Just the Facts: Kanji as One of Several Scripts."

WHAT ARE ALL THOSE SQUIGGLES?

INTRODUCTION

When one sees such oddities as 芝, 包, and 虚偽, one can't help asking, What are all those squiggles? Is there any underlying order to the lines going hither and thither in these characters known as kanji? What function do kanji serve in Japanese?

The kanji system is beautifully intricate, as awe-inspiring in its complexity as the human psyche. Reading the characters brings you face to face with scads of irregularities, but ultimately the system has a deep, solid structure. The more you understand this framework, the easier it is to approach kanji with an organized, calm mind.

The Same Strokes for Different Folks

The underlying structure becomes a bit more apparent once you grasp the concept of stroke order, the sequence with which you should draw lines in each kanji. Remember those charts across the top of first-grade blackboards, the charts showing the proper way to travel around a *w* or an *R?* In Japanese, there's 山 (*SAN, yama:* mountain) instead of *w,* as well as 尺 (*SHAKU, SEKI:* measure, length) instead of *R.* But the same idea exists—to make the shapes look right, you need to draw lines in a certain sequence and direction. See Exhibit 9, "Just the Facts: Drawing 101," for instructions on how to draw these characters.

Even if you don't follow the instructions in Exhibit 9, you can still produce good likenesses of 山 and 尺, which might lead you to wonder why anyone makes a big deal about stroke order. With simple characters, it's largely inconsequential if you deviate from the instructions. But when you draw large conglomerations of strokes such as 勝 (SHŌ, ka•tsu: to win), you'll want some guidance. And if you draw this character as textbooks say you should, you'll see it isn't such a scary conglomeration after all, as it has three sections: 月, 꽁, and 力. When you notice such patterns in kanji, it all feels much more manageable. For more on this, see Exhibit 10, "Just the Facts: Stroke Order."

The Origin of Kanji

But I've gotten ahead of myself. You've begun drawing kanji without any kind of context for these squiggles. They originated in the Yellow River region of China in about 2000 BCE, etched onto turtle shells, animal bones, and clay pots for divination purposes and state inventories. Scholars have identified three thousand characters from the earliest years. By about 200 CE, the number of characters had grown to a staggering fifty thousand.

From China the characters spread to various parts of Asia, including Japan, over perhaps nine hundred years, starting in the third or fourth century CE. Through both miscopying and intentional simplification, the characters have since evolved considerably in both China and Japan. But kanji haven't changed in the same ways in the two countries. Many Chinese and Japanese characters now have different shapes and meanings. Enough similarities remain that Japanese natives can grasp the central ideas in a Chinese newspaper, though not the details.

Chinese natives have the same experience when looking at a Japanese paper, except for one key difference; Chinese has only one script, whereas Japanese texts intertwine four: kanji, hiragana, katakana, and ever so occasionally rōmaji. See Exhibit 11, "Just the Facts: Kanji as One of Several Scripts," for an explanation of how that works. And for a different take on the meaning of the word kanji, see Exhibit 12, "Just the Facts: What Else 'Kanji' Can Be." Exhibit 13, "Just the Facts: How Many Kanji Does It Take?" provides information about how many kanji you need to know for proficiency in reading.

Kanji as Ideographic . . . or Not So Much?

Given that kanji originally represented real-life objects, you may wonder whether characters still have pictorial meanings. With beginners, teachers often tout kanji's pictographic aspects, hoping to make the case that kanji is fun and easy. "Look," they say brightly. "木 (MOKU, ki) is 'tree.' Don't you think 木 looks like a tree?" Yes, it does. But in implying that kanji is usually pictographic, they're flat-out lying. The truth is, only a handful of kanji closely resemble the objects they represent. You'll find more examples of such characters in Exhibit 14, "Just the Facts: Pictograms and Ideograms."

There's no real way to symbolize abstract concepts pictorially. That's why 生 (SEI, i•kiru) doesn't look much like "life," 怒 (DO, ika•ru) comes nowhere close to suggesting "anger," and 世 (SEI, SE, yo) simply doesn't do justice to "world." And yet, on a more micro level, subsections of kanji are often loaded with meaning. For example, 怒 contains three parts, each with its own significance: 女 means "woman," 又 means "hand," and 心 means "heart." However, meanings in kanji are often kaleidoscopic, shifting in dazzling and dizzying ways as the parts combine. It turns out that when you put 女 and 又 together, as in the upper portion of 怒, they form a separate kanji (奴, DO, yatsu) meaning "slave" or "servant." For an explanation of how meaning varies with spacing in this sort of way, see Exhibit 15, "Just the Facts: One Kanji or Two?"

Kanji and the Japanese "Alphabet"

This type of analysis may be difficult for us to grasp if we think in terms of our alphabet. The letters a, d, b, p, and q all contain a circle plus a line. Does that give them meaning, either individually or as a group? Not in the least. Our letters acquire meaning only when we assemble them into words or into units such as un-, neo-, -ed, and so on. Taken individually, English letters are flat and inanimate tools, compared with kanji, which brim with life and significance.

Speaking of letters, you may wonder how one can read 怒 as ika•ru or 奴 as yatsu. Do kanji correspond to letters in the Japanese alphabet, or does each kanji match up with one word? Neither idea is quite right, though they both have elements of truth.

Although kanji can represent whole words (e.g., 奴 as yatsu), the characters frequently represent portions of words, with hiragana finishing the job. Thus, 怒 says ika. The whole word, ikaru, is written as follows: 怒る. This kind of kanji-hiragana hybridization occurs with many adjectives and verbs, as in these examples (in which the kanji appears in bold):

美しい (*utsukushii:* beautiful)
The kanji covers *utsuku,* and the hiragana says *-shii.*

行きます (*ikimasu:* to go)
The kanji covers only *i,* and the hiragana says *-kimasu.*

In the next chapter, Exhibit 18, "Just the Facts: Okurigana," will explain more about hiragana leftovers.

As these examples demonstrate, a single kanji character may be several syllables long (e.g., *utsuku*) or as short as the *i* in *ikimasu.* Note that I said "syllables," not "letters." Japanese is a syllable-based language. Instead of an alphabet, it has a "syllabary." Whereas we write English words by stringing together letters (as in "h-a-t" or "h-a-t-e"), the Japanese write words by stringing together syllables. That is, the Japanese alphabet provides ready-made syllables such as *ra, ri, ru, re,* and *ro.* To write *sushi,* you add the syllable *su* to the syllable *shi.* Similarly, *sake* is *sa* plus *ke.* When I first learned about these ready-made syllables, I wasted considerable mental energy resisting this approach. It's so different from ours that I felt it had to be flawed somehow. It isn't. It's just different. There's no point in raising objections, because that's simply the way the language works.

See Exhibit 16, "Just the Facts: The Japanese Syllables," for an explanation and display of Japanese syllables. As the exhibit shows, most syllables consist of one consonant plus one vowel (e.g., *ka* or *hi*). Some include two consonants followed by a vowel (e.g., *tsu, chi,* and *ryo*). In Japanese, the sound *n* also constitutes a full syllable, as do the vowels *a, i, u, e,* and *o.* Except for *n,* all Japanese syllables end in vowels, making the language sound Hawaiian compared with consonant-heavy English (which yields words such as *schism*).

You can see from Exhibit 16 that each hiragana character equals one syllable. The same is true for katakana. Using hiragana and katakana to write words may therefore make you consider how many syllables each word has. *Ikimasu* has four (いきます, *i-ki-ma-su),* and *utskushii* has five (うつくしい, *u-tsu-ku-shi-i).*

But the word "syllable" is slightly misleading here, given the way we associate it with the number of sounds uttered in a word. In Japanese, the *u* is often silent in various syllables. As a result, *ikimasu* sounds like *ick-key-mahs*—three enunciated syllables. *Utsukushii* includes another silent *u* (this time in *tsu*), as well as a doubled *i,* which means you hold it longer. The word therefore sounds like *oots-koo-sheeee,* again three syllables to the Western ear. A word containing an *n* poses a similar problem, as the sound of the *n* merges with the sound of the previous syllable. For example, *ginkō* (bank) sounds as if it has only two syllables, *gin* and *kō;* one wouldn't dream of enunciating an extra syllable by separating the *gi* and the *n.* For more on pronunciation, see Exhibit 17: "Just the Facts: How to Pronounce Japanese Words."

The linguistics term "mora" (plural "morae") could help us here, as it properly describes Japanese syllabic units in a way that has nothing to do with sound. But "mora" (and certainly "morae") is a bit hardcore for our purposes, so I'll stick with "syllable," deceptive though it is.

But, for the sake of clarity, I will use "mora" just once to make a final point right now. When you can't represent a full word in kanji and you need to tack some hiragana onto it, the hiragana will never start in the middle of a mora. Take, for instance, 速い (*hayai:* fast). The kanji covers *haya* (the syllables *ha* and *ya*), and the hiragana provides the final syllable *i.* It doesn't matter that the ear hears *yai* as one sound. The individual kanji 速 embodies *haya,* determining the way the kanji-hiragana division will play out, almost as genetic material directs a sunflower seed to grow into a sunflower. These rules may seem quirky at times, but the more you know about kanji, the more the behavior of these characters feels genetically determined, deriving from their collective and individual histories.

The way to read Japanese signs nowadays is from left to right. But to understand this old-style sign, you'll need to read from right to left. If you do, perhaps (perhaps!) you can recognize the highly stylized characters as 觀音堂 (Kannon-dō), which means that this is a temple building dedicated to Kannon (the Buddhist deity of mercy). The character 觀 is an old form; the modern form of that kanji is 観. The sign is at the temple Fukuzen-ji in Tomo, Fukuyama City, Hiroshima Prefecture.

觀
観

Drawing 101

To draw 山, start with the central vertical line, drawing it from top to bottom. Next, draw the left-hand vertical line. Without lifting your pen or pencil, turn the corner and create the horizontal line. Finally, draw the right-hand line, bringing it down to meet the horizontal one. And you have yourself a mountain!

To draw 尺, start with the uppermost horizontal line, pulling it across to the right. Without lifting your writing implement, turn the corner and go down a ways. Now pick up your pen or pencil and draw the second horizontal line from left to right, bringing the line to meet the one you left behind. Lift your implement two more times, once to draw the longest vertical line from top to bottom, then to draw the downward-swooping diagonal line. Now you've created . . . what, exactly? A character people rarely use. Not to worry; you'll need it for the common 駅 (eki), where it teams up with the "horse" character 馬 to mean "station."

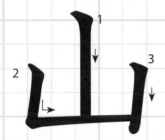

SAN, *yama:* mountain

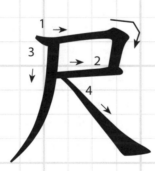

SHAKU: 1 Japanese "foot," a unit of measure

BA, *uma:* horse

eki: station

Stroke Order

You'll find it most natural to draw kanji if you observe these rules (to which there are many exceptions):

- Draw from top to bottom. That is, draw uppermost strokes before lower ones. And when making a vertical line, go from top to bottom, as with the first stroke of a capital *D* in English. To draw 子 (child), move down the character, almost as if drawing a 3, finishing it off with a horizontal line.

- Draw from left to right. You might be tempted to draw ヨ of 良 (good) by extending horizontal lines from the vertical one. Instead, bring the last two horizontal strokes to meet that vertical line.

- Draw enclosures first (e.g., the outermost box in 回 (to turn) and the 門 in 聞 [to listen, ask]), but if there's a bottom closing line (as in 回), draw that last.

- Draw horizontal crossing strokes before vertical crossing strokes. The last lines drawn in 中 (middle) and 用 (to use) are the vertical ones down the middle.

To look up words in kanji dictionaries, you may need to know how to count strokes. This brings us back to the matter of drawing kanji properly, because you count strokes according to the number of times your pen leaves the page. Even if you turn a corner with a line, first drawing left to right and then moving down the page (as in the initial part of ヨ, above), that counts as one stroke, because the motion should be continuous. Here are the stroke counts for the kanji in this exhibit:

子 (2)
良 (7)
回 (6)
聞 (14)
中 (4)
用 (5)

More detailed guidelines about these issues appear inside the front cover of Kenneth Henshall's *Guide to Remembering Japanese Characters*.

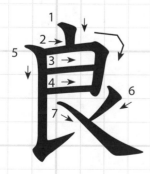

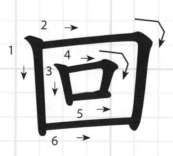

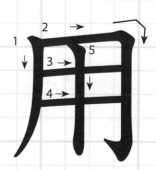

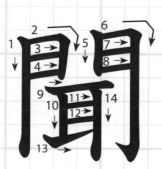

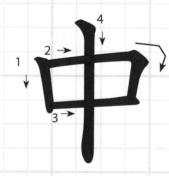

Kanji As One of Several Scripts

Kanji is just one of several scripts interwoven in Japanese texts. Each script plays a different role, as follows:

Kanji: The most complicated-looking of all the scripts (e.g., 議, *GI:* discussion), though some characters are quite tame (e.g., 今, *ima:* now). Kanji can represent all parts of speech (e.g., nouns, verbs, adjectives, and adverbs), as well as place names, people's names, and pronouns.

Hiragana: Loopy, cursive writing (e.g., ひらがな, which says "hiragana") used mainly for grammar but also for kanji that are too difficult to write.

Katakana: Angular writing used for words not of Japanese or Chinese origin (e.g., マクドナルド, which says *Makudonarudo,* meaning "McDonald's").

Collectively, hiragana and katakana are called *kana.* As if all that weren't enough for Japanese schoolchildren to learn, they're also introduced to *rōmaji,* which is the romanized (i.e., our alphabet) rendering of their language. Here's *dog* in all four scripts:

kanji	犬
hiragana	いぬ
katakana	イヌ
rōmaji	*inu*

The following passage incorporates these four types of writing:

私の犬はプードルです。巻毛なので、
Hiraganaという名前です。
Watashi no inu wa pūdoru desu. Makige na node, Hiragana to iu namae desu.
My dog is a poodle. Because he has curly hair, his name is Hiragana.

Here's how the passage breaks down in terms of scripts:

Kanji

私	*watashi:* I
犬	*inu:* dog
巻毛	*makige:* curly hair
名前	*namae:* name

Actually, my dog is a beagle mix named Kanji!

Hiragana

の	*no:* the equivalent of 's
は	*wa:* topic marker
です	*desu:* is
な	*na:* form of *da* (informal *desu*) after a noun and before *node*
ので	*node:* because
という	*to iu:* called

Katakana

プードル	*pūdoru:* poodle

Rōmaji
Hiragana

A typical sentence contains 51 percent hiragana and 36 percent kanji. Japanese text generally alternates between kanji and hiragana, as follows:

私の犬は汚いですが、可愛いですよ。
Watashi no inu wa kitanai desu ga, kawaii desuyo.
My dog is dirty but cute.

But sometimes the kanji-hiragana proportions appear to be out of whack, as when text includes monstrous strings of kanji such as these:

日本建築構造技術者協会九州支部
Nihon Kenchiku Kōzō Gijutsusha Kyōkai Kyūshū Shibu
Architecture and Structural Engineering Association of Japan, Kyushu Branch

次世代育成支援対策推進法
jiseidai ikusei shien taisaku suishin hō
law promoting the governmental policy supporting the rearing of the next generation

Whew! I love kanji, but having fifteen in a row is intense! It feels much better when hiragana provide breathing room between kanji. Then they stand out in contrast, just as a few stalks of bamboo create dramatic beauty in a minimalistic Japanese garden.

What Else "Kanji" Can Be

In this book, *kanji* refers to a concept represented by these characters: 漢字. The first (pronounced *KAN*) means the "Han Dynasty" in China; the second (*JI*) means "character." Japanese also has scads of other words pronounced *kanji*. Here's what these homonyms mean and how they're written:

感じ	perception, impression, feeling
幹事	manager, secretary
監事	inspector, supervisor, auditor
官事	government business
閑事	idleness
甘辞	clever speech, flattery
冠辞	stereotyped epithet
寛治	an era in Japan lasting from 1087 to 1093
寛司	a male given name (e.g., the modern dancer Segawa Kanji, 瀬河寛司)
莞爾	part of the phrase *kanji to shite* (莞爾として), meaning "with a smile."

And then outside Japan, the word has various meanings

- a gnarled Australian tree known as a "kanji bush" or "baderi"
- a city and a dam in Nigeria (Kanji Dam)
- a first name in parts of Africa
- a first or last name in India
- rice gruel in India, related to *congee* in China
- a game reserve in northern India filled with ibex (wild goats); the sole village within that game reserve is also called Kanji
- a manufacturer of "drop shot weights" for fishing; based in Hartsdale, New York, Kanji International uses baits made in Japan

Kanji can also be a shelf! Sammy Engramer designed this 2008 wooden creation (110cm X 130cm X 35cm), which represents 見 (*mi•ru*: to see). A native of France, he calls this the Kanji "Voir"shelf ("voir" is French for "to see").

How Many Kanji Does It Take?

It's much easier now to read Japanese proficiently than it used to be. Until 1946, the Japanese needed to know at least four thousand kanji to read newspapers and magazines. Now, thanks to a series of reforms, people need only half that many. But you may require even less than that, depending on your goals.

If you master the Jōyō kanji, you'll be in great shape. The Jōyō (常用, meaning "ordinary use") are characters that the Japanese Ministry of Education selected for regular use in 1981. At that time, the Jōyō set contained 1,945 characters. However, the list changed in fall 2010, resulting in a set of 2,136 characters. Newspapers and magazines must limit their kanji to this pool, which schools require students to know. Children learn 1,006 of the Jōyō in primary school. These first 1,006 constitute the Gakushū (学習, or "study") kanji. Students may need to learn the remaining 1,130 characters by the end of ninth grade, but now that the Jōyō set has swollen to such a large degree, the rules for the new curriculum remain undetermined at the time of this writing.

As if 2,136 characters weren't enough, 856 more kanji pop up in a group of characters known as the Jinmei-yō (人名用, "used for people's names") set. Jinmei-yō kanji appear in both given and family names.

As for place names, they sometimes feature kanji from the Jōyō and Jinmei-yō sets. But beyond that, scads of other characters appear in the names of towns, streets, rivers, and the like.

Sound daunting? Perhaps. The good news is that if you know the 1,006 Gakushū kanji, you can understand 90 percent of kanji in Japanese publications. The National Language Institute affirmed this fact after analyzing the use of kanji in ninety magazines, working from data about which characters appear most often in texts. For example, the three most frequently used kanji are 一 (*ichi:* one), 日 (*nichi:* sun, day), and 人 (*hito:* person). The researchers deduced the following:

- The 100 most frequent kanji account for 40 percent of kanji used.
- The 200 most frequent kanji account for 50 percent of kanji used.
- The 500 most frequent kanji account for 75 percent of kanji used.

- The 1,000 most frequent kanji account for 90 percent of kanji used.
- The 1,500 most frequent kanji account for 96 to 98 percent of all kanji used.
- The 2,000 most frequent kanji account for 99 percent of all kanji used.

The National Language Institute produced these percentages before the Jōyō set expanded in 2010. It's uncertain how that change might alter these numbers. On the one hand, the most frequently used kanji will appear in print just as often as before. On the other hand, magazines can now use nearly 200 more characters than before, so the calculations could shift slightly. However, I think these percentages still communicate the big picture.

Maybe it'll suit you fine to learn 100 kanji and to grasp two-fifths of what you see, filling in the gaps with good guesses. Or if you want to be able to read kanji in the least violent video games (the ones that are open to anyone, just as a G-rated movie is), you'll need only the 1,006 Gakushū kanji, because the target audience for such games is children. Reading manga is quite a bit easier; they're required to be annotated with small hiragana written underneath, above, or beside kanji, indicating their pronunciations. These hiragana are called furigana. For menus, you'll want to master food-related kanji. Menus will largely present Jōyō kanji. So will the train-station signs that indicate station names. These will often be in rōmaji, as well.

The issue of quantifying the kanji characters in one's repertoire still strikes me as very odd. How many kanji do I know? I haven't the foggiest notion. Back when I used a 500-kanji book that numbered the kanji as we learned them, I had a good sense of the "score." But of course there's no guarantee that just because I've reproduced a kanji on a quiz, I'll actually know it when I see it somewhere else. Some kanji have meaning for me only as parts of words, not when standing on their own. Then there's a nebulous "sort of know" category—the kanji I remember just as soon as I've looked them up for the nth time. This all makes me wonder—when people talk about how many kanji they know, do they fudge the numbers a bit, as many of us do with our weights?

Pictograms and Ideograms

It's worthwhile to notice which kanji are still good likenesses of the objects they represent. In Group A below, you'll find several such characters (line 1), along with their meanings (line 2) and readings (lines 3 and 4):

Pictographic kanji are called 象形文字 (*shōkeimoji*), which also means "Egyptian hieroglyphics."

The pictograms displayed in Group A, below, are common kanji, and once you start learning more obscure characters, you may think you've left pictorial ones far behind. Most likely, yes. But here's one you might stumble upon eventually:

串 *KAN:* to pierce; *kushi:* skewer

This seems quite a clear picture of a shish kebab! Here's another that's almost as pictorial:

傘 *SAN, kasa:* umbrella

The topmost part (ヘ) provides shelter from rain, the cross (十) represents the frame, and the personlike shapes (人) provide further support to the top.

Other names for the same furigana concept include "ruby," "rubi," and "agate." These terms have nothing to do with precious stones. Rather, "ruby" is an old British word for a 5.5-point typeface used to annotate printed documents. In the United States, the same typeface went by "agate." When the Japanese first typed furigana, they used a 7-point typeface. Its similarity to ruby inspired the name ルビ (rubi). See the Glossary for a sample.

A close cousin to the pictogram is the ideogram (指事文字, *shijimoji*). These kanji represent abstract concepts, such as numbers and directions. Group B includes a few common ones.

In the case of 上, the bottom stroke represents a baseline; anything higher than that line is "above." Same with 下; anything beneath the top line is "below."

One supposed ideogram looks like the opposite of its meaning: 円 *(maru•i)* means "round," with "yen" as an associated meaning. If you see nothing round in the orthogonal 円, perhaps the derivation will help. Originally this was 圓, with 囗 indicating roundness. The inner part, 員, meant "round kettle" and emphasized roundness, culminating in the meaning "circle." Did that help? No, I didn't think so.

Let's return to some less common ideograms that actually make sense:

凹 *Ō:* indentation, depression; *kubo:* hollow, depression

凸 *TOTSU:* protrusion, bulge

Notice how nicely these fit together, like two continents that have drifted apart. Ah, if only all kanji were this obvious!

Group A

山	門	火	川	口
mountain	gate	fire	river	mouth, opening
SAN	*MON*	*KA*	*SEN*	*KŌ*
yama	*kado*	*hi*	*kawa*	*kuchi*

Group B

一	二	三	上	下	中	大
one	two	three	above	below	middle	big
ICHI	*NI*	*SAN*	*JŌ*	*GE*	*CHŪ*	*DAI*
hito•tsu	*futa•tsu*	*mi•ttsu*	*ue*	*shita*	*naka*	*ō•kii*

One Kanji or Two?

How many kanji do you see in these examples?

日月	明
重力	動
女子	好

In every row, the left-hand column contains two kanji, whereas the right-hand column contains just one. You can tell because there's more space between the two kanji on the left than between the components on the right. This may seem analogous to treating the roman *o* and *e* as distinct letters (as in *poem*) versus typing them in one fell swoop with the French ligature *œ* (as in *œuvre*). But in Japanese this is no mere typographical matter. The spacing entirely changes the meaning, as follows:

日月	*jitsugetsu:* sun and moon
明	*MEI, aka•rui:* bright
重力	*jūryoku:* gravity
動	*DŌ, ugo•ku:* to move
女子	*joshi:* woman
好	*KŌ, su•ki:* favorite

When I first learned kanji, I could reproduce the correct spacing in 地下鉄 (*chikatetsu:* subway), making 土 and 也 touch each other, as well as 金 and 失. But in my mind, the word had five parts, not three. It

escaped me that by inserting more space, I would be writing different kanji. Instead of this breakdown . . .

地	*CHI, JI:* ground
下	*KA, shita:* below, under
鉄	*TETSU, kurogane:* iron

. . . my characters would have had this meaning:

土	*DO, TO, tsuchi:* earth, soil
也	*YA, nari:* to be
下	*KA, shita:* below, under
金	*KIN, kane:* gold, money
失	*SHITSU, ushina•u:* to lose

If I had written 土也下金失 , it would have meant "to be losing gold under the earth." On second thought, that's pretty much how it feels to buy an overpriced subway ticket!

And how many kanji do you see in this ranking list, known as a *banzuke* (番付)? A banzuke lists sumo wrestlers for a particular tournament, ranking them in accordance with their performance in a previous tournament. The names appear vertically. The top half of the rightmost column says 白鵬 (Hakuhō), but this word bleeds off the right side, obscuring parts of each kanji. To the left of that, we partially see 朝青龍 (Asashōryū), although only the lower half of 朝 appears. These are the names of the Grand Champions. The typeface style is known as *sumōmoji*, a font used for sumo-wrestling posters and programs. For more on typefaces, see Exhibit 57, "Just the Facts: Typefaces."

The Japanese Syllables

Whereas English has an alphabet, Japanese has a syllabary, a collection of syllables. Japanese contains the same vowels as in English (though the order is different: *a, i, u, e, o*). In Japanese, vowels function as full syllables. For instance, the syllabic breakdown of *ukiyoe* (woodblock prints) is as follows: *u-ki-yo-e*. The first and fourth syllables are solely vowel sounds.

Consonants also team up with vowels to form such syllables as *ka, ki, ku, ke,* and *ko*. Therefore, the syllables displayed below mostly come in sets of five.

In each section of the chart, the first line shows the rōmaji (R) reading, the second line reflects the hiragana (H) for that syllable, and the third line contains the katakana (K) for the same syllable.

As the last entry shows, the pronunciation of the *n* syllable varies, depending on the context. Sometimes ん, as in えんぴつ (*enpitsu*: pencil), sounds more like an *m*.

R:	*a*	*i*	*u*	*e*	*o*		R:	*ma*	*mi*	*mu*	*me*	*mo*
H:	あ	い	う	え	お		H:	ま	み	む	め	も
K:	ア	イ	ウ	エ	オ		K:	マ	ミ	ム	メ	モ
R:	*ka*	*ki*	*ku*	*ke*	*ko*		R:	*ya*		*yu*		*yo*
H:	か	き	く	け	こ		H:	や		ゆ		よ
K:	カ	キ	ク	ケ	コ		K:	ヤ		ユ		ヨ
R:	*sa*	*shi*	*su*	*se*	*so*		R:	*ra*	*ri*	*ru*	*re*	*ro*
H:	さ	し	す	せ	そ		H:	ら	り	る	れ	ろ
K:	サ	シ	ス	セ	ソ		K:	ラ	リ	ル	レ	ロ
R:	*ta*	*chi*	*tsu*	*te*	*to*		R:	*wa*				*(w)o*
H:	た	ち	つ	て	と		H:	わ				を
K:	タ	チ	ツ	テ	ト		K:	ワ				ヲ
R:	*na*	*ni*	*nu*	*ne*	*no*		R:	*n/m*				
H:	な	に	ぬ	ね	の		H:	ん				
K:	ナ	ニ	ヌ	ネ	ノ		K:	ン				
R:	*ha*	*hi*	*fu*	*he*	*ho*							
H:	は	ひ	ふ	へ	ほ							
K:	ハ	ヒ	フ	ヘ	ホ							

Small Kana

Although the *y*- line got short shrift, as there are only three *y*- syllables, they serve an important function. When written small and placed after many of the main consonants, *ya, yu,* and *yo* help create "contracted" syllables as follows: きゃ (*kya*).

In the table below, I don't show the katakana version of these diphthongs (called 拗音, *yōon,* meaning "warped sounds"), but they're quite common in katakana words. In fact, katakana has extra *yōon* that enable Japanese to accommodate sounds from foreign languages. For instance, some loanwords (terms that have entered Japanese from any language other than Chinese) include a small *e*, as in チェック (*chekku:* check), and a small *i*, as in フィルム (*firumu:* film). Additional consonants include syllables starting with *f, v, d,* and *ts.*

Tenten and Maru

When the marks ゛ (*tenten* or 点々) and ゜ (*maru* or 丸) follow syllables that start with certain consonants, the sounds of those consonants change. (A syllable including a *tenten* is considered to be "voiced," whereas a syllable with a *maru* is called "plosive.") Although I'll use hiragana here to show how this works, the same rules apply to katakana. Also, when I say *ka*, for instance, that's shorthand for all the syllables in the *ka* series (i.e., *ki, ku, ke,* and *ko*).

Small Kana

き: きゃ きゅ きょ
ki: kya kyu kyo
(e.g., きょう, *kyō:* today)

し: しゃ しゅ しょ
shi: sha shu sho
(e.g., でんしゃ, *densha:* train)

ち: ちゃ ちゅ ちょ
chi: cha chu cho
(e.g., おちゃ, *ocha:* tea)

に: にゃ にゅ にょ
ni: nya nyu nyo
(e.g., にゅうがく, *nyūgaku:* matriculation)

ひ: ひゃ ひゅ ひょ
hi: hya hyu hyo
(e.g., ひゃく, *hyaku:* hundred)

み: みゃ みゅ みょ
mi: mya myu myo
(e.g., だいみょう, *daimyō:* feudal lord)

り: りゃ りゅ りょ
ri: rya ryu ryo
(e.g., りょうり, *ryōri:* cooking, cuisine)

Tenten and Maru

か が
ka ga

きゃ ぎゃ
kya gya

は ば ぱ
ha ba pa

ひゃ びゃ ぴゃ
hya bya pya

さ ざ
sa za

しゃ じゃ
sha ja

た だ
ta da

Doubled Vowels

When speaking Japanese, hold doubled vowels twice as long as single vowels. Rōmaji, hiragana, and katakana all have different conventions for marking "long" vowels. In this book, horizontal bars, "macrons," go above long vowels in rōmaji (as in the word *rōmaji*).

In hiragana, お *(o)* is the most commonly doubled vowel. You usually double お by adding う *(u)*, though on occasion you add another お. Here are examples of each:

ぎんこう	*ginkō:* bank
おおきい	*ōkii:* big

The Japanese pronounce "Tokyo" with two syllables: To-kyo. If you invert these, you get Kyo-to, which again has two syllables. But writing these place names in hiragana and rōmaji reveals a slight difference between the syllables in the two words:

とうきょう	Tōkyō
きょうと	Kyōto

Both o's are long in *Tōkyō*, whereas in *Kyōto* the first o is long and the second is short.

In hiragana, double え *(e)* by adding either another え or more commonly い *(i)*, depending on the word:

おねえさん	*oneesan:* elder sister
れい	*rei:* example

As for doubling the other three vowels, simply repeat the letter in question (as in まあまあ, *māmā:* so-so, passable).

In katakana, show a long vowel with a long dash, as follows:

コーヒー	*kōhī:* coffee
ビール	*bīru:* beer

Note how doubling vowels changes meanings in the following pairs of words:

a:	おばさん	*obasan:* aunt
	おばあさん	*obāsan:* grandmother
e:	げしゃ	*gesha:* disembarking
	げいしゃ	*geisha*
i:	おじさん	*ojisan:* uncle
	おじいさん	*ojiisan:* grandfather

o:	ここ	*koko:* here
	こうこう	*kōkō:* high school
u:	しゅじん	*shujin:* husband
	しゅうじん	*shūjin:* prisoner

One caveat: Just because the same vowel occurs twice in a row doesn't necessarily mean that you hold it longer or double it with a macron in rōmaji. For instance, *ekiin* (station employee) has two adjacent *i*'s because it combines the characters for "station" (駅, *eki*) and "employee" (員, *-in*). Therefore, you need to enunciate *i* twice. To indicate this, there's sometimes an apostrophe between the two *i*'s in rōmaji, though not in this book. Similarly, when a word includes ん *(n)*, you'll sometimes see an apostrophe in the rōmaji version. For example, the apostrophe in *hon'ya* (bookstore) tells you not to read or spell the letters in question as *nya*. The hiragana for *hon'ya* is ほんや, not ほにゃ. In the same way, an apostrophe distinguishes *kin'en* (禁煙, きんえん: no smoking) from *kinen* (記念, きねん: anniversary, memorial). This book does include apostrophes for words where ん precedes a vowel or *y*.

Doubled Consonants

In terms of pronunciation, doubled consonants work the opposite way from doubled vowels. Whereas you hold a doubled vowel longer than a single one, you insert a small pause between doubled consonants. Take *sakka* (作家: writer). Insert a tiny pause between the two *k*'s, much as Brits stop ever so briefly in the middle of *Eddie*. To write a doubled consonant in hiragana or katakana, don't write the consonant twice. Instead, replace the first of the two consonants with a small *tsu* (っ in hiragana, ッ in katakana). Thus, *sakka* becomes さっか, and *chiketto* (ticket) is チケット.

A doubled i is rarely written as ī, because that second i tends to fall at the end of an adjective, changing to something else when you inflect the word. (E.g., *Tanoshii*, "enjoyable," can become *tanoshiku* or *tanoshikatta*.)

How to Pronounce Japanese Words

The five Japanese vowels sound something like the corresponding vowels in the following English words:

a	f**a**ther (e.g., T**a**n**a**k**a**'s r**a**men)
e	**e**gg (e.g., z**e**n)
i	mach**i**ne (e.g., Ak**i**ta)
o	g**o** (e.g., kim**o**n**o**)
u	t**u**ne (e.g., f**u**ton)

When *i* and *u* come between certain consonants, the vowels practically disappear. For example, the *i* in *Yamashita* can be practically silent. If *i* and *u* appear at the end of a word, they can also be silent. That's true when verbs are in the -*masu* form, as in *tabemasu*: (I) eat.

Theoretically, *ai* should be pronounced as two sounds (as in the English word "naive"). Actually, the Japanese *ai* (e.g., *aikidō*) sounds to me more like one syllable, but then again I also don't hear the **e**ggy sound in words such as *deshita*. Instead I hear something more like "d**ay**."

When you double an *e*, it officially acquires that "**ay**" sound (as in *geisha*). The pronunciation of the other vowels doesn't change when you lengthen them.

This is a photo of an *ema*, a small wooden plaque at a Shinto shrine on which worshipers write prayers or wishes. Some *ema* have animals or other Shinto images painted on them. The original image was of a horse, which is the source of the word *ema* (絵馬: drawing + horse). The *ema* in this picture features a treasure ship (*takarabune*: 宝船), a symbol of good tidings to come. The kanji on the sail means "treasure." In typical images or models of *takarabune*, seven gods of fortune sail on the treasure ship. But the image in the photo was a special design for the Year of the Rabbit in 1999. This *ema* appeared at Yushima Seidō, a 17th-century Confucian temple in the Yushima district of Bunkyō Ward in Tokyo.

KANJI IN ALL THEIR GLORIOUS VARIABILITY

1

We've all encountered names we don't know how to pronounce. What do you do with "Anneli" or "Gaije"?

I inevitably balk at "Kirsten," because two acquaintances have this name, and whereas one calls herself *Keer*-stin, the other is *Kurr*-stin. Think how it would be if most words in a language posed these multiple possibilities for pronunciation.

Imagine having circumstances dictate which one you should choose, so that, say, on Monday through Wednesday you'd have to read "Kirsten" as "*Keer*-stin," whereas you'd otherwise say "*Kurr*-stin." Welcome to Japanese in all its variability!

Most kanji present at least two readings. The way you pronounce a kanji often depends on whether it's paired with another one. Take the following sentence:

大学時代には友達が電気代を払う代わりに私が水道代を払いました。

Daigakujidai ni wa tomodachi ga denkidai o harau kawari ni watashi ga suidōdai o haraimashita.

In college, my friend paid the electric bills, and I paid the water bills.

If you underline the kanji, here's how the sentence looks:

<u>大学時代</u>には<u>友達</u>が<u>電気代</u>を<u>払</u>う<u>代</u>わりに<u>私</u>が<u>水道代</u>を<u>払</u>いました。

Omitting the hiragana, we have these eight areas of kanji:

大学時代　友達　電気代　払　代　私　水道代　払
　1　　　　2　　3　　4　5　6　7　　8

Areas 1, 2, 3, and 7 contain compounds of two, three, and even four kanji. In areas 4, 5, 6, and 8, the kanji appear as singletons. What does "singleton" mean? Well, it's by no means an official term. I use it to refer to a lone kanji, one that's not bonded to another. If it helps, you can think of singletons as being like free-floating electrons, whereas compounds contain tight unions of protons and electrons. (Or maybe that brings up bad memories of high school science, in which case forget I said anything about it.)

As you may have noticed, 代 appears four times in the sentence above, once as a singleton (area 5), as well as in three compounds (areas 1, 3, and 7). The words containing this kanji are pronounced as follows:

daigakuji<u>*dai*</u>　*denki*<u>*dai*</u>　*ka*•*wari*　*suidō*<u>*dai*</u>
　1　　　　　3　　　5　　　　7

The singleton 代 is usually pronounced *ka* (as part of the words *kaeru*, "to change or exchange," and *kawaru*, "to take the place of"). In the company of other kanji, 代 almost always becomes *DAI*. The examples above hold true to these patterns.

In the rest of this chapter, we'll examine how such complications developed.

Importing a Writing System

To understand why characters have multiple personalities, you need to know a little about how the Japanese imported kanji. By the way, when I first heard a Japanese native say "import" in reference to kanji, I thought it a wonderfully fanciful use of English. After all, "import" usually refers to merchandise, such as wine, caviar, and cars. We never say that anyone "imported" Latin, Greek, or French words into English. But it turns out that all my English-language reference material about kanji speaks of "importing" it. This is, I suppose, a succinct way of referring to the arrival of kanji in Japan. But beyond that, I think the word points to the great need Japan had for a script, the deliberateness with which they sought one, and the value they've since accorded this writing system that's now the soul of Japan.

That wasn't always the case. Until about fifteen hundred years ago, the Japanese were illiterate. Speaking of words, I'm not sure "illiterate" is the right one. It's not so much that they couldn't read as that there was nothing for them to read. Imagine how that must have shaped daily life. No signs over shops—only pictures perhaps. No way of writing an address. No postal workers, because there was no mail to deliver. No detailed way to record plans for the future or memories of the past. What a problem!

Fortunately, in about the fourth century CE, migrants from neighboring Korea shared their knowledge of kanji and of Buddhism with the Japanese people. Koreans had borrowed both kanji and Buddhism from China, an adjacent land mass. The kanji that Japan imported from Korea are called 呉音, *go'on*. The first character (呉, *go*) refers to the Go region in China. And 音, *on*, which roughly rhymes with "bone," means "sound."

During the eighth century, many Japanese students studied in China, and along with other elite Japanese tourists in China, these students brought a second round of kanji back to Japan. Chinese envoys and scholars also shared kanji with the Japanese. The characters that entered Japan during this era are called 漢音, *kan'on*, named for the Han tribe in China.

Four hundred years later it happened again. In the late twelfth century, Japanese priests studied Zen and Confucianism in China. Chinese priests also traveled to Japan. The kanji introduced to Japan during this era go by the name of 唐音, *tō'on*, because at that time the Japanese referred to China as 唐 *(Tō)*.

The kanji that entered Japan during these eras originated in various regions of China, ensuring different pronunciations of the same characters. As dynasties changed, so did the rulers' dialects, which also altered the sounds of characters. These facts help explain why 月 (moon, month) has the similar-sounding pronunciations of *GATSU* (*go'on*) and *GETSU* (*kan'on*). Sometimes, multiple Chinese-inspired readings are much further apart, as is the case below, with the third pronunciation of 行:

go'on: *GYŌ*, as in 一行 (*ichigyō:* first line of text) and 行事 (*gyōji:* event)

kan'on: *KŌ*, as in 銀行 (*ginkō:* bank) and 旅行 (*ryokō:* travel)

tō'on: *AN*, as in 行脚 (*angya:* pilgrimage, travel on foot)

Dictionaries for native Japanese speakers indicate the era in which each reading originated; this information is still relevant to native speakers' grasp of the language. The rest of us needn't learn kanji at such a microscopic level. But this type of analysis does provide a fascinating slice through the layers of the language, a geological cross-section as beautiful as the multicolored striations in the Grand Canyon. Over and over, the study of kanji reveals itself to be a study of linguistic evolution, and if etymology excites you, you'll have a ball with kanji.

Assigning Japanese Words to Symbols

The Japanese call imported readings *on-yomi* (音読み). Rhyming with "foamy," *yomi* means "reading"—that is, a way of reading a particular character. Some people refer to *on-yomi* as Chinese readings, but that's somewhat misleading. From the time they were imported, Chinese pronunciations changed in Japanese mouths. Plus, in both China and Japan, these sounds have evolved over the millennia. So we'll use the term *on-yomi*. Nevertheless, it's crucial to remember their Chinese origins, because that affects a great deal that we'll explore.

Meanwhile, *kun-yomi* (訓読み) are the "Japanese" way of reading kanji. (*Kun* more or less rhymes with "noon" and means "teachings.") Again, this nomenclature creates potential confusion, because both on-yomi and kun-yomi have long been integral parts of the Japanese language. But kun-yomi are called Japanese because they refer to the language spoken in Japan before kanji arrived.

And now we've hit on a key issue that the Japanese confronted when they imported characters. They already had a complete spoken language. How were they to match their native vocabulary with symbols for Chinese words? Those symbols, after all, came with their own sounds. For instance, the Japanese word for "new" is *atarashii*. The Chinese write "new" as 新, which has an on-yomi of *SHIN*. (In this book, we've represented on-yomi with small capital italics. By contrast, kun-yomi appear in lowercase italics.)

How could this kanji accommodate Japanese grammar? Not easily. Matching native Japanese vocabulary with Chinese characters turned out to be like jamming the proverbial square peg into a round hole.

In the face of a dilemma, many people use an either-or mentality. But the Japanese opted for a both-and approach. To continue with the example of *atarashii*, the Japanese decided to keep that word in the lexicon while also absorbing *SHIN* into the language. They would associate both readings with 新. When it came to writing

atarashii, they decided that this kanji would represent the root *atara*. They would use hiragana to write any parts of the word that had grammatical significance. In *atarashii*, the *shi* has grammatical significance; it's known as an "infix." And the final *i* of *atarashii* can change (e.g., to *ku* or *katta*), depending on the situation. In other words, the Japanese began to write *atarashii* in this hybridized way: 新しい. As you can see, the hiragana are like long legs that stick out over the end of the kanji "bed."

These "long legs" become particularly apparent when we write the yomi of 新しい in romanized letters. The portion representing hiragana is known as *okurigana,* and the convention is to put parentheses around that part of the word, yielding *atara(shii)*. In this book, you'll see a raised dot instead of parentheses. The raised dot is an alternate convention. *Atara(shii)* means the same as *atara•shii*. For more on how trailing hiragana work with kanji, see Exhibit 18, "Just the Facts: Okurigana."

When the Japanese imported 新, that character represented the whole sound *SHIN,* so they didn't need to worry that any leftover syllables would trail behind this on-yomi. That's true for all on-yomi.

And because they come with no parts sticking out, grammatically speaking, on-yomi can fit together in a neat, modular way. Whereas kun-yomi are like spiky snowflakes that would jab each other if you tried to unite them, on-yomi are more like hexagons that lie alongside one another with smooth joints.

In fact, on-yomi generally *must* pair off with each other; they rarely stand alone. Exceptions include 茶 (*cha:* tea), 絵 (*e:* picture), and 福 (*fuku:* good fortune). But it's not as if the Japanese had to figure out which on-yomi could fit together. In many cases, the Japanese imported whole kanji compounds from Chinese, especially when those words expressed concepts that didn't yet exist in Japanese or that said something better than any native Japanese term could.

On and *Kun* Rules of Thumb

When you see a kanji by itself, you should probably use kun-yomi. When two or more kanji have "bonded" into a compound, then you're pretty safe in trying their on-yomi. Of course there are exceptions. What would a language be without exceptions?! But the rule illuminates why we read the sentence about electric and water bills as we did. Here are all eight groups again, followed by an analysis of the yomi:

大学時代　友達　電気代　払　代　私　水道代　払
　　1　　　　2　　3　　4　5　6　　7　　8

1. 大学　　*daigaku:* university
This compound links two on-yomi, DAI (big) and GAKU (study).

　時代　　*jidai:* era
This compound joins two on-yomi, JI (time) and DAI (which can mean "era").

Daigaku and *jidai* are two separate words, but because the Japanese often use them together, they place these kanji compounds side by side with no interstitial grammar.

2. 友達　　*tomodachi:* friend
This compound breaks the rule, combining the kun-yomi *tomo* (friend) with the kun-yomi *tachi* (a suffix meaning "plural").

3. 電気代　*denkidai:* electricity fee
This compound joins three on-yomi: DEN (electricity), KI (air, atmosphere), and DAI, which means "fee" here.

4. 払　　　*hara•u:* to pay
This singleton uses the kun-yomi, not the on-yomi FUTSU.

5. 代　　　*ka•wari:* substitute
This singleton uses the kun-yomi, not the on-yomi DAI.

6. 私　　　*watashi:* I
This singleton uses the kun-yomi, not the on-yomi SHI.

7. 水道代　*suidōdai:* water service fee
This compound joins the on-yomi SUI (water) and DŌ (way). Once again, the on-yomi DAI means "fee."

8. 払　　　Same as 4.

As you can see, most of these kanji follow the rule: singletons use kun-yomi, compounds use on-yomi.

For practice with identifying kun-yomi and on-yomi, try your hand at Exhibit 19, "Game: *Kun* or *On?*" For more on the mutability of yomi, see Exhibit 20, "Just the Facts: The Empty Sky and Other Variable Meanings," as well as "Game: One Kanji, So Many Yomi." On the subject of mutability, see Exhibit 21, "Just the Facts: Shape Shifters," to learn how even the shapes of kanji can vary, depending on the situation. And while you're thinking about the shapes of characters, you'll want to check out Exhibit 22, "Just the Facts: Kana from Kanji," to learn how both hiragana and katakana evolved from kanji shapes.

How to Know *Kun* from *On*

Given that the rules don't always hold, you may wonder how to determine whether you're seeing kun-yomi or on-yomi when you consider a word such as 友達 (*tomodachi:* friend) in area 2. A number of resources can supply the answer.

1. Kanji dictionaries or other kanji reference books: The index will represent the two types of yomi differently, and the entries in the main part of the book should do the same. Many books represent on-yomi with katakana and kun-yomi with hiragana. Other books use capital letters for on-yomi versus lowercase for kun-yomi.

2. Sound: Kun-yomi and on-yomi often sound as different as *atarashii* and SHIN. Native Japanese words can be quite long, whereas SHITSU is the longest on-yomi that exists. By "long," I mean both the number of romanized letters and the syllable count; on-yomi never exceed two syllables. For this reason, one Japanese teacher I know believes that on-yomi sound "crispier," having staccato sounds such as KU. In *The Japanese Language,* linguist Haruhiko Kinda-ichi supports this view, saying that on-yomi generally have "clear sounds" (清音, *seion*) involving such consonants as *k, s, ts, t, h,* and *ch.* By contrast, he says, kun-yomi tend to use "unclear sounds" (濁音, *dakuon*) or so-called voiced versions of the same consonants: *g, z, d, b,* and *j.* For more on the sounds of kun-yomi and on-yomi, see Chapter 3 for Exhibit 46, "Thematic Explorations: Syllabic Similarity."

3. *Suru* as a clue: Verbs involving *suru* (to do) are sure to be on-yomi compounds, as in 勉強する (*benkyō suru:* to study) and 食事する (*shokuji suru:* to dine).

4. Experience and context: After a while, you can often sense which yomi are *on* and which are *kun,* simply from context.

Okurigana

When you use a kanji dictionary, you'll find such puzzling entries as *mō(shi)ko(mi)*. This looks like a complicated algebraic formula! What's with all the parentheses?

As noted earlier, you'll see raised dots rather than parentheses to demarcate okurigana in this book. That is, you'll see words such as *sema•i*, "narrow," rather than *sema(i)*. The raised dot enables us to avoid an excess of parentheses.

Both conventions have to do with a concept called *okurigana*, 送り仮名. The *-gana* (仮名) part of *okurigana* refers to kana (that is, hiragana and katakana collectively). In the past, okurigana were often written in katakana. Now, however, people write them in hiragana. The first character, 送, means "to send," and according to Michael Pye in *The Study of Kanji*, that's because okurigana "send" a word off into the right inflection. Okurigana are the hiragana that trail after kanji, though they can also pop up between kanji, as in the very word *okurigana*, 送り仮名.

Back when the Japanese imported kanji, they tried to marry their spoken language with the written symbols of the Chinese. In many ways it was an awkward fit. The Japanese could match most nouns entirely with kanji (e.g., 犬, *inu*: dog), except for verbal nouns such as 食べ物 (*tabemono*: food), as we'll see shortly. But they couldn't make a complete match with verbs (e.g., 行く, *iku*: to go) or *-i* adjectives (e.g., 高い, *takai*: tall, expensive), because these have conjugations (or "inflections," as they say in terms of Japanese). With verbs and adjectives, kanji supply only the main idea of the word, and okurigana trail afterward, providing details. Another take on this: kanji provide the topic of the story, and okurigana tell you how it ends!

Okurigana prove helpful in several ways. For one thing, just by glancing at text that interweaves kanji and okurigana, we know we're reading Japanese, not Chinese.

For another thing, okurigana provide inflections. Look at these forms of the adjective 長:

長い	*nagai:* long
長くない	*nagakunai:* not long
長かった	*nagakatta:* was long
長くなかった	*nagakunakatta:* was not long

The kanji says "long," and the okurigana completes the picture by qualifying that statement. The same is true with okurigana verb endings:

買う	*kau:* to buy
買います	*kaimasu:* (I) buy
買っていて	*katte ite:* (I) am buying
買わない	*kawanai:* does not buy
買わなかった	*kawanakatta:* did not buy
買える	*kaeru:* to be able to buy
買わせる	*kawaseru:* to make someone buy
買われる	*kawareru:* to be bought
買おう	*kaō:* let's buy!

With 来る (to come), okurigana even tell you how to pronounce the kanji verb stem, which changes as you conjugate from the dictionary form 来る (*kuru*) to the negative 来ない (*konai*) to the past tense 来ました (*kimashita*).

Here's a third benefit—a huge one. When kanji have multiple pronunciations, okurigana help you determine whether to use kun-yomi or on-yomi. Consider these words:

明るい 明かり 明らか 明ける 明白

In your kanji dictionary, you'll see these as some of the many readings of 明:

MEI: light; MYŌ: light, next, following; MIN: Ming (dynasty) **aka•rui:** bright; **a•kari:** light, clearness; **aki•raka:** clear; **a•keru:** to become light

Now return to the list of kanji containing 明. The first four contain hiragana, the last one doesn't. The general rule of thumb is that if okurigana follow singleton kanji, you should go with the kun-yomi. If two kanji stand side by side with no okurigana in sight, you'll usually use the on-yomi for both characters.

Knowing that, we can look at the line of rōmaji readings starting with *aka•rui* and know that these are all kun-yomi. If we match the okurigana -るい, -かり, -らか, and -ける with the letters after the raised dots, we can find the right reading: 明るい is *akarui*, 明かり is *akari*, and so forth.

The last word in the list of kanji is hardest, because

we don't know which of the three on-yomi to use for 明. By contrast, 白 (shiro: white) is more straightforward, its on-yomi almost invariably being HAKU. Turns out that in the case of 明白, the first on-yomi of 明 is right, yielding meihaku, which means "clear, unmistakable."

Okurigana prove particularly useful in differentiating groups of kun-yomi with similar and therefore easily confused meanings:

話	hanashi: a talk, story
話す	hanasu: to talk
入れる	ireru: to insert
入る	hairu: to enter
入る	iru: to enter

Here again we see that a noun such as hanashi has no okurigana, whereas a verb such as hanasu can't function without it. Alas, even okurigana can't help with the last two kanji in the 入 list or with this tricky pair:

注ぐ	sosogu: to pour
注ぐ	tsugu: to pour a drink

To figure out which reading to use, you need to consider the context. Sosogu is the broader word, used literally for pouring liquids, as well as metaphorically (as in "pouring" one's attention into a task). Tsugu is the more common word. In any case, it's rare to have identical kanji and identical okurigana in this way.

When okurigana emerge in the middle of a word, they present a different sort of trickiness, throwing off the rhythm that develops as you read word after word with kanji followed by hiragana. On seeing 買い物, for instance, you may approach 買い as one entity and 物 as another. Not knowing where a word starts or ends makes it harder to look things up in a dictionary. But when you realize that 物 can't stand on its own in this instance, you'll figure out that these characters collectively say kaimono, "shopping." These interstitial bits of hiragana tend to occur in verb compounds:

考え易い	kangaeyasui: easy to think
焼き鳥	yakitori: grilled or roasted chicken
申し込み	mōshikomi: application

All these words begin with the pre-masu forms of verbs. The "pre-masu form" is what you have when you take a verb such as iku (行く: to go), inflect it as ikimasu, and delete -masu, leaving iki. In the above list, the pre-masu forms are as follows: kangaeru (考える: to think) becomes kangae, yaku (焼く: to grill or roast) becomes yaki, and mōsu (申す: the humble form of "to say") becomes mōshi. Appendages change these pre-masu verb forms into other parts of speech.

This discussion of inflections and appendages brings us back to the parentheses mentioned in the beginning of this exhibit. Kanji dictionaries such as the one by Mark Spahn and Wolfgang Hadamitzky (hereafter referred to simply as "Spahn") provide readings for just the kanji in a word, not the hiragana. You won't actually find a listing for 申し込み. Instead, under the character 申, Spahn presents the compound 申込 as if this were a viable word. (It took me ages to realize otherwise.) You need to look at the rōmaji rendering mō(shi)ko(mu) to understand the role that hiragana play in this word; anything in parentheses should be in hiragana.

Even that's not the end of the story; you need to make the leap that mōshikomu is a verb (to propose, apply for), not the noun (application) that brought you to this listing in the first place. Though Spahn never mentions it, the noun form has the hiragana み instead of the verb ending む. Spahn has presented the bare bones, the stem that pertains to kanji. The hiragana details fall into a different realm.

This approach reminds me of lowest common denominators (LCDs) in math. When you have pairs of transitive and intransitive verbs, such as tomeru and tomaru, they often differ by just one vowel. The kanji covers the word only up to the point before that fork in the woods. Thus, we have 止める (tomeru, "to stop something," as in "I stopped the car") and 止まる (tomaru, "to come to a stop," as in "the car stops"). It doesn't matter how long the word is; even with the mouthful yomaserareru, "to be made to read," the kanji only represents the initial yo: 読ませられる. That's because the same yo stands for the stem of the much simpler dictionary form 読む, yo•mu, "to read," and must be able to cover all forms of that verb.

When I first started learning kanji, I was perplexed about words such as 行きます (ikimasu: [I] go), for which one had to draw quite a bit of hiragana after going to the trouble of producing a kanji. Then I grasped the LCD concept that explained this. After that, I couldn't see why adjectives such as 楽しい (tanoshii:

Specifically, adding *yasui* (-易 い), an adjectival suffix meaning "easy," creates *kangaeyasui*, also an adjective. Adding *tori* (鳥), a noun meaning "bird," gives you *yakitori*, also a noun. And adding *-komi* (-込み) produces *mōshikomi*, a noun. (Incidentally, *-komi* seems to defy neat grammatical classification. Opinions vary as to whether *-komi* is a suffix that lacks meaning unto itself, a part of a noun, a verbal noun [that is, a gerund], or an inflection of the verb *komu*. When used in a compound verb such as in *mōshikomu*, "to apply," *komu* means "to go inside.")

enjoyable) and 難しい (*muzukashii*: difficult) had more than just い hanging off of them. It turns out that the し (*-shi*) tucked just before the final い (*-i*) serves a function; this "infix" (the proper grammatical term) indicates something (usually human emotion) that one cannot objectively measure. So these adjectives aren't inefficiently written after all.

But several verbs *are* inefficient—namely, 食べる (*taberu*: to eat), 終わる (*owaru*: to finish), 教える (*oshieru*: to teach), and 考える (*kangaeru*: to think). In each word, the kanji could have covered one more hiragana character. It can be tough to remember these exceptions when writing. When I write by hand, I always have to look up 分かる (*wakaru*: to understand) to figure out whether or not I'm supposed to write the か. But it turns out that *wakaru* isn't an exception; this intransitive verb has a transitive twin, 分ける (*wakeru*: to divide). Fortunately, when you type Japanese on a computer, the software rescues you from much of this uncertainty, converting certain syllables into kanji and leaving the rest as okurigana.

But never fear—the world of kanji offers plenty more inconsistencies. For that reason, you may see the following words written in multiple ways:

お見舞い　お見舞
Both are *omimai*, "visiting a sick person."

気持ち　　気持
Both are *kimochi*, "feelings."

具合　　　具合い
Both are *guai*, "condition."

空揚げ　　空揚
Both are *karaage*, "fried food."

折り紙　　折紙
Both are *origami*, "artistic paper folding."

買い物　　買物
Both are *kaimono*, "shopping."

In every case, the official reading appears in the left-hand column. Academics might sneer at the other, informal versions, but they do appear nonetheless, possibly as part of a contemporary trend.

On the subject of inconsistencies, here are some words with unexpected, hard-to-remember, or even inexplicable okurigana:

同じ	*onaji*: same
盛ん	*sakan*: active, enthusiastic
赤ん坊	*akanbō*: baby
軟らかい, 柔らかい	both are *yawarakai*: soft

It seems that these words should have worn longer kanji to cover up more of their legs.

申し込み

Kun or On?

Kanji change each other alchemically. You generally read a character one way unless it's positioned next to another kanji. Then both of them change.

For example, without the influence of other kanji, 大 (big) has the reading *ō*, and 変 (to change) has the reading *ka*. Both of these readings are kun-yomi. But put these kanji together, and presto! Now 大変 says *taihen* (serious, terrible, very). That is, you use the on-yomi of both 大 and 変 (respectively, *TAI* and *HEN*). This adds a surprise element to kanji, to say the least. (Another surprise: Uniting these two kanji doesn't yield "big change.")

In each of the following examples, the first line presents a kanji with its on-yomi in small cap italics, followed by the kun-yomi in lowercase italics. In the next line, you'll find a sentence using this kanji at least twice, employing multiple readings. You'll then see the same sentence in hiragana, rōmaji, and English. Write the kun-yomi and the on-yomi in the order in which they appear in the sentence, then indicate *kun* or *on*. For example:

日 (*NICHI, hi, bi, ka*: sun, day)
四日は日曜日です。
よっか は にちようび です。
Yokka wa nichi-yōbi desu.
The 4th (of the month) is Sunday.

日 yomi in this sentence:
a. *ka* (kun)
b. *NICHI* (on)
c. *bi* (kun)

Answers appear in the Answer Key. *Ganbatte kudasai!* (Good luck!)

1. 山 (*SAN, yama:* mountain)

   あの山は富士山です。
   あの やま は ふじさん です。
   Ano yama wa Fuji-san desu.
   That mountain is Mount Fuji.

   山 yomi in this sentence:
   a.
   b.

2. 車 (*SHA, kuruma:* car)

   どうやって行きますか。車ですか。電車ですか。
   どう やって いきます か。 くるま です か。 でんしゃ です か。
   Dō yatte ikimasu ka. Kuruma desu ka. Densha desu ka.
   How will you go? By car? By train?

   車 yomi in this sentence:
   a.
   b.

3. 高 (*KŌ, taka•i:* high, tall)

   あの高校の授業料 (*jugyōryō:* tuition) が高いです。
   あの こうこう の じゅぎょうりょう が たかい です。
   Ano kōkō no jugyōryō ga takai desu.
   The tuition for that high school is expensive.

   高 yomi in this sentence:
   a.
   b.

4. 月 (*GETSU, GATSU, tsuki:* moon, month)

   来月は十月ですね。月は二回満月になります。
   らいげつ は じゅうがつ です ね。 つき は にかい まんげつ に なります。
   Raigetsu wa jūgatsu desu ne. Tsuki wa nikai mangetsu ni narimasu.
   Next month is October, right? There will be two full moons.

   月 yomi in this sentence:
   a.
   b.
   c.
   d.

The Empty Sky and Other Variable Meanings

Recall how I said in the main chapter text that, as a singleton, 代 is usually *ka,* the beginning of *kaeru* (to change or exchange) or *kawaru* (to take the place of)? Two more possible readings include *yo* (generation) and *shiro* (price, substitution, materials). And remember how I said that 代 almost always becomes DAI when grouped with other kanji? True, but it can also be TAI (e.g., 交代, *kōtai:* to work in shifts). If kanji rules were consistent, then 代代 should be read as *daidai,* and it is. But it can also be read as *yoyo.* Both readings mean "from generation to generation." And that's not all! If you insert a little hiragana (e.g., 代わる代わる or 代わり代わり), the same pair of kanji can even be read as *kawarugawaru* or *kawarigawari,* both meaning "by turns, alternately."

Of course, all languages have exceptions, particularly English, which demands different pronunciations for "tough," "cough," and "bough." But that doesn't come close to the changeability of 下, which has meanings related to "lower" or "under" and has thirteen possible readings: *KA, GE, shita, shimo, moto, sa•geru, sa•garu, kuda•ru, kuda•ranai, kuda•saru, kuda•sai, kuda•su,* and *o•riru.* This state of affairs can be frustrating, for sure. But once you accept such vacillations as a fact of kanji life, they can inspire wonderment. Consider the following facts about kanji mutability.

· The kun-yomi and on-yomi can have vastly different meanings. Here's how Spahn defines the following yomi:

安   AN: peacefulness
      yasu•i: cheap, inexpensive

点   TEN: point
      tomo•ru, tomo•su: to burn
      tsu•ku: to catch (fire), be lit

· There can be multiple kun-yomi, as in the last example. That's especially true of the next two kanji:

空   KŪ: sky, empty
      a•keru: to empty, leave blank
      kara, kara•ppo: empty
      muna•shii: empty, vain, futile
      sora: sky

      su•ku, a•ku: to be empty or unoccupied
      utsuke: empty-headed
      utsu•ro: hollow, blank

生   SEI: birth, life, student
      SHŌ: birth, life
      -fu: grassy place, woods
      ha•eru, ha•yasu: to grow
      i•kasu: to let live, revise, make the best use of
      i•keru: to be living, be alive, arrange flowers
      iki, i•ki: living, fresh
      i•kiru: to live, be alive
      ki-: pure, undiluted, genuine, raw, crude
      mu•su: to grow
      nama: raw, fresh, unprocessed, inexperienced
      na•ru: to grow (on a plant), bear (fruit)
      na•su: to bear (a child)
      o•u: to grow
      ubu: naive
      u•mare, umare: birth, origin, lineage, birthplace
      u•mareru: to be born
      u•mi: childbirth, bearing a child
      u•mu: to give birth to, bear, produce, yield (interest)

But that's not all! One dictionary also provides the following readings of 生, readings that even native speakers struggle to define:

ai	*asa*	*chiru*	*e*	*gose*	*gyū*
ike	*iku*	JŌ	*kurumi*	*mi*	*mō*
naba	*niu*	*nyū*	*o•i*	*ryū*	*sa*
so	SŌ	*sugi*	*u-*	*umai*	*yoi*

I present this plethora simply to drive home how variable kanji can be. The variability is indeed confusing. But it also allows us to concoct fun phrases such as 空の空 (*kara no sora:* the empty sky) and 夫の夫 (*sono otto:* that ex-husband of mine).

· Multiple kun-yomi can have widely disparate meanings, as the following example shows:

着   *CHAKU, JAKU:* to arrive at, put on, wear
        tsu•ku: to arrive at
        ki•ru, tsu•keru: to put on, wear
        ki•seru: to clothe, dress, put on

You might wonder how all this developed. Why such large and occasionally mismatched collections of yomi for one kanji? When the Japanese matched kanji to their spoken language, they gathered together abstract words such as "life." They then used only one kanji (生) to express such related concepts as "to be born" (*u•mareru*), "to be living" or "to arrange flowers" (*i•keru*), "raw" (*nama*), and "to grow" (*ha•eru*), among many others. What once may have seemed convenient has since complicated the process of decoding sentences.

Furthermore, when the Japanese imported kanji, they sometimes attached synonyms to the same kanji. In that way, *higashi* and *azuma* (both "east") came to be the kun-yomi for 東. But even contradictory words can congregate around one kanji, as in this case:

先   *SEN:* the future, priority, precedence
        saki: tip, point, end, (in the) lead, first priority, ahead, the future, previous, recent, objective, destination, sequel, the rest, the other party
        ma•zu: first (of all), nearly, anyway, well

I've noticed that obscure words tend to show up in groups of kun-yomi associated with one kanji, as is true for this character:

縦   *JŪ, tate:* height, length; vertical
        hoshiimama: self-indulgent
        yo•shi: even if

This kanji isn't used much in the last two ways indicated.

Game: *One Kanji, So Many Yomi*   Kana Needed: Y / Kanji Level: 0 / Difficulty Level: 3

Now you're ready for a game, providing the hiragana or rōmaji for kanji such as 空の空. Some of the kanji below have more yomi than you see here, but to simplify the game I've presented a limited number. Each yomi appears at least once in the Japanese sentence. Answers appear in the Answer Key. *Ganbatte kudasai!*

1. 和
   WA: peace, harmony, Japan(ese)
   a•eru: to dress (food with vinegar, miso, sesame seeds, etc.)
   nago•yaka: mild, gentle, congenial
   yawa•ragu: to feel calm

和やかな女の人は和食に味噌を和えると、気持ちが和らぎます。

_____

_____

   Additional kanji and vocabulary:
   女の人 (*onna no hito:* woman)
   食 (*SHOKU:* food)
   味噌 (*miso:* fermented bean paste)
   気持ち (*kimochi:* feeling)

2. 脱
   DATSU: to omit, escape
   nu•gu: to take off clothes

彼は服を脱いで、世界から脱して、脱俗になりました。

_____

_____

   Additional kanji and vocabulary:
   彼 (*kare:* he)
   服 (*fuku:* clothes)
   世界 (*sekai:* world)
   俗 (*ZOKU:* worldliness)

3. 精
   SEI, SHŌ: spirit, energy, vitality, semen, precise, to refine, polish (rice)
   kuwa•shii: in detail, full

彼は精力的に米の精製法を精しく説明しました。

_____

_____

_____

Additional kanji and vocabulary:
彼 (*kare:* he)
力 (*RYOKU:* power, force)
的 (*TEKI:* suffix such as -ic, -al, -tive to make *-na* adjective)
米 (*kome:* rice)
製 (*SEI:* to make, manufacture)
法 (*HŌ:* method)
説明 (*setsumei:* explanation)

4. 実

   JITSU: actual, real, true; sincerity
   makoto: sincerity
   mi: fruit, nut
   mino•ru: to bear fruit

彼は、実際に、実の心で全部の木に果物と木の実が実ると言いました。

_____

_____

_____

Additional kanji and vocabulary:
彼 (*kare:* he)
際 (*SAI:* time, occasion)
心で (*kokoro de:* sincerely)
全部 (*zenbu:* all)
木 (*ki:* tree)
果物 (*kudamono:* fruit)
言 (*i•u:* to say)

5. 生

   SEI: birth, life, student
   SHŌ: birth, life
   ha•yasu: to grow
   i•keru: to be living, be alive, arrange flowers
   u•mareru: to be born

花の野原で生まれて、あの学生は、生け花をするのと実生を生やすのが好きです。

_____

_____

_____

_____

Additional kanji and vocabulary:
花 (*hana:* flower)
野原 (*nohara:* field)
学 (*GAKU:* learning)
実 (*JITSU:* actual, real, true; sincerity)
好 (*su•ki:* fondness, favorite)

6. 直

   CHOKU, JIKI: straight, immediate, direct, correct
   jika•ni: directly, in person
   nao•ru: to return to normal, be fixed, recover
   nao•su: to fix, correct, revise, convert into, do over
   su•gu: immediately, readily, easily, right (near)
   tada•chini: immediately

自転車が直せないと困っていた子供がいました。青年が来て「すぐ直るよ」と、地面に直に座って直ちに作業に掛かり、「直に家に帰れるからね」と優しく言いました。

_____

_____

_____

_____

Additional kanji and vocabulary:
自転車 (*jitensha:* bicycle)
困 (*koma•ru:* to have a problem, be in trouble)
子供 (*kodomo:* child)
青年 (*seinen:* young man)
来 (*ku•ru:* to come)
地面 (*jimen:* ground)
座 (*suwa•ru:* to sit)
作業 (*sagyō:* work)
掛 (*ka•karu:* to get to work)
家 (*ie:* house, home)
帰 (*kae•ru:* to return home)
優 (*yasa•shii:* kind)
言 (*i•u:* to say)

Shape Shifters

It can be mystifying to copy a kanji from a dictionary, only to have a teacher strike through the shape and draw something different. The discrepancy may come from the fact that certain kanji look one way when typed and another way when handwritten. This is true in English, too; when we write *g* by hand, it looks nothing like a typewritten *g*.

The handwritten style of kanji is called *kaisho* (楷書) or *kaishotai* (楷書体), meaning "standard script." Developed in China along with cursive and semi-cursive styles in the third century CE, this handwritten style allows people to write kanji more quickly than if they tried to imitate the printed style, which is called *minchō kaisho* (明朝楷書). *Minchō* means "Ming Dynasty." During that era (1368–1644), *minchō kaisho* was created, and printing with movable type flourished in China. (For more on typefaces, see Chapter 5 for Exhibit 57, "Just the Facts: Typefaces.")

The kanji in the following lists differ when typed and when handwritten. I've supplied just one reading for each character.

Reading and Meaning	Typed	Handwritten
hito: person	人	人
hai•ru: to enter	入	入
HACHI: eight	八	八

In the first two rows, the characters resemble inverted **V**s when typed but look like inverted **Y**s when handwritten. In rows 2 and 3, eliminate hooks when writing by hand. This also applies to such forms as 込 (*ko•mu:* to be crowded).

Reading and Meaning	Typed	Handwritten
i•u: to say	言	言
suzu: bell	鈴	鈴
kota•e: answer	答	答

Take a different slant to these kanji when writing them. In row 1, angle the first stroke of 言. This applies to any kanji containing 言, such as 話 (*WA, hanashi:* talk) and 語 (*GO:* word). In row 2, the 卩 component below the right-hand 个 takes on a new angle when handwritten. The same change occurs in writing kanji such as 冷 (*REI, tsume•tai:* cold). And in row 3, the last stroke of the bamboo on top (⺮) should point back toward the left when drawn. That is, the two pieces of bamboo should cease to be identical. That's true for any kanji with bamboo on top, such as 笑 (*wara•u:* to laugh, smile).

Reading and Meaning	Typed	Handwritten
kokoro: heart	心	心
ie: house	家	家

When drawing *kokoro*, reorganize the parts of the character as shown. When drawing *ie,* consolidate the two "trunks" (the two long vertical parts) into one.

Reading and Meaning	Typed	Handwritten
te: hand	手	手
ko: child	子	子
ito: thread	糸	糸

With this group, loosen up the strokes when drawing them. It feels good to draw 手 with a rakish tilt at top and a little pizzazz to the form—so good that one wonders about other stiff kanji such as 系, 印, 臣, and 舟. Are we supposed to relax their shapes, too? Yes on the first two, as follows:

Reading and Meaning	Typed	Handwritten
KEI: system, group	系	系
shirushi: sign	印	印

As you can see, the 卩 in 印 doesn't relax nearly as much as the similar form in 鈴 did. As to the other rigid characters I mentioned, you can see here that they need to stay relatively rigid when drawn:

Reading and Meaning	Typed	Handwritten
SHIN: vassal, subject	臣	臣
kita: north	北	北
fune: boat	舟	舟
kata: one (of two)	片	片
ke: hair	毛	毛

Reading and Meaning	Typed	Handwritten
KŌ: public	公	公
KYO: to leave, pass	去	去
ta·beru: to eat	食	食
kura·beru: to compare	比	比
koromo: garment	衣	衣
arawa·su: to express	表	表

In the lower left-hand part of these typed kanji, the lowest line juts out to the left, possibly making you think you should pick up your pencil to draw a separate stroke. In reality, the bottom line in the handwritten versions continues a fluid **V** formation or is merely a hook at the base of a vertical stroke. Go by the handwritten version when counting strokes. An exception is 以 (*I:* by means of), which does require the lower overlap and therefore takes five strokes.

* * *

These lists are not exhaustive. To find the proper handwritten forms of other shape-shifting characters, you could consult various resources:

- Kanji textbooks generally show stroke order, stroke direction, and the proper handwritten form.
- Websites such as "Jim Breen's Japanese Page" have videos showing how to draw each kanji.
- *The Kodansha Kanji Learner's Dictionary* shows stroke order and handwritten variants for each kanji included.
- For what it's worth, Chinese computer fonts generally match the look of Japanese handwritten kanji, so if you want to type handwritten shapes, there's your solution.

The characters on the cover of this notebook say "karate." The first kanji, 空, means "empty." The second one, 手, means "hand." See the rakish tilt at the top of 手? These characters (drawn with a silver Sharpie and a stencil on a Moleskine) are full of vitality. The notebook lies on top of karate gear—a sword and a uniform.

Kana from Kanji

For centuries the Japanese have struggled with kanji. Initially, as they tried to represent their spoken language with imported Chinese characters, they grew frustrated with the phonetic and grammatical differences, so the Japanese thought up various solutions, including the creation of kana (hiragana and katakana) in the eighth or ninth century.

The idea behind kana was to make writing more efficient. A contraction of the term *kari na*, the word *kana* (仮名) means "false name" or "borrowed name," because kana were offshoots of kanji, the real deal. (Kanji also go by 真名, *mana*, which means "true name.")

Learning kanji required a rigorous education, a privilege reserved for noblemen. Therefore, noblewomen and commoners began using hiragana (平仮名, meaning "ordinary kana"). This script sometimes went by the names 女手 (*onnade:* by women's hand), 女文字 (*onna moji:* female lettering), and 女仮名 (*onna-gana:* female lettering). Hiragana evolved from the cursive writing of kanji known as 草書, *sōsho* (grass script). The first character, 草, means "loose and sketchy," as well as "grass," and these are apt descriptions for this quickly written, hard-to-read calligraphy. Because *sōsho* bears so little resemblance to the kanji that most learners know, it can be tough to see the links between kanji and hiragana in Table 2 on page 50.

Visually, katakana has a more obvious link, and this makes sense, given its origins. Elite men looked down on those who used hiragana. Wanting to set themselves apart while still hoping to avail themselves of a simpler alternative to kanji, these men developed their own kana by breaking off parts of kanji. The *kata* of *katakana* (片仮名) means "partial" or "fragmentary." Considered suitable for men, katakana acquired the alternative moniker 男手 (*otokote:* by men's hand).

But the kanji-katakana connection is not as obvious as you might think. I always figured that オ *(o)* evolved from 閉, just as ム *(mu)* must have come from 払. I also had a hunch that タ *(ta)* or ト *(to)* derived from 外. None of that turned out to be true!

The tables on the following pages show the real origins of the kana. In Table 1, you can read columns 3, 4, and 5 as an evolutionary process. Start with the kanji in column 3. Then look at column 4 to see which part of the kanji turned into the katakana in column 5.

In a sense, columns 1 and 7 also go together. Column 1 gives the on-yomi of the kanji. (Column 2 provides its meaning, which is irrelevant to this kanji-to-kana study but has been supplied to satisfy curiosity.) Column 7 lists the yomi of the kana. Notice where columns 1 and 7 match (e.g., the first three rows) and where they deviate (e.g., the fourth row).

You may wonder why the on-yomi would be closely linked to the kana yomi and why the kun-yomi doesn't matter. The Japanese consider the on-yomi to be the purest sound of kanji, as that pronunciation is close to the original Chinese reading. But in a few cases below (i.e., those with the kana yomi of *e, to, mi, me,* and *wi*), the kun-yomi do sound like the kana yomi. That may be because, in the early days of kanji usage in Japan, the Japanese used the kun-yomi of those kanji more frequently than the particular on-yomi.

The tables include two kana that might be unfamiliar to you: *wi* and *we*. Historically, four kana started with *w: wa, wi, we,* and *wo* (but not *wu*). Japanese pronunciation changed over the centuries, and by modern times the *w* had become silent in the last three kana, creating redundancy with the vowels *i, e,* and *o*. In 1946, as part of a general postwar orthographic reform, the Japanese rendered *wi* and *we* obsolete. In the case of katakana, they also jettisoned *wo*. But they retained the hiragana *wo*, を, as the "object *o*," because it performs the distinct function of marking direct objects.

As for hiragana, Table 1 shows that most derive from the kanji listed in column 3. For instance, when it comes to the kana yomi of *u*, う comes from 宇 (*u:* heavens, roof), just as ウ does.

But sixteen hiragana derive from other kanji. Table 2 lists only those mavericks. Lacking information about exactly which part of each kanji gave rise to these hiragana, I have omitted the column called "Key Part."

TABLE 1: ORIGINS OF ALL KATAKANA AND MOST HIRAGANA

1. On-Yomi	2. Kanji Meaning	3. Kanji	4. Key Part	5. Katakana	6. Hiragana	7. Kana Yomi
A, O	to flatter	阿	阝	ア	一	a
I	that one	伊	イ	イ	一	i
U	heavens, roof	宇	宀	ウ	う	u
KŌ	inlet, bay	江	エ	エ (kun-yomi: *e*)	一	e
O	at, in, on	於	方	オ	お	o
KA	to add	加	カ	カ	か	ka
KI	how many	幾	戈	キ	き	ki
KYŪ, KŪ	long	久	ク	ク	く	ku
KAI	to mediate, shellfish	介	介	ケ	一	ke
KO, KI	oneself	己	コ	コ	こ	ko
SAN	to scatter	散	艹	サ	一	sa
SHI	this	之	之	シ	し	shi
SU, SHU	should	須	八	ス	一	su
SEI, SE	generation, world	世	乜	セ	せ	se
SO, SŌ	once, former	曾	丷	ソ	そ	so
TA	many	多	タ	タ	一	ta
SEN	thousand	千	千	チ	一	chi
SEN	river	川	川	ツ	つ	tsu
TEN	sky, heavens	天	テ	テ	て	te
SHI	to stop	止	ト	と (kun-yomi: *to•maru*)	と	to
NA	what?, how?	奈	ナ	ナ	な	na
JIN, NI	virtue, man	仁	二	ニ	に	ni
DO, NU	slave, fellow	奴	又	ヌ	ぬ	nu
DEI, NE	ancestral shrine	祢	ネ	ネ	ね	ne
DAI, NAI	your	乃	ノ	ノ	の	no
HACHI, HATSU	eight	八	ハ	ハ	一	ha
HI	to compare	比	ヒ	ヒ	ひ	hi
FU, BU	not, -un	不	フ	フ	ふ	fu
BE	department, part	部	阝	ヘ	へ	he
HO, HŌ	to preserve	保	木	ホ	ほ	ho
MATSU, BATSU	end	末	ニ	マ	ま	ma
SAN	three	三	三	ミ	一 (kun-yomi: *mit•tsu* or *mi-*)	mi
MU, BŌ	mooing	牟	ム	ム	む	mu
JO, NYO, NYŌ	woman but one	女	メ	メ	め (kun-yomi: *me-*)	me
MŌ	hair, tiny amount	毛	モ	モ	も	mo

#22 JUST THE FACTS

1. On-Yomi	2. Kanji Meaning	3. Kanji	4. Key Part	5. Katakana	6. Hiragana	7. Kana Yomi
YA	to be, is	也	ヤ	ヤ	や	*ya*
YU, YŪ, YUI	to be based on, due to	由	ユ	ユ	ゆ	*yu*
YO	palanquin	輿	ヨ	ヨ	よ	*yo*
RYŌ	good	良	ㄱ	ラ	ら	*ra*
RI	advantage	利	刂	リ	り	*ri*
RYŪ, RU	flow, style	流	儿	ル	—	*ru*
REI, RAI	courtesy	礼	し	レ	れ	*re*
RO, RYO	backbone	呂	口 (top box)	ロ	ろ	*ro*
WA, O	peace, harmony, Japan(ese)	和	冂	ワ	わ	*wa*
SEI, SHŌ	well (water)	井	?	ヰ (kun-yomi: *i*)	—	*(w)i*
KEI, E	wise, astute	慧	?	ヱ	—	*(w)e*
HEI, BYŌ	flat, average	平	ㅠ	ヲ	—	*(w)o*
JI, NI	thou, in that way	尓	𠂉	ン	—	*n*

TABLE 2: ORIGINS OF "MAVERICK" HIRAGANA

1. On-Yomi	2. Kanji Meaning	3. Kanji	4. Hiragana	5. Kana Yomi
AN	peacefulness	安	あ	*a*
I	by means of	以	い	*i*
I, E	garment	衣	え	*e*
KEI	measure, plan	計	け	*ke*
SA	left	左	さ	*sa*
SUN	small amount, inch	寸	す	*su*
TAI, TA	plump, thick	太	た	*ta*
CHI	to know	知	ち	*chi*
HA	wave	波	は	*ha*
BI, MI	beauty	美	み	*mi*
BU, MU	military	武	む	*mu*
RYŪ, RU	to stop, keep	留	る	*ru*
I	to do	爲	ゐ	*(w)i*
KEI, E	to bless	惠	ゑ	*(w)e*
EN, ON	far	遠	を	*(w)o*
MU, BU	without	无	ん	*n*

THE ARCHITECTURE OF A CHARACTER

2

I've mentioned that Michael Rowley's *Kanji Pict-o-Graphix* makes kanji both fun and manageable by identifying the ingredients in each character. When I started studying kanji, I followed his lead, creating diagrams such as this one:

時 (hour) ➤ 日 (sun)
➤ 寺 (temple) ➤ 土 (soil)
➤ 寸 (inch)

After doing this type of analysis, I felt that I understood a character down to its bones, almost as if I'd seen an X ray of its anatomy.

I *did* gain an in-depth understanding of characters this way . . . but at the same time I missed a big chunk of context—namely, that just a limited group of kanji have the kind of structure in which little bits of meaning add up to one larger meaning. Other characters contain pieces that contribute sound.

Far from being random collections of strokes, kanji have distinct parts that serve purposes, much as walls, ceilings, and floors contribute to a building's functionality. Let's tour a character so we can understand its architecture.

Components

Every kanji consists of one or more components (also known as "elements"). The character 秋 (*SHŪ, aki:* autumn) has two: 禾 (which represents "rice plant") and 火 (which symbolizes "fire"). And 照 (*SHŌ, te•ru:* to illuminate) contains four: 日 (sun, day), 刀 (sword), 口 (opening), and 灬 (another way of representing "fire"). By contrast, 木 (*MOKU, ki:* tree) has just one component: 木 (which means "tree," not surprisingly). When I say "component," I'm referring to an indivisible unit of meaning. Of course, you could break 灬 into four pieces, but as separate lines they don't mean anything. For some fun with components, see Exhibit 23, "Thematic Explorations: Kanji of a Feather Flock Together."

Radicals

Every kanji includes a radical, a component that helps us locate that kanji within the vast library of characters, much as the Dewey Decimal System makes it easier to find books. The radical may be a component with a clear meaning, such as 艹 (grass), 宀 (roof), or 刂 (sword), but that meaning may have little to do with the significance of the whole kanji. For instance, it's hard to see how grass figures semantically into 荷 (*KA, ni:* load, baggage), how a roof pertains to 字 (*JI:* character, letter), or what a sword has to do with 到 (*TŌ:* to arrive). Rather than looking at how a radical adds meaning to a character, consider the way it allows us to group all kanji with that shared feature. For example, the hand radical 扌 appears in 押, 払, 持, and 指 (respectively, *o•su:* to push; *hara•u:* to pay; *mo•tsu:* to possess; and *yubi:* finger). For much more on radicals, see Exhibit 24, "Just the Facts: A Radical Concept," as well as "Game: Radicals." See also Exhibit 25, "Thematic Explorations: The Hill and the Village."

Phonetics

Kanji are pictures plus sounds. It's as if kanji can stream audio and video, compared with the mere audio function of kana or roman letters. The phonetic component (also simply called the phonetic) tells us how a character sounds. Not all kanji contain phonetics, but at least two-thirds do. When you can split a kanji into left-hand and right-hand sides, the radical will typically be on the left, the phonetic on the right. The on-yomi of the phonetic may tell you the *on* reading of the whole kanji. However, the kun-yomi of the phonetic is irrelevant to the kun-yomi of the entire character. Returning to the example at the beginning of this chapter, we see that the left side of 時 is the radical 日. Its meaning of "sun" does indeed relate to the meaning of 時, which is "hour" or "time." The phonetic 寺 is the remainder. Its meaning, "temple," is irrelevant here. But its sound is important. Because 寺 has the on-yomi *JI,* the bigger kanji 時 does, too. For much more on phonetics and characters with shared shapes, see Exhibit 26, "Just the Facts: The *On*-Echo"; Exhibit 27, "Just the Facts: Easily Confused Kanji"; Exhibit 28, "Game: Which Is Which?"; and Exhibit 29, "Thematic Explorations: Strategies for Conquering Look-Alikes."

Putting the Pieces Together

So there you have it, the building blocks of a character: radicals, phonetics, and components. Some kanji include all three, but others lack a phonetic. Exhibit 30, "Just the Facts: Classification of Characters," explains the four basic ways in which these building blocks can fit together, creating different types of kanji "architecture."

In only type (*kaiimoji,* Type 3 in Exhibit 30) do the smaller bits of meaning add up to a larger meaning. The deconstructive approach I adopted via Rowley is appropriate with just 25 percent of characters. And yet I confess that I haven't shaken the habit. It's just too much fun to break down characters and to discover what secrets they contain. You'll find these kinds of investigations in Exhibit 31, "Thematic Explorations: Elegant Etymology"; Exhibit 32, "Thematic Explorations: Charmingly Illogical Characters"; and Exhibit 33, "Thematic Explorations: Just Add Water."

It's also fun to do the opposite—to assemble and rearrange components until you've formed kanji. Try your hand at that in Exhibit 34, "Game: The Missing Link," and Exhibit 35, "Game: Create a Kanji."

Kanji of a Feather Flock Together

It's not uncommon to see a component repeated within a kanji character. Take, for example, 多 (ō•i: many). Many kanji contain doubled components, but they usually come with extra strokes or components. For instance, 暗 (kura•i: dark) includes 日 twice but also contains 立. Characters such as 儡 (RAI: doll, puppet, defeat) and 器 (KI, utsuwa: container, tool) go so far as to triple or quadruple certain components, but once again, extra elements ruin the neat pattern. "Pure" forms of these multiples are rare. A few things to notice about the list of triples below:

- Sometimes tripling greatly changes the meaning. Or the tripled kanji just means "more of the same."
- In the Triple column, notice the similarities among on-yomi. I don't know if it's significant that so many have -ō sounds, particularly SHŌ, but that trend might help you figure out the on-yomi if you ever encounter these kanji.
- The kanji 蟲 (CHŪ, mushi: insect) does not qualify because this is simply an alternate writing of 虫 (CHŪ, mushi: insect). Japan simplified many kanji right after World War II, and this triple hails from the prewar period.
- The last triple, 姦, is controversial in Japan. According to author Kittredge Cherry in Womans-

word: What Japanese Words Say About Women, feminists resent the suggestion that three women are thought to produce something as negative as noisiness (indicated by the kun-yomi). Cherry notes that no kanji shows a trio of "men"; presumably such a gathering would seem normal, not heinous. (In fact, the male ideogram 男 rarely appears in other kanji.) The on-yomi for 姦 has even worse connotations than noisiness; defined as "wicked or immoral," this syllable factors into such words as 姦する (kansuru: to seduce, assault, rape), 強姦 (gōkan: rape), and 姦通 (kantsū: adultery).

Kanji triples are rare, but quadruples are more so:

    TETSU: garrulous, verbose

I suppose when four dragons get together, they have a lot to discuss.

What about five or six of a kind? Until now we've examined singletons with repeated components. The only way to see five or six together is in a compound:

森林	*shinrin:* forest
森森	*shinshin:* deeply forested
轟轟	*gōgō•to:* thunderously, with a rumble
犇犇	*hishihishi:* firmly, tightly, thronging

Single		**Triple**	
一	*ICHI, hito•tsu:* one	三	*SAN, mi•ttsu:* three
牛	*GYŪ, ushi:* cow	犇	*HON, hishime•ku:* to jostle
貝	*BAI, kai:* shell	贔	*HII, HI:* favor, patronage
口	*KŌ, KU, kuchi:* mouth	品	*HIN, shina:* item, goods, refinement
木	*MOKU, BOKU, ki:* tree	森	*SHIN, mori:* forest
車	*SHA, kuruma:* car	轟	*GŌ, todoro•ku:* to roar, thunder
水	*SUI, mizu:* water	淼	*BYŌ:* vast (expanse of water)
馬	*BA, uma:* horse	驫	*SHŌ:* many horses
日	*NICHI, hi:* sun, day	晶	*SHŌ:* clear, crystal
耳	*JI, mimi:* ear	聶	*JŌ, SHŌ, sasa•yaku:* to whisper
鹿	*ROKU, shika:* deer	麤	*SO, ara•i:* rough
龍	*RYŪ, RYŌ, tatsu:* dragon	龘	*DŌ, TŌ:* dragons on the move
石	*SEKI, ishi:* stone	磊	*RAI:* many stones, easygoing
直	*CHOKU:* straight; *nao•su:* to correct	矗	*CHOKU:* standing straight or tall
女	*JO, onna:* woman	姦	*KAN:* wicked, immoral; *kashima•shii:* noisy

A Radical Concept

Imagine an enormous, messy storeroom in a house. The only hope of creating order would be to devise categories: sports equipment over here, suitcases over there, paint cans in the corner, and so forth. In the vast "storeroom" of Chinese characters, radicals (部首, *bushu*) enable us to categorize kanji and therefore to look them up in dictionaries.

Here are some radicals: 冫 儿 匚 广 女. Many can't stand on their own; they only exist as parts of characters. That's true of the first four here. If a kanji consists of just one component (e.g., 女), the whole kanji functions as the radical.

When there are multiple components, the radical tends to be one of them. I say "tends to be" because a radical isn't always as small as a component. The kanji 魚 (*sakana:* fish) contains three meaningful components: ク (to crouch), 田 (field), and 灬 (fire). Nevertheless, 魚 serves in its entirety as a radical.

It would be nice if you could determine the radical based on whether components were connected or autonomous, but radicals such as 冫, 氵, 儿, and 魚 have disconnected pieces. Conversely, kanji consisting of interconnected lines may conceal a kanji made of fewer strokes. The radical 戈 (halberd) underlies 栽 (SAI: "planting," as in *bonsai*) and 幾 (KI, iku-: "how much, how many," as in *ikutsu:* "how many").

You can determine the radical by finding components corresponding to those in your dictionary's radical chart. But the challenge doesn't end there. Both 低 and 宿 (respectively, TEI, hiku•i: low; and SHUKU, yado: lodging) contain the component 亻 (person). You might think this is the radical for each. Not so;

亻 is the radical in 低, whereas the radical in 宿 is 宀 (roof).

Even if all the components in a character are classifiable as radicals, only one radical at a time is "on duty." The others are just along for the ride, adding meaning or sound but contributing nothing to the classification scheme. In the kanji displayed in the box, all components can serve as radicals. I've listed the on-duty radical as it appears in Spahn. Note that the kanji in the first two lines share 亻 and 貝 but have different radicals. The kanji in the last two lines share 攵, which serves as the radical only once.

Determining radicals is hit-or-miss, but when there are several choices, these pointers should help:

- **Start big and work down:** Determine whether the entire character constitutes a radical. If not, maybe a significant chunk of the kanji does. In Spahn, these are all radicals:

  酉 頁 金 食 馬

  Look for the most inclusive radical, rather than finding 一 (ICHI, hito•tsu: one) in nearly every kanji.

- **Left and right:** If the kanji divides neatly into a left and right side, look first on the left. That's where you'll find the radicals of these characters:

kanji:	体	明	情
radical:	亻	日	忄 (a variant of 心)

  If the left side isn't a radical, then the right side must be, as in these:

kanji:	政	別	都
radical:	攵	刂	阝

	Yomi and Meaning	On-Duty Radical	Radicals Along for the Ride
貸	TAI, ka•su: to lend	貝 (shell, money)	亻 (person), 弋 (stake)
側	SOKU, kawa: side	亻 (person)	貝 (shell, money), 刂 (sword)
簡	KAN: simple, brief	竹 (bamboo)	門 (gate), 日 (sun, day)
箱	SŌ, hako: box	竹 (bamboo)	木 (tree), 目 (eye)
数	SŪ, SU, kazu: number	攵 (to strike)	米 (rice), 女 (woman)
驚	KYŌ, odoro•ku: to be surprised	馬 (horse)	艹 (grass), 口 (mouth), 攵 (to strike)

- **Up and down:** If the kanji divides neatly into upper and lower parts, look first on top. The upper portion can be a radical only if the component fully stretches across the character, as in these kanji:

kanji:	会	高	寝
radical:	个 (var. of 人)	亠	宀

  By contrast, the bottom parts of the next characters are radicals because the topmost parts never exist as radicals:

kanji:	無	悪	祭
radical:	灬 (var. of 火)	心	示

- **Enclosures:** If a component encloses the rest of the character on at least two sides, you've found your radical:

kanji:	区	原	進
radical:	匚	厂	辶

As I've said, Spahn presents these as the radicals for the characters in question, but other dictionaries categorize these kanji differently. This discrepancy has a historical context. In 1716, the Chinese grouped about 42,000 kanji into 214 radical categories. Japan followed suit. Then in 1946, the Japanese simplified several aspects of their language, including the classification and shapes of many radicals. (The idea was to make it easier for children to learn and easier for adults to read literature and periodicals.) Spahn's dictionary features just 79 radicals, whereas other dictionaries retain the 214-radical system as an organizing principle. Dictionaries for native speakers vary, too; one has 245 radicals, whereas another has 257.

As a consequence of simplification, 人 came to have the "variant" forms 亻 and 个. All mean "person," and all appear as components in kanji (or as an autonomous kanji in the case of 人). Although life has become simpler with the 79-radical system, in some ways you still need to know older forms and how they correspond to characters today. This isn't an entirely bad thing; meanings were often more apparent in older radicals. For instance, it's easier to grasp that 羊 signifies "sheep" than to see that symbolized solely in the top two strokes, which now represent that radical.

As long as we're discussing mutability, it's useful to note how components change their shapes accord-ing to their position in kanji. Take the simple form 木 (tree). See how it changes in these configurations:

wide on the top	李	(RI, *sumomo:* plum)
wide on the bottom	栗	(RITSU, *kuri:* chestnut)
skinny on the left	机	(KI, *tsukue:* desk)
skinny in a pair	林	(RIN, *hayashi:* forest)
practically invisible	鬱	(UTSU, *fusa•gu:* depression)

Although it's nearly impossible to tell, the last character contains two trees, among many other things.

And on the subject of positions within a kanji, there are seven such positions for radicals:

- **Positions 1–2:** When a kanji divides neatly into left and right sides, the left is *hen* (偏: side) and the right is *tsukuri* (旁: side).
- **Positions 3–4:** For top-and-bottom-divided characters, the top is *kanmuri* (冠: crown) and the bottom is *ashi* (脚: foot).
- **Positions 5–7:** Enclosing elements are usually *kamae* (構え: structure), but there are two exceptions. *Tare* (垂れ: to sag) enclosures go down the lower left and across the top (e.g., 广), whereas *nyō* (遶: to surround) enclosures go down the lower left and across the bottom (e.g., 辶).

As if all that terminology weren't enough, each radical has a name. Usually (but not always) the name combines its yomi and its position within the kanji. Here's how this plays out for certain radicals:

- *hen:* 牛 (*ushihen*), 土 (*tsuchihen*), and 貝 (*kaihen*)
- *kanmuri:* 艹 (*kusakanmuri*), 竹 (*takekanmuri*), and 雨 (*amekanmuri*)
- *kamae:* 門 (*mongamae*) and 囗 (*kunigamae*)

Game: *Radicals*

Kana Needed: N
Kanji Level: 0
Difficulty Level: 2

Give your radical muscles a workout:

1. Of the kanji for the seven radical positions, how many match their own descriptions? For example, does the kanji for *hen* (偏) depict a *hen* radical?

2. What's the radical of 導?

Answers appear in the Answer Key. *Ganbatte kudasai.*

#25 THEMATIC EXPLORATIONS

The Hill and the Village

According to Michael Rowley's *Kanji Pict-o-Graphix*, the radical 阝 means "hill" when on the left side of a character and "village" when on the right. Let's see how this plays out:

Left: Hill

院 (*IN:* institute), as in 病院 (*byōin:* hospital)
降 (*fu•ru:* to fall [e.g., rain]; *o•riru:* to come down)
階 (*KAI:* stairs), as in 階段 (*kaidan:* stairs)
際 (*SAI:* time), as in 国際 (*kokusai:* international)
障 (*SHŌ:* to hinder), as in 障子 (*shōji:* sliding door with paper panes)
隣 (*RIN, tonari:* next door, adjoining)

Right: Village

都 (*TO, miyako:* capital), as in 京都 (*Kyōto*)
郊 (*KŌ:* suburbs), as in 郊外 (*kōgai:* suburbs)
郵 (*YŪ:* mail), as in 郵便局 (*yūbinkyoku:* post office)
部 (*BU:* part), as in 部分 (*bubun:* part)

I can see the hill connection in 降 (*o•riru:* to come down) and 階 (*KAI:* stairs). And the village theme connects to 都 (*TO, miyako:* capital), 郊 (*KŌ:* suburbs), and possibly 郵 (*YŪ:* mail). But mostly these bits of meaning disappear in the shadow of other semantic parts. So even when it's perfectly appropriate to assess the meaning of a component (as it is in the case of a radical), this type of analysis may not prove helpful.

A final note: Some dictionaries say that characters such as 院 and 都 have different radicals because 阝 has changed position. Other authorities consider 阝 on the left and 阝 on the right to be different radicals not only because of their positions but also because of their original shapes (埠 for the left-hand version, 邑 for the right-hand one). Both 埠 and 邑 mean "village," although the primary meaning of 埠 is hill. Because of this shared meaning, still more experts say that 阝 is just one radical, no matter where you locate it. Finally, the Nelson dictionary says that 阝 symbolizes a small village when on the left and a large one when on the right. A Japanese-language teacher told me that this is because you can build only a small village on a hill.

Here are two of Michael Rowley's illustrative mnemonics for kanji with the 阝 radical. In each case, he has represented this radical with a flag, and for good measure he has planted both flags on hills, helping the twin associations stick in readers' minds.

In the left-hand drawing, the "flag" appears on the right, so 阝 means "village" here. As I mentioned above, "village" correlates with the meaning of 郊 (*KŌ:* suburbs).

And in the right-hand illustration, the "flag" shows up on the left, so it means "hill." The kanji is 陛 (*HEI:* majesty), which did not appear in the above list. It's certainly hard to see a semantic connection between "majesty" and "hill."

By the way, those of you who own Rowley's *Kanji Pict-o-Graphix* might notice that the illustrations here don't match the ones in that book. These new drawings come from a set of flash cards that Rowley has produced.

The *On*-Echo

If you've ever wished kanji were more logical, your wish may have come true. One pattern reveals order in the chaos. Consider these characters:

安	AN: peacefulness; *yasu·i:* cheap
案	AN: plan, proposal
按	AN: to hold, consider, investigate
鮟	AN: anglerfish

Notice any commonalities? These kanji share not only the component 安 but also the on-yomi AN. Here's a handy rule of thumb: When a character shows up as a component in other kanji (e.g., 安 in 案, 按, and 鮟), they may well share an on-yomi. You might not know anything about 鞍 and 晏, but if you guessed that their on-yomi was AN, you'd be right!

There doesn't appear to be a name for this phenomenon. The concept often arises during linguistic discussions of the "semantic-phonetic principle" or "semantic-phonetic compounds," also called "phonetic compounds" (形声文字, *keiseimoji*, in Japanese). But I haven't heard a term referring just to this rule. To rectify matters, I've dubbed it the "*on*-echo," because the on-yomi reverberates through kanji containing a common element.

Note that this shared shape may have no bearing on meaning. The first two kanji listed above share a radical (宀), which might seem to place them in the same semantic category (i.e., things concerning roofs), but that doesn't prove true. And "anglerfish" is a world away from "proposal." Nor do the characters' kun-yomi matter at all; in fact, just three of the six kanji have kun-yomi, and the only one shown above (*yasu·i:* cheap) tends to have a different meaning from the on-yomi of that character. The *on*-echo is all about shape as related to sound.

This pattern relates to events that occurred two millennia ago. Before that, the Chinese had tried to create a pictographic system, representing mountain with 山 and so on. This was nice as far as it went, but it didn't go very far, particularly in terms of depicting abstract concepts or names. For that reason, some words had no characters and existed only in speech. The written language was in a state of chaos, consisting of thousands of characters that had evolved with little rhyme or reason. So in the second century CE, the Chinese set about reforming kanji.

Rather than hammering out still more characters, the Chinese rounded up words with identical or similar sounds and matched them to characters that had common elements. The reformers went about this in three ways, according to John DeFrancis in *The Chinese Language: Fact and Fantasy*.

For example, 然 originally meant "to burn." The Chinese then made this character serve double-duty; for a time, it also represented the abstract concept "thus, so," which had the same pronunciation as the word for "to burn." (Hence, this was a "phonetic loan.") Having the same pronunciation and the same character for two words guaranteed confusion. To differentiate the two, the Chinese decided to use 然 for "thus, so." Adding the fire radical 火 to that character, the Chinese produced a new writing for "burn": 燃. In Japanese, these characters still mean "so" and "to burn," and they share an on-yomi of NEN, though 然 can also be read as ZEN.

In other cases (called semantic extensions), the Chinese assigned characters to words with similar meanings. For instance, 方 meant "square" in a general sense. The reformers added the semantic element 土, creating 坊 (square, marketplace). They left 方 with its original meaning. Sometimes, as in this case, the newly associated word (also called the derived word) took the semantic element (that is, the radical). Other times, the original word took the new radical.

With the third kind of change, the Chinese took an unwritten word and matched it to a character that had a sound but no meaning (a pure phonetic). "Sugar" had no character, and 唐 had no meaning, only a sound. They made a perfect pair. But every character needed a semantic category, so the Chinese added the grain element 米 as a radical, and 糖 became the new way of writing "sugar." That's what it means in Japanese, too. It's pronounced TŌ, as in 砂糖, *satō*, the full word for "sugar."

With all three types of reform, the Chinese created "semantic-phonetic compounds." That's the official term for such singletons, but let's call them "composites" so we can differentiate them from kanji compounds (unions of two or more kanji). At any rate, each of these "semantic-phonetic" composites combines one radical (the semantic aspect) and one phonetic (governing pronunciation). From then on, the Chinese structured virtually all new kanji accordingly. In *Asia's Orthographic Dilemma,* William C. Hannas sums up the significance of that shift: "Chinese writing moved decisively and irrevocably away from iconicity and toward phonetics as the dominant principle governing the creation of new character forms."

This is no minor statement. The popular way of looking at kanji is to emphasize that they all mean something and to overlook their phonetic aspects. In light of that misconception, one statement by DeFrancis sounds particularly startling. When it comes to semantic-phonetic composites, he says, the phonetic came first and the radical was added later. He says the term "radical" is misleading "since the semantic element is not the basic root but a later accretion to the really basic phonetic."

Clearly, the phonetic aspect of kanji is essential. And the *on*-echo is amazingly widespread. In *The Study of Kanji,* Michael Pye extracted 600 *on*-echoes from the 3,000 most common kanji. In other words, 20 percent of ordinary kanji have *on*-echoes.

It's astounding, then, that the *on*-echo remains relatively unexplored and unnamed. One reason may be that it's full of exceptions, enough to make it unreliable as a predictor of pronunciation. But when you're staring blankly at an unknown kanji, the *on*-echo is a better tool than nothing.

Given how many *on*-echoes there are, I can't list them comprehensively in this exhibit. Section 1 below contains the kanji with the most echoes, and Section 2 presents echoes for the most frequently used kanji. To save space, I've omitted meanings and kun-yomi, but you can easily look these up if you want, using the on-yomi supplied.

A few notes:

- I've isolated the "purest" element (that is, the one reverberating in the others). Usually this is a whole kanji, but occasionally it's only part of one. I've marked such exceptions.
- An *on*-echo series can contain "neutral" and "voiced" consonant pairs (e.g., *HŌ* and *BŌ, KAKU* and *GAKU*). When this is the case, I've classified the series under the neutral reading.
- Oddly, *on*-echoes starting with *k* (e.g., *KAN, KŌ,* etc.) predominate in the following pages.
- For further displays of *on*-echoes, see the out-of-print (and hard-to-find) *Study of Kanji* by Michael Pye or *Let's Learn More Kanji: Family Groups, Learning Strategies, and 300 Complex Kanji,* in which authors Richard Glenn Covington, Joyce Yumi Mitamura, and Yasuko Kosaka Mitamura refer to *on*-echo series as "family groups."

The word 音楽 *(ongaku)* means "music." The first kanji, 音, means "sound." This same *on* shows up in the term *on-yomi,* 音読み. From this, we get *on*-echoes, or 音-echoes, one could say. This photo is of a poster hanging in a Tokyo subway station.

SECTION 1: MOST ECHOES PER KANJI

In the following *on-echo* series, I've arranged kanji according to where the common component lies within the character. The numbers of echoes are quite high but could have been even higher had I included extremely rare kanji within the series. To compile the lists below, I worked from Pye, Covington, Spahn, and computerized component displays supplied by Microsoft Word. Even so, my lists may be incomplete.

KO: 古 (25 echoes)

Boxed:	固 個 涸 痼 箇 錮
Centered:	湖 餬 瑚 楜 糊 蝴
Right:	估 沽 姑 怙 枯 蛄 詁
Left:	故 胡 鴣
Bottom:	居
Bottom Left:	葫

HŌ, BŌ: 方 (20 echoes)

Centered:	倣
Right:	防 彷 妨 坊 肪 紡 訪 魴
Left:	放
Bottom:	芳 房 旁 蒡
Bottom Right:	傍 滂 榜 膀 謗

KŌ: 工 (16 echoes)

Centered:	鴻
Right:	江 杠 肛 紅 虹 訌
Left:	功 巧 項 攻
Top:	貢
Bottom Right:	倥 控 腔

KAN: 干 (15 echoes)

Right:	汗 奸 肝 鼾
Left:	刊
Top:	栞
Bottom:	旱 竿
Bottom Right:	稈 捍 悍 桿 幹 駻

HAKU: 白 (12 echoes)

Right:	伯 迫 拍 泊 狛 柏 珀 粕 舶
Left:	魄
Top:	帛
Bottom Right:	箔

Runners-Up for the High Score

HAN:	反 板 飯 etc.
HO:	甫 補 浦 etc.
HŌ:	包 砲 抱 etc.
JI:	寺 時 持 etc.
KA:	可 何 荷 歌 etc.
KAKU, GAKU:	各 客 格 額 etc.
KEN:	僉 (not a complete kanji). It appears in 験, 険, and 検, among others.
KEN, GEN:	幺 (not a complete kanji). It appears in 玄 and 幻, among others. The series has nothing to do with the form 糸.
KI:	己 記 起 紀 etc.
KI, GI:	其 期 基 旗 etc.
KŌ:	厶 (not a complete kanji). It appears in 公 and 広, among others.
KŌ:	交 校 効 etc.
SHŌ:	肖 消 宵 etc.
SO:	且 組 祖 etc.

SECTION 2: MOST FREQUENTLY USED KANJI

Spahn lists the 100 most frequently used kanji. Of these, 49 have *on*-echoes, as listed below. The most frequently used kanji may be the actual shape that echoes through the series. If not, the echoing shape doesn't necessarily have the same yomi as the kanji that contain the shape. And the echoing shape may not be a complete kanji at all, in which case it has no sound. The listing has 51 items because 2 of the 49 have multiple echoes; 生 "reverberates" through other characters as both *SEI* and *SHŌ,* and 成 does so as both *SEI* and *JŌ.*

On-Yomi	Echoing Shape	Most Freq. Used Kanji	Related Kanji
CHI	也	地	池 馳
			Echoing shape is not pronounced *CHI.*
CHI	知	知	痴
CHŌ	長	長	帳 張 脹
CHŪ	中	中	虫 忠 仲
DAI	弟	第	弟
DŌ	動	動	働 慟
FU	付	府	符 腐 附 俯
FUN	分	分	粉 紛
GI	義	議	儀 犠 艤 蟻
GO	五	五	語 悟 吾 伍 齬
HATSU, HA·TTSU	発	発	溌 撥
HI	皮	彼	被 疲 披
HŌ, BŌ	方	方	防 芳 彷 妨 坊 放 肪 房 倣 紡 旄 旁 訪 傍 滂 蒡 榜 膀 磅 謗 魴
HŌ	法	法	琺
IN	員	員	韻
JI	寺	時	持 侍 峙 痔
JO	女	女	如
JŌ	成	成	城 盛
			See also 成 (*SEI*).
JŪ	十	十	汁 什
KA	化	化	花 貨 訛
KA	家	家	嫁 稼
KAI	会	会	絵
KAN	門	間	関 簡 閑 癇
			Echoing shape is not pronounced *KAN.*
KEN	見	見	現 硯
KEN	県	県	懸
KI	气	気	汽
KIN, GIN	今	今	琴 矜 吟
KIN, GIN	金	金	銀 欽 錦
KŌ	行	行	衡
KŌ, GŌ	高	高	稿 敲 嚆 膏
KYŌ	亡	京	亨 哀 享
KYŪ	九	九	究 仇 鳩
MEI	名	名	銘
NI	二	二	弐
SA, SAKU	乍	作	昨 酢 窄 搾 詐 炸
SEI	生	生	性 姓 星 牲 醒
			See also 生 (*SHŌ*).
SEI	成	成	誠 盛
			See also 成 (*JŌ*).
SEN, ZEN	前	前	煎 剪
SHA	者	者	煮 奢
SHI	子	子	仔
SHŌ	小	小	少 省 渉 抄
SHŌ	生	生	性 姓 星
			See also 生 (*SEI*).
TAI	大	大	太
TAI	寸	対	耐
			Echoing shape is not pronounced *TAI.*
TAI, DAI	代	代	貸 袋
TEI	正	定	提 堤 碇
TŌ	⺌	当	党 堂 瞠
TŌ	東	東	凍 棟
TŌ, DŌ	同	同	桐 筒 銅 胴 洞
TSŪ	通	通	痛
YŌ	用	用	踊 慂

#27 JUST THE FACTS

Easily Confused Kanji

Countless kanji look alike. Can you tell these characters apart?

I.	水	氷	永	泳
II.	氏	民	眼	眠
III.	城	域		
IV.	置	直	植	値

Right now, when you're presumably calm and clear, I bet you can pick out differences, and you may even recognize these as follows:

I.	水	*SUI, mizu:* water
	氷	*HYŌ, kōri, hi:* ice
	永	*EI, naga•i:* eternal
	泳	*EI, oyo•gu:* to swim
II.	氏	*SHI, uji:* family name
	民	*MIN, tami:* people, subjects
	眼	*GAN, GEN, manako:* eye
	眠	*MIN, nemu•ru:* to sleep
III.	城	*JŌ, shiro:* castle
	域	*IKI:* boundary, region
IV.	置	*CHI, o•ku:* to put, place
	直	*CHOKU, JIKI:* direct; *nao•ru, nao•su:* to fix
	植	*SHOKU, u•eru:* to plant, set type
	値	*CHI, atai:* value; *ne, atai:* price

Looking at these characters when they're "standing still" is one thing. But reading a string of kanji is another matter altogether. It's absurdly easy to glance too quickly, to lose your bearings, to overlook a stroke, and thereby to confuse two kanji.

Once, when I encountered 伺, I was somehow unable to take in the line over the internal box. Positive that the kanji was 何 (*nan, nani:* what), I couldn't make sense of the subsequent okurigana, *tte.* Why would it say *nantte?* Was this one of those *-tte* constructions signaling a quotation? Increasingly muddled, I flipped through books, researching grammar and any kanji formed with 何 *(nan).* After fifteen frustrating minutes, I revisited 伺, scrutinizing its shape and at last noticing the extra stroke. The kanji is *ukaga•u,* "to visit" or "to ask." As I'd never seen it before, my brain had translated the form into something I thought I knew.

Unfortunately, once you've mistaken one character for another and panicked about a nonsensical reading, it's hard to reason your way out of confusion. Ideally in such a state, you could conjure up rows of look-alikes, such as 日, 白, 百, 目, 自, 首, 道, thinking about individual meanings and readings and realizing where you went astray. But it's rare to see look-alikes displayed together, so you don't tend to internalize them as such. (Also, once you panic, it's hard to reason your way through pretty much anything.)

To imprint such line-ups on your brain, look at the following examples. For each example, the last two rows present words containing the particular kanji.

了	予	子	字
RYŌ	*YO*	*SHI, SU*	*JI*
—	*arakaji•me*	*ko*	*aza*
to complete, finish	previously	child	character
完了 *(kanryō)*	予約 *(yoyaku)*	子供 *(kodomo)*	漢字 *(kanji)*
to finish	reservations	child	Chinese characters
大	犬	太	
DAI, TAI	*KEN*	*TAI, TA*	
ō•kii	*inu*	*futo•i*	
big	dog	fat	
大半 *(taihan)*	負け犬 *(makeinu)*	太陽 *(taiyō)*	
majority	loser	sun	

木
BOKU, MOKU
ki
tree, wood
丸木 *(maruki)*
log (lit., round wood)

本
HON
moto
origin, root, book
本当 *(hontō)*
true, real

休
KYŪ
yasu•mu
to rest
休火山 *(kyūkazan)*
dormant volcano

体
TAI
karada
body
体内 *(tainai)*
inside the body

力
RYOKU, RIKI
chikara
power, force, ability
馬力 *(bariki)*
horsepower

刀
TŌ
katana
sword
執刀 *(shittō)*
performing surgery

万
MAN, BAN
—
10,000, all, every
万歳 *(banzai)*
hurrah!

方
HŌ
kata
direction, way, means
方法 *(hōhō)*
method

米
BEI
kome
rice, America
日米 *(Nichi-Bei)*
Japan-U.S.

来
RAI
ku•ru
to come
来日 *(rainichi)*
to come to Japan

番
BAN
tsuga•i
number
二番目 *(nibanme)*
second, number 2

老
RŌ
oi•ru
to grow old
老人 *(rōjin)*
elderly person
(impolite)

考
KŌ
kanga•eru
to think, consider
考え方 *(kangaekata)*
way of thinking

孝
KŌ
—
filial piety
孝行 *(kōkō)*
filial piety

教
KYŌ
oshi•eru
to teach
教会 *(kyōkai)*
church

天
TEN
ame
sky
天才 *(tensai)*
genius

夫
FU, FŪ
otto
my husband
夫婦 *(fūfu)*
husband and wife

末
MATSU
sue
end
週末 *(shūmatsu)*
weekend

未
MI
ma•da
not yet
未亡人 *(mibōjin)*
widow (lit., not
yet dead person!)

味
MI
aji
taste, flavor
味噌 *(miso)*
fermented
bean paste

寺
JI
tera
temple
大寺院 *(daijiin)*
large temple

待
TAI
ma•tsu
to wait
招待 *(shōtai)*
invitation

持
JI
mo•tsu
to hold, have
持病 *(jibyō)*
chronic illness

特
TOKU
—
special
特色 *(tokushoku)*
characteristic

度
DO
tabi
times, degree
温度計 *(ondokei)*
thermometer

席
SEKI
—
seat, place
出席 *(shusseki)*
attendance

渡
TO
wata•ru
to cross
渡り鳥 *(wataridori)*
migratory bird

> GYOKU is a rare on-yomi, as it can stand on its own to mean "gem" or "jewel" (though GYOKU also combines with other yomi in compounds). By contrast, *tama* means "ball."

主
SHU, SU
omo, nushi
main
主人 *(shujin)*
master, husband

王
Ō
—
king
王様 *(ōsama)*
king

玉
GYOKU
tama
gem, ball
目玉 *(medama)*
eyeball

国
KOKU
kuni
country
外国人 *(gaikokujin)*
foreigner

史
SHI
—
history
歴史 *(rekishi)*
history

吏
RI
—
an official
官吏 *(kanri)*
govt. official

束
SOKU
taba, tsuka
bundle
約束 *(yakusoku)*
promise, appt.

速
SOKU
haya•i
fast
高速 *(kōsoku)*
high-speed

東
TŌ
higashi
east
東洋 *(tōyō)*
the Orient

貝
BAI
kai
shellfish, shell
貝殻 *(kaigara)*
seashell

具
GU
sona•eru
equipment
道具 *(dōgu)*
tool

員
IN
—
member
金員 *(kin'in)*
money

買
BAI
ka•u
to buy, purchase
売買 *(baibai)*
buying and selling

困
KON
koma•ru
to be in trouble
困難 *(konnan)*
difficulty

因
IN
yo•ru
to be based on, cause
原因 *(gen'in)*
cause

囚
SHŪ
—
to confine
囚人 *(shūjin)*
prisoner

Which Is Which?

In the sentences below, can you distinguish between the look-alike kanji displayed in Exhibit 27? Some of the vocabulary supplied in that chart will come in handy here, too. Write each sentence in hiragana or rōmaji. The Answer Key supplies solutions in both scripts, as well as translations. *Ganbatte kudasai!*

1. 大きくて太った犬ですね。

_____

_____

2. 特別な物を持って、お寺で待っています。

_____

_____

Additional kanji and vocabulary:
別 (*BETSU*: extra, specially)
物 (*mono*: thing)

3. セミナーで私は着席しましたが、友達は欠席したので、とうとう外に出て、もう一度道路を渡りました。

_____

_____

Additional kanji and vocabulary:
私 (*watashi*: I)
着 (*CHAKU*: to arrive)
友達 (*tomodachi*: friend)
欠 (*KETSU*: lack)
外 (*soto*: outside)
出 (*de•ru*: to leave)
道路 (*dōro*: street)

4. この週末、未だ、夫が見つかっていません。

_____

_____

Additional kanji and vocabulary:
見 (*mi•tsukaru*: to be found)

5. 体を休めたいので、この木の下で休憩して、本を読みます。

_____

_____

Additional kanji and vocabulary:
下 (*shita*: below)
憩 (*KEI*: recess, rest)
読 (*yo•mu*: to read)

6. 暴動の原因はあの囚人でした。今みんな困っています。

_____

_____

Additional kanji and vocabulary:
暴動 (*bōdō*: riot)
今 (*ima*: now)

7. 力をもってそれをするためには、刀を持っている人を一万人集める事です。

_____

_____

Additional kanji and vocabulary:
人 (*NIN, hito*: person)
集 (*atsu•meru*: to assemble)
事 (*koto*: thing)

8. 過去、貝は道具でも金員でもありました。貝で、物を買えました。

_____

_____

Additional kanji and vocabulary:
過去 (*kako*: past)
物 (*mono*: thing)

Strategies for Conquering Look-Alikes

In *Decoding Kanji: A Practical Approach to Learning Look-Alike Characters,* Yaeko Habein explains why there are so many look-alikes. Quite a few characters were intentionally created equal, so to speak. Someone added strokes to 大, resulting in the characters 天 and 夫. Adding dots to 大 produced 太 and 犬. This last character, representing "dog," replaced the ancient form, which looked much more like a dog. Over many centuries of kanji usage, such simplifications occurred to accommodate people who needed an easier script. This led to further confusing resemblances. Habein notes, for example, that 男 (*DAN, NAN, otoko*: man), 思 (*SHI, omo•u*: to think), and 胃 (*I*: stomach) look as if they contain 田 (field), but only 男 does. In the other two, the same shape came from elsewhere; the top part of 思 originally meant "head," and the same grid in 胃 meant "food in stomach."

The brain makes distinctions by searching for differences. When characters differ only slightly, the brain may find too few differences to tell them apart. It's easy to mix up 運 and 連 (respectively, *UN, hako•bu*: to carry, fate; and *REN, tsu•reru*: pair, link), because one notices only the similar aspects of each kanji, ignoring the part that's different. The brain works in mysterious, self-defeating ways.

It can also be hard to differentiate between characters that combine identical components in similar layouts. I struggle with all these pairs:

選 (*SEN, era•bu*: to choose), as in 選手 (*senshu*: player [on a sports team])
港 (*KŌ, minato*: port), as in 空港 (*kūkō*: airport)

資 (*SHI*: capital, fund), as in 投資 (*tōshi*: investment)
貸 (*TAI, ka•su*: to lend, rent), as in 貸本 (*kashihon*: book for lending out)

料 (*RYŌ*: ingredients, fare), as in 料理 (*ryōri*: cooking)
科 (*KA*: branch, division), as in 教科書 (*kyōkasho*: textbook)

歩 (*HO, BU, aru•ku*: to walk), as in 歩行者 (*hokōsha*: pedestrian)
走 (*SŌ, hashi•ru*: to run), as in 走者 (*sōsha*: runner)

I'm often surprised the last pair confounds me, but their related meanings add to the confusion.

What's a kanji student to do about the vexing problem of look-alikes? Habein lays out a five-step strategy. The first three steps may not be too encouraging, relying as they do on memorization, but an unusual approach emerges in the fourth. Unfortunately, beginners will lack the prerequisite knowledge to benefit fully from her ideas. Habein's way of thinking is most suitable for intermediate or advanced students.

The Five Steps

Step One

Memorize the simplest kanji, such as:

小	*SHŌ, chii•sai, ko, o*: small
用	*YŌ, mochi•iru*: to use
県	*KEN*: prefecture

Since Habein wrote her book and since the first printing of *Crazy for Kanji,* the Jōyō list has lost 5 characters and gained 191. Thus, Habein's percentages may no longer be accurate.

One can trace these characters back to ancient pictures. As such, they're "indivisible" into smaller kanji. Thus, Habein calls these "single-unit kanji." Accounting for 9 percent of the 1,945 Jōyō kanji (discussed in Exhibit 13, "Just the Facts: How Many Kanji Does It Take?"), single-unit kanji appear in many complicated characters. Therefore, knowing the forms and meanings of basic ones will help you distinguish complex kanji. Habein notes, for example, that recognizing 犬 as "dog" will prove handy when you study 伏 (*FUKU, fu•seru*: to lie prostrate, hide), affording the mnemonic "a dog which shows submission by lying prostrate."

Step Two

Nearly a quarter of Jōyō kanji are "semantic" composites, or *kaiimoji* (会意文字), in which all parts contribute to the meaning. The components never relate to the pronunciation. According to Habein, in 解 (*KAI, GE, to•ku, hodo•ku*) the components 角 (animal horn), 刀 (sword or edged tool), and 牛 (cow) collectively create the meaning of "horn separated from an ox with an edged tool." In other words, 解 means "to take apart." To make such analyses, she recommends memorizing the meanings of all components and even their etymology. (Easier said than done.)

Step Three

Habein believes you should learn common radicals and their variant forms, as well as any variations in their meanings. Note, for instance, that 人 turns into イ (as in 傾, *KEI, katamu•ku:* to incline) or even 𠆢 (as in 企, *KI, kuwada•teru:* to plan). Knowing such variants will help you analyze all types of kanji.

Step Four

Habein says that 67 percent of Jōyō kanji are "phonetic" composites, or *keiseimoji* (形声文字). That is, one component (the radical or the "semantic component") relates to the meaning of the whole character, whereas the "phonetic component" relates to the on-yomi. As we saw in Exhibit 26, the following kanji contain the component 寺, which can also stand alone, meaning "temple" *(JI, tera):*

侍	*JI, samurai:* samurai
時	*JI, toki:* hour, time
持	*JI, mo•tsu:* to possess
峙	*JI, sobata•tsu:* to tower, soar
痔	*JI:* hemorrhoids
詩	*SHI:* poetry
待	*TAI, ma•tsu:* to wait
特	*TOKU:* special
等	*TŌ, hito•shii:* equal rank

Exhibit 26 showed that if you know the on-yomi of the phonetic component, you can sometimes determine the reading of the whole kanji. In this list, the *on*-echo *JI* applies two-thirds of the time, including in 詩 *(SHI),* which is what we might call an "approximate echo," since the sounds *JI* and *SHI* are so close. (Writing them in hiragana as じ *(JI)* and し *(SHI)* makes the similarity more obvious.)

This much is familiar. But Habein takes her strategy further, suggesting that you do two things:

a. Memorize all on-yomi. According to Habein, about 98 percent of Jōyō kanji have on-yomi. Approximately 40 percent of Jōyō have *only* on-yomi, no kun-yomi. Given the prevalence of on-yomi and the possibility of an *on*-echo, mastering on-yomi will help you guess the readings of kanji you've never seen. (Again, much easier said than done.)

b. Learn to identify phonetic components within kanji. Here are a few things to look for:

- The single-unit kanji hidden inside: If you see a simple kanji tucked within a more complex one, the simple one could be your phonetic. With the kanji in the list above, however, the phonetic 寺 is not a single-unit kanji. Instead, it's made of two indivisible components: 土 (*DO, tsuchi:* soil) and 寸 (*SUN:* inch). Habein calls 寸 the "semantic component" of 寺.
- Position within the kanji: As you know, the phonetic component often appears on the right-hand side, with the radical to the left.
- Process of elimination: If you determine the semantic component, then you've narrowed down the choices for the phonetic component. In 持, the radical is 扌, which gives the meaning of "hand." So 寺 must be the phonetic.

Step Five

Finally, Habein thinks you should learn how the sound of a phonetic component can change as it pops up in kanji that share approximate echoes. For example, the phonetic 加 has an on-yomi of *KA.* When this simple kanji becomes part of a more complex character, it may retain its on-yomi (as in 架, *KA, kake•ru:* to lay across), or the sound may mutate from *KA* to *GA* (as in 賀, *GA:* to congratulate). Changing *k* to *g* is a simple act of "voicing," or *nigori* (濁り). *Nigori* occurs when one adds a *tenten* (゛) to certain neutral syllables. So it is that *HŌ* and *BŌ* share a series in Exhibit 26, as do *SEN* and *ZEN*, as well as *TAI* and *DAI.* But, as Habein points out, the linked sounds in an on-echo series don't always follow typical voicing patterns. Here are some of the many aberrations she lists:

- *m* and *b* coexist in a series (possibly with *k*)
  e.g., *MAI, BAI,* and *KAI* are readings for kanji with the echoing shape 毎
- *s* and *t/ch* coexist in a series
  e.g., *SHITSU, TETSU,* and *CHITSU* are readings for kanji with the echoing shape 失
- *k* and *r* coexist in a series
  e.g., *KA* and *RA* are readings for kanji with the echoing shape 果

Testing the Theory

So there you have it, the nuts and bolts of Habein's strategy. Now, let's see it in action with a few examples. Can you identify the phonetic and semantic components in the following characters?

究　　汁　　視　　政

Not so easy, huh? Here's how they break down, using Habein's methods and conclusions:

究 (*KYŪ, kiwa•meru:* to study exhaustively)
Phonetic: 九 (*KYŪ:* nine), giving this character the on-yomi of *KYŪ*
Semantic: 宀 (roof)
Reasoning: If you recognize this character as the *kyū* in *kenkyū* (research), then you know the on-yomi you're looking for, and you can recognize 九 as the phonetic. But if you already knew how to read 究, you wouldn't need to bother with Habein's strategy. The other way to reason through this is to know that, of the three components represented therein (宀, 儿, and 九), only the first two can be radicals. If they can never be phonetics (which is true in this case), then 九 would have to be the phonetic. If you remember this phonetic from Exhibit 26, you may already have known that.

汁 (*JŪ, shiru, tsuyu:* juice)
Phonetic: 十 (*JŪ:* ten)
Semantic: 氵 (water, liquid)
Reasoning: This one is easier, as 氵 is a radical and 十 isn't. Plus, the phonetic is in the standard position on the right. And again, you saw this phonetic in Exhibit 26.

視 (*SHI:* to see, look at)
Phonetic: 礻 (*SHI, JI:* altar). This is a variant of 示.
Semantic: 見 (to see). This component clearly lends its meaning to 視.
Reasoning: It might look as if 見 could break down further to 目 (eye) and 儿, and indeed Spahn identifies 目 as the radical in 見. But Habein calls 見 a radical. Unfortunately, 礻 can also be a radical, which makes this example really tricky. If you already knew the on-yomi of 視, then you might realize that it doesn't match the on-yomi of 見, *KEN,* which you saw in Exhibit 26. But if you did know how to read 視, you wouldn't need this analysis.

Similarly, if you knew from context that 視 meant "to see," then you'd conclude that 見 must be the semantic, as it has a related meaning. That would make 礻 the phonetic. If you had none of that information, though, Habein's strategy wouldn't seem to serve you here.

政 (*SEI, SHŌ:* government)
Phonetic: 正 (*SEI, SHŌ:* correct)
Semantic: 攵 (to strike)
Reasoning: If you happen to know the on-yomi of 正 and 政, then you're all set to draw the right conclusions. But again, that gets the process backward. Just know that 攵 is a radical and that 正 isn't (though the similar-looking 止 is).

This analysis is all very well and good if we know a character to be a phonetic composite (or *keiseimoji*). But what if it's a semantic composite (or *kaiimoji*), as a quarter of the Jōyō are? How can we figure out which type a kanji is? If you split up a character into the major parts (usually two or three) and those parts can all stand on their own as kanji, you likely have a semantic composite. For instance, in 虹 (*niji:* rainbow), both 虫 (*CHŪ, mushi:* insect) and 工 (*KŌ:* construction) are characters. By contrast, in a phonetic composite such as 汁, the water radical can't stand alone as a kanji. That's the general clue, though there are exceptions.

Confusing matters more, Habein notes that certain components sometimes act as phonetics, sometimes as semantics. In 韻 (*IN:* rhyme, elegant), 員 serves as a phonetic, affording an *on*-echo. But in 損 (*SON:* loss, damage; *sokona•u:* to harm), 員 is a semantic and means "round, tripod kettle."

That inconsistency is certainly bothersome. But it's just a blip in the larger picture. And as I look at that picture, I can't help but ask whether all of this can truly help us distinguish look-alikes. It must help people who can think as Habein does. I'm not one of them. The only thing that helps me identify radicals, phonetics, and *on*-echoes and to distinguish two look-alike kanji is to have a solid grasp of that information. Habein is certainly advocating that, but in a more abstract way that one can use to generalize to the unknown. Her method may not work for everyone, but it opens up a broad perspective on kanji, allowing us to analyze them on a whole other level if we're so inclined.

Classification of Characters

We've seen several ways in which the parts of a character can relate to one another. Scholars have identified six types of character composition, calling these categories the *rikusho* (六書: six + writing). But two are so fuzzily defined that even experts sound ill at ease when discussing them. And then there's *kokuji,* a seventh type pertaining only to Japan. If you choose to concern yourself with these categories (and you can actually live a full, satisfying life without doing so!), don't get too hung up on their definitions and differences, because there's considerable overlap.

Four Basic Types

Type 1: *Shōkeimoji* (象形文字), pictograms

Definition: Simple characters resembling the objects they represent.

Example: 門 (*MON, kado:* gate).

What the category name means: *Shōkei* (象形) means "hieroglyphics" and breaks down as "image" + "shape." *Moji* (文字) breaks down as "character" + "character" and means "character." So *shōkeimoji* are characters derived from the shapes of objects.

Where this type appears in the book: The main text of the Introduction; Exhibit 14, "Just the Facts: Pictograms and Ideograms."

Type 2: *Shijimoji* (指事文字), ideograms

Definition: Characters symbolizing abstract concepts (e.g., numbers and directions).

Example: 上 (*JŌ, ue:* above).

What the category name means: As 指 means "to point to" and 事 means "thing, matter," *shiji* means "pointing to a thing."

Where this type appears in the book: Exhibit 14, "Just the Facts: Pictograms and Ideograms."

Frequency of usage: In *Decoding Kanji,* Habein collectively refers to Types 1 and 2 as "single-unit" kanji and says they account for about 9 percent of all characters. However, the numbers go up when you consider the 200 most commonly used characters; Habein says about 32 percent are single-unit kanji.

Type 3: *Kaiimoji* (会意文字), semantic composites

Definition: Characters in which all components contribute to the meaning.

Example: 花 (*KA, KE, hana:* flower), since a flower is grass (艹) that changes (化).

What the category name means: "Meeting" (会) + "meaning" (意). Components meet within a kanji and create a joint meaning.

Where this type appears in the book: Exhibit 29, "Thematic Explorations: Strategies for Conquering Look-Alikes"; Exhibit 31, "Thematic Explorations: Elegant Etymology."

Frequency of usage: Habein says 24 percent of all kanji are *kaiimoji.*

Type 4: *Keiseimoji* (形声文字), semantic-phonetic composites

Definition: Characters that combine a radical (the semantic aspect) and a component governing the sound (the phonetic).

Example: 組 (*SO, kumi:* group, set), as in 番組 (*bangumi:* program). In 組, the component 糸 lends the meaning of "thread," whereas 且 contributes the sound *SO.* In keeping with the *on*-echo principle, the autonomous kanji 且 (furthermore, besides) also has the on-yomi of *SO* or *SHO.*

What the category name means: "Shape" (形) + "voice" (声). In other words, the shape (形) of one component relates to the meaning, whereas another component relates to the sound (声) of the kanji.

Where this type appears in the book: Exhibit 26, "Just the Facts: The *On*-Echo"; Exhibit 29, "Thematic Explorations: Strategies for Conquering Look-Alikes."

Frequency of usage: Most characters are Type 4. Habein estimates that 67 percent of characters fall into this category, whereas Kenneth Henshall puts the figure at a whopping 85 percent in *A Guide to Remembering Japanese Characters.* That's quite a discrepancy, and it must come down to fuzzy boundaries between these categories.

Special note: There's such a thing as *kaii-keiseimoji,* a category spanning Types 3 and 4. This kind of kanji evolved as other *keiseimoji* did. That is, the Chinese formed such a character by joining two components.

One affected the meaning of the new kanji, and the other influenced both the sound and the meaning. For example, when the "sickness" radical 疒 and 皮 combined to form 疲 (HI, tsuka•reru: to be tired), 皮 (HI, kawa) contributed both its sound (HI) and its meaning (skin). Hence, 疲 breaks down as "sick" + "skin," approximating "tiredness." This kanji qualifies not only as *keiseimoji* but also as *kaiimoji*, so it's considered to be *kaii-keiseimoji*.

Three More Types

The next two categories relate to things that have happened to characters post-creation, rather than relating to the actual creation process.

Type 5: *Tenchūmoji* (転注文字), **characters with borrowed or derived meanings or pronunciations**

Definition: Characters reassigned to represent new and possibly associated concepts. In this process, many kanji have undergone changes in meaning or pronunciation or both.

Example: 鳴 (MEI, na•ku, na•ru: nonhuman cry). When read as *na•ku*, this kanji (which combines "mouth" and "bird" in a *kaiimoji* fashion) originally referred to a bird's chirping. Later it came to symbolize the cries of other animals. Now, when read as *na•ru,* 鳴 stands for the chiming of a doorbell, the ringing of a phone, or sounds from other machines.

What the category name means: If you recognize 転 from 自転車 (*jitensha:* bicycle), you may recall that this kanji means "to roll, turn." And 注 means "to pour." Perhaps meaning rolls or pours from one character to another, turning into something new.

Where this type appears in the book: Nowhere specific.

Frequency of usage: Unknown (at least to me).

Special note: Henshall's introduction has the best information I've found on this. He says that since "the majority of characters have undergone some change of meaning, now often displaying extended or associated meanings in addition to or in place of their original meanings . . . , and since a very large number have also experienced a change in pronunciation, any category based upon such changes is now in effect pointless, though it may have had some relevance in the second century" (xviii).

Type 6: *Kashamoji* or *kashakumoji* (仮借文字), **phonetically borrowed characters**

Definition: Characters used just for their sounds, regardless of the original meanings.

Example: In China, the pictogram 来 meant "wheat." The word for "wheat" sounded just like the word for "to come," so 来 also became the character for that verb. This process continued in Japan, notably when the Japanese chose kanji to represent country names. For example, 亜米利加 (*a-me-ri-ka*) stands for "America," and the Japanese made this match purely on the basis of phonetics, with no regard for the meanings of the kanji.

What the category name means: "Temporary" or "false" (仮) + "borrow" (借).

Where this type appears in the book: Exhibit 36, "Just the Facts: Doesn't Sound the Way It's Spelled," Type 1; Exhibit 52, "Just the Facts: Country Kanji."

Frequency of usage: Unknown to me.

Type 7: *Kokuji* (国字), **literally "national characters," also known as** 和製漢字 (*wasei kanji:* **Chinese characters made in Japan)**

Definition: Kanji invented in Japan. The components came from China, but the arrangement and composite meaning are strictly Japanese. *Kokuji* only have kun-yomi, never on-yomi, as on-yomi come from China. But there's one exception; 働 (to work) has the kun-yomi of *hatara•ku* and the on-yomi of DŌ.

Example: 峠 (*tōge:* mountain pass, the mountain itself), which combines 山 (mountain) with 上 (up) and 下 (down). Other examples include 畑 (*hatake:* field of crops) and 辻 (*tsuji:* crossroads, street).

What the category name means: 国 (KOKU, kuni) is "country," so these are the characters of Japan.

Where this type appears in the book: Nowhere specific.

Frequency of usage: Henshall says only a dozen or so kokuji exist, most of them ideographic. Another source claims that there are hundreds, though many are rarely used. Kanji for fish and plant names are often of Japanese origin.

Special note: See Exhibit 36, "Just the Facts: Doesn't Sound the Way It's Spelled," for a discussion of *kokkun,* a concept somewhat related to *kokuji.*

Elegant Etymology

A kanji such as 薬 (*YAKU, kusuri:* medicine) breaks down in the neatest of ways: 艹 means "grass," and 楽 (*RAKU, tano•shii*) means "pleasure." Pleasurable grass as medicine! It can be tempting to break down all singletons this way, looking for built-in lyricism or wittiness. But then there's the matter of sound. As we've seen in several exhibits (such as 26, "Just the Facts: The *On*-Echo," and 29, "Thematic Explorations: Strategies for Conquering Look-Alikes"), the majority of kanji contain phonetic components, pieces that determine pronunciation and contribute nothing to the meaning. Mindful of this, we might conclude that we're never to look at kanji in terms of how the parts add up to a larger meaning. But by thinking so restrictively, we'd miss out on a lot of fun, because the additive approach *does* work with a quarter of singleton kanji.

As we've seen, these are called "semantic" composites, or *kaiimoji*, 会意文字. This term breaks down as "meeting" + "meaning" + "characters" (or components that create new meanings when joined in a character). Let's examine some characters to see what they reveal. A list of the kanji used here, along with readings and meanings, appears at the end of the exhibit.

1. 働 (to work)　　　　イ + 動
　　　　　　　　　　　person + to move

   A further breakdown looks like this:

   動 (to move)　　　　重 + 力
   　　　　　　　　　　heavy + power

   Putting it all together, work happens when a person does heavy lifting.

2. 花 (flower)　　　　　艹 + 化
   　　　　　　　　　　grass + to change

   A flower is grass that changes. A further breakdown looks like this:

   化 (to change)　　　　イ + ヒ
   　　　　　　　　　　person + fallen person

   If a person turns into a fallen person, there has indeed been a change.

3. 困 (to be in trouble)　口 + 木
   　　　　　　　　　　　box + tree

A tree growing inside a box would be in trouble.

4. 妹 (younger sister)　　女 + 未
   　　　　　　　　　　woman + not yet

Younger sisters unite in outrage! This kanji implies that we're not yet women! Originally, though, 未 just meant "small."

5. 炒 (to stir-fry)　　　火 + 少
   　　　　　　　　　　fire + a little

With a little fire under the pan, you can stir-fry.

6. 趣 (tendency)　　　　走 + 取
   　　　　　　　　　　to run + to take

According to Henshall, 趣 originally referred to running after something to take hold of it. Then this character came to mean "go in a certain direction." Now it means "incline toward" or "tendency." A further breakdown:

取 (to take)　　　　耳 + 又
　　　　　　　　　ear + hand

Henshall says this likely refers to taking control of an animal by seizing its ear (to avoid being bitten).

7. 製 (to manufacture)　制 + 衣
   　　　　　　　　　　control + garment

Clothes manufacturing involves the control of garments, or whipping fabric into shape.

8. 貧 (poor)　　　　　　分 + 貝
   　　　　　　　　　　to divide + money

When you divide money too many ways, there's little left, and people are poor.

9. 痴 (foolish)　　　　　疒 + 知
   　　　　　　　　　　sickness + to know

This breakdown seems apt, as 痴 appears in 痴漢, *chikan,* a pervert who frequents crowded trains. A further breakdown looks like this:

知 (to know)　　　　矢 + 口
　　　　　　　　　　arrow, dart + mouth

As Dartmouth College is a source of knowledge, this is easy to remember.

10. 盲 (blind)　　　　亡 + 目
　　　　　　　　　　to die + eye

If your eye "died," it would leave you blind.

11. 劣 (to be inferior)　　少 + 力
　　　　　　　　　　a little + power

Feeling inferior involves feeling powerless, so although Henshall interprets 劣 as "little strength," I see no reason not to go with the usual meaning of 力 as "power" or "ability."

Kanji Used in This Exhibit

Notice the *on*-echoes in this list:

1. 働　*DŌ, hatara•ku:* to work
   イ　This isn't an autonomous kanji but a radical meaning "person."
   動　*DŌ, ugo•ku:* to move
   重　*JŪ, CHŌ, omo•i:* heavy, serious
   力　*RYOKU, RIKI, chikara:* power

2. 花　*KA, KE, hana:* flower
   艹　This isn't an autonomous kanji but a radical meaning "grass."
   化　*KA:* to make into, transform; *KE, ba•kasu:* to bewitch, enchant, deceive
   イ　This isn't an autonomous kanji but a radical meaning "person."
   ヒ　This isn't an autonomous kanji but a component meaning "fallen person."

3. 困　*KON, koma•ru:* to be in trouble
   囗　As a radical, this means "enclosure."
   木　*BOKU, MOKU, ki:* tree, wood

4. 妹　*MAI, imōto:* younger sister
   女　*JO, onna:* woman, female
   未　*MI, mada, ima•da:* not yet, still

5. 炒　*SHŌ, SŌ, i•ru:* to roast, toast, stir-fry; *ita•meru:* to stir-fry
   火　*KA, hi:* fire
   少　*SHŌ, suko•shi, suku•nai:* a little, few

6. 趣　*SHU, omomuki:* purport, gist, taste, elegance
   走　*SŌ, hashi•ru:* to run
   取　*SHU, to•ru:* to take, control
   耳　*JI, mimi:* ear
   又　As an autonomous kanji, this is pronounced *mata* and means "again." As a component in a larger kanji such as 趣 and 取, it means "right hand."

7. 製　*SEI:* to manufacture
   制　*SEI:* control, system, with the associated meaning here of "to cut to shape"
   衣　*I, koromo:* garment

8. 貧　*HIN, BIN, mazu•shii:* poor, meager
   分　*BUN, wa•keru:* to divide
   貝　*kai:* shell, with the associated meaning of "money"

9. 痴　*CHI:* foolish
   疒　This isn't an autonomous kanji but a radical meaning "sickness."
   知　*CHI, shi•ru:* to know
   矢　*SHI, ya:* arrow, dart
   口　*KŌ, KU, kuchi:* mouth

10. 盲　*MO, BŌ, mekura, meshii:* blind
    亡　*BŌ, MŌ:* dead; *na•kunaru:* to die
    目　*MOKU, BOKU, me:* eye

11. 劣　*RETSU, oto•ru:* to be inferior
    少　*SHŌ, suko•shi, suku•nai:* a little, few
    力　*RYOKU, RIKI, chikara:* power, ability

Charmingly Illogical Characters

For every character that makes you marvel at its elegant etymology, plenty more leave you smiling with bemusement. Some can legitimately be read as semantic composites (*kaiimoji*, as explored in Exhibits 30 and 31); others can't. But I recommend putting all such considerations aside for now and just enjoying the illogic of these composites. A full explanation of each kanji appears at the end of the exhibit.

1. 虹 (rainbow)　　　虫 + 工
   insect + construction

   Did someone think that insects constructed rainbows as colorful "webs"?

2. 像 (image)　　　イ + 象
   person + elephant

   What a strange self-image that person has, seeing himself as elephantine!

3. 道 (road, way)　　　辶 + 首
   movement + neck

   A moving neck makes me think of a bobblehead!

4. 静 (quiet, peaceful)　　　青 + 争
   blue, green + dispute

   Can a dispute of any color be quiet and peaceful? The Japanese tend not to differentiate blue and green, so they are interchangeable here. Interestingly, 争 means "dispute" but helps form this "peaceful" kanji. A further breakdown of 青 looks like this:

   青 (blue, green)　　　生 + 月
   life + moon

   Blue is the color of life on the moon!

5. 盗 (to steal)　　　次 + 皿
   next + plate

   Careful—the thief will steal your plate next! Here's a further breakdown:

   次 (next)　　　冫 + 欠
   ice + lack

   Next, after stealing the plate, he'll lament the lack of ice.

6. 家 (house)　　　宀 + 豕
   roof + pig

   Put a pig under a roof, and it will really feel like a house!

7. 泊 (to stay overnight) 氵 + 白
   water + white

   If you go white-water rafting, there's a great place to stay overnight.

8. 姉 (elder sister)　　　女 + 市
   woman + city

   Her elder sister is a woman of the city.

9. 齢 (age)　　　歯 + 令
   tooth + order

   As you age, it's important to keep your teeth in order.

10. 件 (matter, item, case) イ + 牛
    person + cow

    What's the matter with that person and cow?!

Kanji Used in This Exhibit

Once again, notice *on*-echoes in these *yomi*:

1. 虹　*KŌ, niji:* rainbow
   虫　*CHŪ, mushi:* insect
   工　*KŌ:* artisan, construction, craft, skill

2. 像　*ZŌ, SHŌ, katachi:* image
   イ　This isn't an autonomous kanji but a radical meaning "person."
   象　*ZŌ:* elephant; *SHŌ:* image; *katado•ru:* to pattern after, imitate

3. 道　*DŌ, TŌ, michi:* road, way
   辶　This isn't an autonomous kanji but a radical meaning "movement."
   首　*SHU, kubi:* neck, head, beginning

4. 静　*SEI, JŌ, shizu•ka:* quiet, peaceful, calm
　　青　*SEI, SHŌ, ao•i:* blue, green, unripe
　　争　*SŌ, araso•u:* to dispute, argue, contend for
　　生　*SEI, SHŌ:* life; *i•kiru:* to live
　　月　*GETSU, GATSU, tsuki:* moon, month

5. 盗　*TŌ, nusu•mu:* to steal
　　次　*JI, SHI, tsugi:* next
　　皿　*BEI, sara:* plate, dish
　　ン　This isn't an autonomous kanji but a radical meaning "ice."
　　欠　*KETSU, ka•ku:* lack

6. 家　*KA:* house, family, profession; *ie:* house
　　宀　This isn't an autonomous kanji but a radical meaning "roof."
　　豕　*SHI, inoko:* pig

7. 泊　*HAKU, to•maru:* to stay overnight
　　氵　This isn't an autonomous kanji but a radical meaning "water."
　　白　*HAKU, shiro•i:* white

8. 姉　*SHI, ane:* elder sister
　　女　*JO, onna:* woman
　　市　*SHI:* city, town; market; *ichi:* market, fair

9. 齢　*REI, yowai:* age
　　歯　*SHI, ha:* tooth
　　令　*REI, RYŌ:* order, command, good

10. 件　*KEN:* matter, item, case
　　イ　This isn't an autonomous kanji but a radical meaning "person."
　　牛　*GYŪ, ushi:* cow

Every year, on February 15 and 16, Yokote City in the northern Japanese prefecture of Akita holds a festival called Kamakura. For this four-hundred-year-old festival, people make more than a hundred *kamakura*. A *kamakura* is a room carved out of a mound of snow. Children sit in the snow houses, inviting passers-by to come in and enjoy sweet sake and snacks. The city hall has a permanent *kamakura* displayed in a freezing-cold room that visitors can enter. The photo is of a City Hall plaque with information about the festival. The plaque explains the origin of the name "Yokote."

Just Add Water

To how many things can you add water, creating a new substance? Water + powder = soapsuds. And water + dirt = mud. But in Japan it works differently, in terms of kanji, anyway. When the water radical 氵 combines with certain kanji, it produces new and sometimes surprising characters.

1. 洗   *SEN, ara•u*
   water + previous = to wash

   The kanji 洗 appears in お手洗い (*otearai:* bathroom), 洗脳 (*sennō:* brainwashing), and 丸洗い (*maruarai:* washing a kimono without taking it apart).

2. 洋   *YŌ*
   water + sheep = ocean, with an associated meaning of "Western"

   The kanji 洋 appears in 太平洋 (*Taiheiyō:* Pacific Ocean), 東洋 (*tōyō:* the Orient), and 洋食 (*yōshoku:* Western food).

3. 海   *KAI, umi*
   water + every = sea

   The kanji 海 appears in 海水 (*kaisui:* seawater), 海員 (*kaiin:* sailor), 海馬 (*kaiba:* seahorse), and 海坊主 (*umibōzu:* sea monster).

4. 汗   *KAN, ase*
   water + dry = sweat

   The kanji 汗 appears in 汗顔 (*kangan:* sweating from shame).

5. 法   *HŌ, nori*
   water + to leave = method, law

   The kanji 法 appears in 文法 (*bunpō:* grammar), 方法 (*hōhō:* method), and 法律 (*hōritsu:* law). The character is also in 法皇 (*hōō:* ex-emperor who has become a monk), as well as 一寸法師, *issunbōshi*, translated as "dwarf, midget, Tom Thumb."

6. 油   *YU, YŪ, abura*
   water + reason = oil

   The kanji 油 appears in 油絵 (*aburae:* oil painting) and 醤油 (*shōyu:* soy sauce).

7. 決   *KETSU, ki•meru*
   water + to pull apart = to decide

   The kanji 決 appears in 決定 (*kettei:* decision, determination), 決起 (*kekki:* springing to one's feet with renewed resolve), 決勝点 (*kesshōten:* goal, finish line), and the rhyming word 決裂 (*ketsuretsu:* breakdown, rupture, collapse).

8. 泣   *KYŪ, na•ku*
   water + to stand = to cry

   These components prompted an older male classmate of mine to say, "I usually sit down to cry." The kanji 泣 appears in 男泣き (*otokonaki:* weeping in spite of being a man), 泣き笑い (*nakiwarai:* smiling through tears), 泣き腫 (*nakiha•rasu:* to get swollen eyes from crying), 泣き上戸 (*nakijōgo:* maudlin drinker), and 嬉し泣き (*ureshinaki:* crying for joy).

9. 注   *CHŪ, soso•gu*
   water + master = to pour

   The kanji 注 appears in 注文 (*chūmon:* [food] order) and 注意 (*chūi:* attention, warning, caution).

10. 治   *SHI, JI, nao•su, nao•ru*
    water + platform, self = to govern, heal

    The kanji 治 appears in 政治家 (*seijika:* politician) and 明治 (*Meiji:* the era from 1868 to 1912).

11. 濃   *NŌ, ko•i*
    water + farming = thick, deep, rich

    Shouldn't wet farming produce the kanji for "rice"? The character 濃 has to do with the concentration of liquids and colors, as in 濃度 (*nōdo:* degree of concentration) and 濃紫 (*komurasaki:* deep purple).

12. 活   *KATSU, i•kiru*
    water + tongue = life, activity

    If your tongue isn't wet, you're no longer alive! The kanji 活 appears in 生活 (*seikatsu:* life), 活力 (*katsuryoku:* vitality, vigor) , and 活動 (*katsudō:* activity).

The Missing Link

In the following chain, each kanji builds on the previous one in terms of shape:

十	田	由	油
JŪ, tō	*DEN, ta*	*YU, yoshi*	*YU, abura*
ten	rice field	reason	oil

When kanji books depict the evolution of characters, they show how the pictograph of, say, a horse has changed over time, becoming the unhorselike 馬 used today. This game isn't about that. Instead, it's a bit of fun with similar-looking kanji that may not have evolved from the same pictograph. (In some cases, the kanji *are* related and have *on*-echoes. For instance, 由 and 油 both have on-yomi of *YU*.) Below you'll find kanji chains with "missing links," as in this one:

上	____	正
JŌ	*SHI*	*SHŌ*
ue	to•maru	tada•shii
above	to stop	correct

Your task is to fill in the omitted information. The completed chain looks like this:

上	止	正

Answers appear in the Answer Key. *Ganbatte kudasai!*

1.
小	____	歩	渉
SHŌ	*SHŌ*	*HO*	*SHŌ*
chii•sai, ko	suku•nai	aru•ku	wata•ru
small	few	to walk	to go across

2.
小	____	景	影
SHŌ	*KYŌ, KEI*	*KE, KEI*	*EI*
chii•sai, ko	—	—	kage
small	capital	view	shadow

3.
目	____	首	道
MOKU, me	*JI, mizuka•ra*	*SHU, kubi*	*DŌ, michi*
eye	self	neck	way

4.
日	白	____	薬
NICHI	*HAKU*	*RAKU*	*YAKU*
hi	shiro•i	tano•shii	kusuri
sun, day	white	enjoyable	medicine

5.
日	____	簡
NICHI	*KAN*	*KAN*
hi	aida	—
sun, day	between	simple

6.
人	____	次	資
JIN	*KETSU*	*JI*	*SHI*
hito	ka•keru	tsugi	—
person	to lack	next	capital, fund

7.
口	____	俗
KŌ, KU	*KOKU*	*ZOKU*
kuchi	tani	—
mouth	valley	worldliness, vulgarity

8.
口	____	苦
KŌ, KU	*KO*	*KU*
kuchi	furu•i	niga•i, kuru•shii
mouth	old	bitter, painful, to suffer

9.
口	____	若	匿
KŌ, KU	*U, YŪ*	*JAKU*	*TOKU*
kuchi	migi	waka•i	—
mouth	right	young	to hide

10.
口	____	格
KŌ, KU	*KAKU*	*KAKU*
kuchi	ono•ono	—
mouth	each	structure, frame, rank

11.
雨	____	電
U	*RAI*	*DEN*
ame	kaminari	—
rain	thunder, lightning	electricity

12.
木	____	凍
MOKU	*TŌ*	*TŌ*
ki	higashi	kogo•eru
tree	east	to freeze

13.
米	____	齢
BEI	*SHI*	*REI*
kome	ha	yowai
raw rice	tooth	age

14.
耳	____	趣
JI	*SHU*	*SHU*
mimi	to•ru	omomuki
ear	to take	meaning, gist, taste

15.
立	____	竜	滝
RITSU	*ON*	*RYŪ*	—
ta•tsu	oto	tatsu	taki
to stand	sound	dragon	waterfall

Kana Needed: N / Kanji Level: 0 / Difficulty Level: 2

Create a Kanji

Drawing from the pool of components below, assemble as many characters as you can. For example, with 門 and 日, you could form 間.

Write each character in a blank below. A few tips are in order:

• If you've completed Exhibit 34, look there for inspiration. The Answer Key lists eight answers for Exhibit 35, all of which come from the kanji displayed in the completed version of Exhibit 34. Other answers for Exhibit 35 are possible, but they're not included in the Answer Key.

• Use components only once within a character, but feel free to use them again whenever you create new kanji.

• Don't take one of the components below as an answer. That is, 小 and 少 aren't answers, because that would be too easy!

Ganbatte kudasai!

一　し　ノ　亠　十　夂　小　口　日　少　立　竹　門　止

Kanji	On-Yomi	Kun-Yomi	Meaning
1. _____	_____	_____	_____
2. _____	_____	_____	_____
3. _____	_____	_____	_____
4. _____	_____	_____	_____
5. _____	_____	_____	_____
6. _____	_____	_____	_____
7. _____	_____	_____	_____
8. _____	_____	_____	_____

COMPOUNDING THE PLEASURE

3

If you slice an English word in two and invert it, the resulting word is meaningless. Let's try this with the word "English":

> eng lish
> lish eng

We've produced gibberish. By contrast, if you cut a Japanese word between its kanji and invert it, you're more likely to produce a real word:

> 会社 (*kai-sha:* company)
> 社会 (*sha-kai:* society)

These characters are truly an odd couple; 会 means "to meet," and 社 means "shrine." But both combinations produce words.

This experiment drives home how syllables are the foundation of Japanese compounds. It also shows how compounds have distinct parts loaded with meaning. By contrast, English words (such as "English") are strings of individual letters, and unless they have prefixes, suffixes, or clear roots in another language, they disintegrate into mush during dissection. Syllabic divisions are certainly beside the point in words such as "laundry," "blizzard," and "picture," to take a random sampling.

If you invert the syllables in Japanese compounds, there are four possible outcomes:

1. The meanings of the compounds and the syllabic sounds stay the same:

> 練 (to refine, train) and 習 (to learn, train)
> • 練習 (*ren-shū:* practice, exercise)
> • 習練 (*shū-ren:* training, discipline, drill)

平 (flat, even, calm) and 和 (peace, Japan)
- 平和 (*hei-wa:* peace)
- 和平 (*wa-hei:* peace)

Heiwa and *wahei* have slightly different meanings. *Heiwa* is more abstract, whereas *wahei* means something akin to "cease-fire."

2. Both the sounds and the meanings change:

花 (flower) and 落 (to drop, fall)
- 花落 (*hana-o•chi:* part of a plant where a flower has fallen off)
- 落花 (*rak-ka:* falling or scattered petals)

These syllables undergo a massive alteration in sound. In *hanaochi,* both halves are kun-yomi, whereas *rakka* combines two on-yomi. (Exhibit 36, "Just the Facts: Doesn't Sound the Way It's Spelled," shows how this second compound changes in a fascinating way with the addition of one common kanji. The exhibit then takes this thinking in the opposite direction with a discussion of ateji.)

3. The sound stays the same, but the meaning changes:

理 (reason, logic) and 論 (to discuss, debate)
- 理論 (*ri-ron:* theory)
- 論理 (*ron-ri:* logic)

数 (number) and 人 (people)
- 数人 (*sū-nin:* several people)
- 人数 (*nin-zū:* the number of people)

Sū and *zū* are the same on-yomi, but *zū* has been voiced.

始 (to begin, first) and 終 (to finish)
- 始終 (*shi-jū:* always, all the time)
- 終始 (*shū-shi:* from beginning to end)

Again, *shū* and *jū* are the same on-yomi, but *jū* has been voiced.

演 (to perform) and 出 (to go out)
- 演出 (*en-shutsu:* direction in a film or play)
- 出演 (*shutsu-en:* acting in a film or play)

4. The meaning stays the same but the pronunciation changes:

腹 (belly, guts) and 切 (to cut)
- 腹切 (*hara-ki•ri:* ritual suicide by disembowelment)
- 切腹 (*sep-puku:* ritual suicide by disembowelment)

Before seeing this pair of compounds, I'd wondered why there were two words for this concept. Japanese abounds in synonyms, but they seemed unnecessary in this case. I now realize that the two words are fundamentally the same, though you'd never know it to hear them. The first compound, 腹切, uses the kun-yomi of *hara* and *ki•ri,* whereas the second compound, 切腹, uses the on-yomi of *SETSU* and *FUKU.*

Compounds often work with a clean, mathematical logic, much as if they were equations. For example:

電車 (*densha:* train) = electricity + car
電話 (*denwa:* phone) = electricity + conversation
電池 (*denchi:* battery) = electricity + reservoir

For other elegant constructions, see Exhibit 37, "Compound Interest: Cool Compounds."

Of course, not all Japanese words are kanji compounds. Some words contain one character, such as 猫 (*neko:* cat) and 次 (*tsugi:* next). Other words have no kanji at all, such as particles (similar to English prepositions), which are written in hiragana. But the majority of Japanese words are indeed compounds. And that's great news for those of us who love seeing the wonderful ways in which kanji combine. Sometimes they also combine in crazy ways, as in Exhibit 38, "Compound Interest: Crazy Compounds."

Ground Rules for Compounds

Compounds (known as *jukugo,* 熟語, or "matured" + "language") are one part of the kanji world that's relatively straightforward and free from irregularities. You don't need too much information to feel comfortable with compounds, but these pointers should help.

- As you know, compounds generally combine on-yomi. To learn when that's *not* the case, see Exhibit 39, "Just the Facts: Combinational Exceptions."
- After kanji arrived in Japan, the Japanese attached their spoken language to compounds in various ways, as explained in Exhibit 40, "Just the Facts: *Wago, Kango,* and *Kokugo.*" As a result of that process, one compound could have multiple pronunciations (e.g., kun-kun combinations versus on-on combinations), usually with different meanings. For more on this, see Exhibit 41, "Just the Facts: Multiple Readings of Certain Compounds."
- Generally, a character can take any position in a

compound. That is, 化 (*KA, KE:* to transform) takes first position in 化生 (*kasei:* metamorphosis), second position in 道化師 (*dōkeshi:* clown), and third position in 有機化学 (*yūki kagaku:* organic chemistry). In all cases, the kanji imparts its meaning to the word. However, some kanji also serve as prefixes or suffixes (collectively, "affixes"), including 化. At the end of a word, 化 means "-ization," as in 専門化 (*senmonka:* specialization). You may be shocked by the plethora of affixes in Japanese. To learn more, see Exhibit 42, "Just the Facts: Helping Hands."

- When a kanji doesn't occupy the first position of a compound, the yomi sometimes undergoes slight spelling changes. Take, for instance, 力強い (*chikara-zuyoi:* forceful, vigorous, emboldened). The *tsu* of *tsuyoi* has become *zu*. This voicing can also happen when on-yomi combine, as we noted with 人数 (*ninzū:* number of people) and 始終 (*shijū:* always, all the time). Remember this changeability when searching for yomi in a dictionary. You may need to look under *shi,* not *ji,* and so on. Some voicing patterns appeared in Exhibit 26, "Just the Facts: The *On*-Echo," and Exhibit 29, "Thematic Explorations: Strategies for Conquering Look-Alikes." But the best reference for this is the section "*Tenten* and *Maru*" in Exhibit 16, "Just the Facts: The Japanese Syllables," from the Introduction.

- The kanji within a word relate to each other in different ways, creating various categories of compounds. To find out about this, see Exhibit 43, "Just the Facts: How Kanji Modify Each Other in Compounds."

So that's it! There's not an encyclopedic amount to know. You just yoke a couple of kanji together and form a word, right? Not so fast! Exhibit 44, "Game: Will the Real Compound Please Stand Up?" may well change that way of thinking.

Sound-Alikes and Look-Alikes

Having grasped the fundamentals of compounds, we can now tackle the homonym problem mentioned in the Preface. How can kanji help us make sense of the scads of Japanese compounds that sound alike? To find out, see Exhibit 45, "Thematic Explorations: Homonyms and Near Homonyms," as well as "Game: Homonym Match-Up." To find out why there are so many Japanese homonyms in the first place, read Exhibit 46, "Thematic Explorations: Syllabic Similarity."

Apart from sounding alike, kanji compounds can also look alike! That's right, we didn't leave behind look-alike characters when we moved from singletons to compounds. Whole compounds can resemble each other. They can also contain look-alike characters. Check this out in Exhibit 47, "Thematic Explorations: Look-Alikes in Compounds."

The Thrill of a Good Breakdown

It's frightfully easy to overlook the crucial thing to do with compounds—enjoy them! Take them apart and see what they mean. Find the puns or elegance hidden in words. Such discoveries will make all your work with kanji worthwhile!

Now, you may not find definitive answers about why compounds mean what they do. It's easier to find reference material in English about the breakdown of characters than about the etymology of compounds. This is strange, because most characters predated compounds by a good many years and should therefore be more shrouded in mystery. But on the bright side, this leaves you lots of room to interpret compounds as you wish, with no one informing you that you're wrong!

Most Japanese people don't analyze compounds much; being so close to their own language, native speakers often miss the sheer delight of it. But you don't have to miss a thing. Exhibit 48, "Compound Interest: Wonderful Words," will get you off to a running start.

Doesn't Sound the Way It's Spelled

Here's a riddle for you. If 花 (flower) and 落 (to fall) combine in 落花 (rakka) to mean "falling or scattered petals," then what do you get when you add 生 (SEI: life), resulting in 落花生 (rakkasei)? Falling live petals? A life of scattering petals? Life is like a box of scattered petals? Wrong in all cases. *Rakkasei* means "peanut"!

How did this come to be? Well, it all started when the peanut arrived in China long ago. Not knowing what to call it, the Chinese decided to observe the plant closely before choosing a name. (Imagine a group of people huddled around a plant, watching, waiting, hoping it will do something!)

This perceptive bunch realized that the peanut plant develops flowers quite close to the the ground. After a peanut flower pollinates itself, its petals fall. The fertilized ovary grows down away from the plant, forming a stem that enables the ovary to penetrate the soil. The ovary becomes a peanut, and because it grows underground, it seems as if the peanut plant has given birth to a new life. Or rather, according to the kanji that the Chinese chose, "Dropped flowers (create) life."

Now, what's the opposite of peanuts? Umm . . . jelly? Butter? Popcorn? No, figs! Whereas the peanut arrived in China before anyone had devised a name for it or had matched the concept of "peanut" to the characters 落花生, sometimes the process worked the other way around, as with the fig.

The preliterate Japanese called the fig *ichijiku*. After importing kanji, they assigned Chinese characters to the words in their language (including *ichijiku*). But the Japanese took their time choosing the right kanji. Just as the Chinese did with the peanut, the Japanese observed the fig closely. And they noticed that you can't see flowers on the exterior of a fig plant because the small white flowers grow inside the fruit. To represent *ichijiku*, a fruit with no flower, they chose 無花果, or "not" + "flower" + "fruit."

Here's the kicker—none of these kanji carries the sounds *i, chi, ji,* or *ku*. Those who are proficient in kanji know not to sound out the word (which would yield *mukaka,* if one went strictly by on-yomi). Instead, Japanese people see this word holistically as *ichijiku,* much as some teachers encourage children to do with the "whole-language" approach to reading (rather than sounding out words phonetically). That is, with this word and many others, native speakers think in terms of meaning, not sound. In English we do the same thing when we read "lb." as "pound" or "e.g." as "for example," but this phenomenon exists only on a small scale, whereas it pervades Japanese.

Japanese people are comfortable with this imprecision, which they call *ateji* (当て字: assigned characters). They may not always know how to pronounce a word created with ateji, but they can usually figure out what it means. If it's hard to imagine their making that kind of leap, just consider that the whole kanji system is a wriggling, imprecise mass of variability and that the Japanese accommodate this in a relaxed, accepting manner.

This is a harder state for non-natives to achieve. Instead, I bog down in frustration and bewilderment when I search a dictionary's yomi index for a sound I believe a kanji to have (such as *hi, hito, tode,* or *de* in 海星, *hitode:* starfish), only to find no such listing. Then when I locate the character via the radical chart, the yomi I'm seeking isn't listed as an option. What's going on? Who changed the rules?! Oh, no! Ateji has gotten me again!

I recover my good humor about it whenever I associate this mismatch with a scene from the TV show *Cheers.* When the pompous psychiatrist Frasier Crane introduces his bride to the gang at the bar, he announces proudly, "This is Lilith Sternin-Crane—M.D., Ph.D.," and at least one more degree. Woody, the dim-witted bartender, responds in bewilderment, "Gee, it sure doesn't sound the way it's spelled." That's ateji for you. Actually, I'm not positive about the quotations here, but just treat them as another type of ateji—a loose interpretation, a stand-in for the most accurate version, or, as someone once said of ateji, "poetic license."

Types of Ateji

There are several types of ateji.

Type 1: Kanji that were chosen for their sound, with no regard to their meaning

A good example of this is *sushi*. As one account has it, *sushi* originally referred to vinegary rice (not fish), so an appropriate kanji would likely include 酸 (*SAN*: acid), which isn't terribly appetizing. The Japanese needed to choose a character that says *SU* and another that says *SHI*. Ideally, the chosen kanji would also have pertinent meanings, as opposed to, say, the nonsense word 数止, which would say *sushi* but would mean "number stop." Many (but not all!) Japanese write *sushi* as 寿司. The first character (*JU, SU, kotobuki*: longevity, congratulations) carries an auspicious meaning. Similarly, 司 (*SHI, tsukasado•ru*: to govern) can be interpreted as "to preside over," which also has a positive connotation.

The Japanese use ateji for some "loanwords" (terms that have entered the lexicon from some language

羅 (*RA*) means "silk gauze" but is always used phonetically (that is, as ateji). This compound requires so many strokes that you'll often see it written as 天ぷら, even in dictionaries.

Type 2: Kanji that were chosen for their meaning, with no regard to their sound

Along with tempura, the Portuguese priests brought tobacco. Nowadays we usually see *tabako* as タバコ or たばこ, but when the Japanese set this word to kanji music, they came up with 煙草, which breaks down as "smoke" (*EN, kemuri*) + "grass" (*SŌ, kusa*). Clearly, this is a match of meanings, not of sounds. Many refer to this type of ateji as *jukujikun*, 熟字訓 (matured + character + teachings).

A classic example of *jukujikun* is 今日, *kyō*, "today." The compound breaks down as "the present" (or "this" or "now") + "day," yielding a perfectly suitable meaning. Neither 今 (*KON, KIN, ima*) nor 日 (*NICHI, hi*) has official yomi corresponding to the sound of *kyō*; that aspect has been ignored.

Type 2 Ateji	Formal Reading	Casual Reading	Meaning
一昨日	*issakujitsu*	*ototoi*	day before yesterday
昨日	*sakujitsu*	*kinō*	yesterday
今日	*konnichi*	*kyō*	today
明日	*myōnichi*	*ashita, asu*	tomorrow
明後日	*myōgonichi*	*asatte*	day after tomorrow

Asu is a synonym for ashita. Asu is more formal than ashita but less formal than the synonym myōnichi. Even though asu looks like a verb whose past tense would be ashita, nothing of the sort has happened here etymologically, especially because "tomorrow" can't be in the past tense!

other than Chinese). Typically, the Japanese render these in katakana. But in the past, people felt a need to represent them in kanji, attempting to match either the meaning or the sound (or both, if they could swing it). To represent *tenpura* (or "tempura," which Portuguese Jesuit priests brought to Japan in the fifteenth and sixteenth centuries), the Japanese chose 天麩羅 primarily for its sounds. The meanings of the first two kanji also make fairly good matches; 天 (*TEN, ame*) means "heaven," and 麩 (*FU, fusuma*) is "wheat bran." Meanwhile,

Several other words concerning relative time are also ateji: *ototoi* (一昨日: the day before yesterday), *kinō* (昨日: yesterday), *ashita* or *asu* (明日: tomorrow), and *asatte* (明後日: the day after tomorrow). All these words (including *kyō*) existed before kanji arrived in Japan. To create compounds, the Japanese then mixed and matched characters that represented particular concepts. Meanwhile, the Japanese overlooked the sounds of those kanji. So far so good—your standard Type 2 ateji process.

But then there was a twist. For awhile, China and Chinese creations carried prestige in Japan, much as certain Americans embrace anything French. When speaking formally, prestige-minded Japanese started pronouncing these kanji words according to their on-yomi, as shown in the Formal Reading column in the table.

If you're wondering about the undefined kanji in the table, here they are: 一 (ICHI: one), 昨 (SAKU: yesterday, past), 明 (MEI, MYŌ: clear, open, bright), and 後 (GO, KŌ: after). All these kanji present logical matches for the vocabulary at hand, except perhaps 明.

Type 3: Characters used for proper names

When lesser-known yomi are used for people's names and place names, these readings are called *nanori*, 名乗り (name + ride), because the name "rides" on the kanji. These lesser-known yomi may simply be kun-yomi, rather than the on-yomi much more commonly associated with a particular kanji compound. For example, 大木 *(taiboku)* usually combines two on-yomi and means "big tree," unless it's a family name, in which case it's read as *Ōki*, uniting the kun-yomi of both kanji.

For more on kun-kun constructions, see Exhibit 39, "Just the Facts: Combinational Exceptions." And for more on place-name kanji, see Exhibit 52, "Just the Facts: Country Kanji."

Type 4: Chinese characters to which the Japanese assigned new meanings

The type of kanji known as *kokkun*, 国訓 (nation + teachings), involved a mini-rebellion by the Japanese. Usually, they adopted kanji on an "as-is" basis from China, no matter how odd the grouping of components seemed. But in some cases the Japanese hit a reset button and redefined characters more logically. For example, 沖 *(CHŪ, oki)* looked to the Japanese like the middle of the water, so it became "offshore," rather than "to rinse," as it meant in China. And, they reasoned, why should 森 *(SHIN, mori)* mean "gloomy, majestic, luxuriant growth" when it obviously represents a forest?

Which Words Are Ateji?

When I discussed ateji with a Japanese-language teacher, he mused for a moment, then exclaimed with sudden insight that the Japanese assigned all kun-yomi to kanji in an ateji-like way. He commented that

if there had been a perfect match between the native Japanese vocabulary and the reading of a Chinese compound, "It would have to have been a *huge* coincidence."

That is, in assigning indigenous vocabulary to Chinese characters, the Japanese temporarily disregarded the accompanying on-yomi. For instance, 鉄 (iron, steel) had the sound of *TETSU*, and the Japanese planned to keep that. But they already had a word for "iron," namely *kurogane* (literally, black metal). So they attached their word to 鉄, as well. *Kurogane* is now the official kun-yomi of the character; this reading is in no way ateji. But the origiNal process was like ateji, involving as it did an acceptance that *kurogane* sounded nothing like *TETSU* and that the mismatch in sounds was nevertheless OK. It seems that the Japanese shrugged off the inconsistency as something that people would have to figure out for themselves. From that perspective, then, a massive number of native Japanese words are ateji.

But if we return to the usual ways of considering ateji, where does it tend to lie in the Japanese lexicon? I've realized that food terms often have ateji. Consider these:

人参 *(ninjin:* carrot) = person + to go, come, visit
The yomi are appropriate, but the meanings of the kanji are unexpected. This odd compound came into play when the Korean carrot arrived in Japan. Shaped like an upside-down **Y**, it reminded the Japanese of the kanji 人. With lots of small roots dangling down, the carrot also inspired the use of 参, which originally meant "many."

山葵 *(wasabi:* Japanese horseradish) = mountain + hollyhock
Forget about the usual yomi here (*SAN* and *yama* for 山, *KI* and *aoi* for 葵). The characters refer to "mountain" and "hollyhock," a plant that the wasabi leaves resemble. In addition, the wasabi plant can grow on shady hillsides, so "mountain" is appropriate.

茄子 *(nasubi:* eggplant) = eggplant + object
The meanings of the characters (eggplant + object) apply, but the yomi for 茄 *(KA)* and 子 *(SHI, SU, ko)* do not.

烏賊 (*ika:* squid) = crow, raven + burglar
The reading *ika* has nothing to do with the actual yomi: 烏 *(U, O, karasu)* and 賊 *(ZOKU).* Given the meanings (crow, raven + burglar), the *ika* must act in some way like a dark, winged burglar!

Certain kanji seem to inspire a great deal of ateji. Although 海 *(KAI, umi:* sea) usually functions in a regular way, it also produces many irregularities, some of which are again food-related:

海老 (*ebi:* shrimp) = sea + old (man)
With whiskers and curved backs, shrimp resemble old men!

海月 (*kurage:* jellyfish) = sea + moon
In both color and shape, the jellyfish looks like the moon of the sea.

海豹 (*azarashi:* seal [the animal]) = sea + leopard
Because of their spots, seals look like aquatic leopards.

海苔 (*nori:* an edible seaweed) = sea + moss
It's easy to imagine how people viewed seaweed as marine moss.

海女 (*ama:* woman pearl diver) = sea + woman
For two millennia, by some estimates, women have been the ones to dive for pearls in Japan, perhaps because female bodies naturally have more fat than male bodies, enabling women to stay warmer in cold water.

Other prominent examples of ateji include the following, with the normal yomi and meanings listed below each one:

田舎 (*inaka:* countryside, rural)
DEN, ta: rice field + *SHA:* building, inn

土産 (*miyage:* souvenir)
DŌ, tsuchi: soil, earth + *SAN, umu:* birth, to produce

貴方 (*anata:* you)
KI, tattoi: precious, revered + *HŌ, kata:* person, side, way

比島 (*Hitō, Firipin:* Philippines)
HI, kura•beru: to compare + *TŌ, shima:* island

Japanese lacks the sound *fi,* so *hi* stands as a substitute and as an abbreviation for "Philippines." As we'll see in Exhibit 52, "Just the Facts: Country Kanji," almost all country kanji are ateji, because the meanings of the kanji never match the meanings of the names, except in the case of "Vietnam." The example of 比島 above shows that if only one of the kanji in a compound doesn't match the meaning or the sound, the whole word can be considered ateji.

Ah, but this introduces another bit of confusion. I assumed that 部屋 (*heya:* room) was ateji, because the first kanji should be read as *BU.* However, as it turns out, 部 once had the yomi *BU* and *BE.* Then *BE* morphed into *HE* before disappearing as an option. *Heya* is a legacy of that period. So 部屋 isn't ateji. But not to worry—many Japanese words are, and you'll eventually encounter ateji, whether you want to or not!

In the discussion of Type 2 ateji, we saw that 煙草 (*tabako:* tobacco) is ateji and that it breaks down as "smoke" *(EN, kemuri)* + "grass" *(SŌ, kusa).* Clearly, the standard sounds of the kanji have been disregarded in 煙草. The sign in the photo contains one of these kanji. The sign (from a Kyoto temple) says 禁煙, *kin'en,* "No Smoking." In this case, 煙 keeps its usual sound *(EN)* and its meaning, as does 禁 *(KIN:* prohibition).

Cool Compounds

For endless entertainment and insights, there's nothing like examining the meanings of kanji compounds. Many have the same verbal logic as equivalent words in English. (I don't know why that seems so charming, but it does!) Here's a sampling of such compounds:

馬力 (*bariki:* horsepower) = horse + power
金魚 (*kingyo:* goldfish) = gold + fish
下着 (*shitagi:* underwear) = under + to wear

After a Moment's Reflection . . .

The following words make sense if you think about them. I've passed on a few interpretations that I've heard, and I've tried my hand at other explanations.

上手 (*jōzu:* skilled) = up + hand
Having the upper hand means that one is skilled.

向上 (*kōjō:* improvement) = facing + up
When things are looking up, it's an improvement.

文化 (*bunka:* culture) = writing + change
Among several early meanings, 文 (*bun*) originally referred to things that humans produced. Now it means sentences, compositions, and literature. Whichever meaning one attributes to 文 here, it's fascinating to think that creative output causes cultural change.

文明 (*bunmei:* civilization) = writing + light
According to William C. Hannas in *Asia's Orthographic Dilemma*, 文明 means "enlightenment through writing."

人気 (*ninki:* popular) = people + spirit
Whatever is popular reflects the spirit of the people.

動物園 (*dōbutsuen:* zoo) = animals + garden
A garden of animals—how lovely! Here's a further breakdown:

動物 (*dōbutsu:* animals) = to move + things
A zoo is a garden of moving things! Incidentally, 動 (DŌ, *ugo•ku:* to move) breaks down as "heavy" + "power."

瞬間 (*shunkan:* moment) = to wink + interval
A moment is the time it takes to wink.

落胆 (*rakutan:* disappointment) = to fall + courage
After disappointment, hope and courage crash to the ground.

日食 (*nisshoku:* solar eclipse) = sun + to eat
月食 (*gesshoku:* lunar eclipse) = moon + to eat
In an eclipse, it looks as if something is eating the sun or moon!

名声 (*meisei:* prestige) = famous, name + voice
Prestige gives a "voice" to a name, or else it makes people "voice" that name.

先入感 (*sen'nyūkan:* prejudice, bias) = before + to enter + feeling
"Prejudice" refers to feelings one has before entering a situation.

Lyrical Simplicity

The next compounds are self-explanatory and are wonderful in their lyrical simplicity:

化石 (*kaseki:* fossil) = to change + stone

半島 (*hantō:* peninsula) = half + island

舌戦 (*zessen:* war of words) = tongue + war

無口 (*mukuchi:* reticence) = no + mouth

口外 (*kōgai:* telling a secret) = mouth + outside

消毒 (*shōdoku:* disinfection) = to erase + poison

同情 (*dōjō:* sympathy) = same + feelings

悪化 (*akka:* deterioration) = bad + to change

恥骨 (*chikotsu:* pubic bone) = shame + bone

救急車 (*kyūkyūsha:* ambulance) = to rescue + to hurry + car

調味料 (*chōmiryō:* seasoning) = to adjust + flavor + ingredients

手袋 (*tebukuro:* glove) = hand + bag

工場 (*kōjō:* factory) = manufacturing + place

山崩れ (*yamakuzure:* landslide) = mountain + to fall to pieces

Crazy Compounds

Certain compounds show a shocking and delightful lack of logic. Or it seems that way if we don't know the stories behind them. Consider the following:

馬鹿 (*baka:* fool) = horse + deer

八百屋 (*yaoya:* vegetable store) = 800 (1st 2 chars.) + store

切手 (*kitte:* stamp) = to cut + hand

大変 (*taihen:* difficult, very) = big + strange

空恥 (*soraha•zukashii:* feeling ashamed without knowing why) = sky + shame

泥棒 (*dorobō:* thief) = mud + stick, pole
This is certainly different from our term "stick in the mud." A further breakdown:

棒 (*Bō:* stick, pole) = tree + respectful

迷惑 (*meiwaku:* annoyance) = perplexed + bewildered

皮肉 (*hiniku:* sarcasm, irony) = skin + flesh

茶化 (*chaka•su:* to make fun of) = tea + to change

物見高 (*monomidaka•i:* burning with curiosity) = thing + to see + tall, high

怪我 (*kega:* injury) = weird + self

不動産 (*fudōsan:* real estate) = not + to move + wealth
It sounds as if this compound were created during a massive economic depression when properties weren't moving at all! But this compound refers instead to wealth that literally doesn't budge—namely, real estate.

赤道 (*sekidō:* equator) = red + way
The ancient Chinese organized their understanding of the world around the five elements: trees, fire, earth, gold, and water. These elements became associated with colors and directions; "fire" went with "red" and "south." Located south of China, the equator therefore became associated with redness.

This sign, which comes from a building site at the Imperial Palace East Gardens in Tokyo, is full of compounds, with nary a kana in sight! On the whole, these compounds are more cool than crazy. Here's how they break down:

- 関係者 (*kankeisha:* authorized people, or literally, people with a connection) = to be connected + to connect + person
- 以外 (*igai:* except for) = intention + beyond
- 立入禁止 (*tachiiri kinshi:* No trespassing!) = prefix for emphasis + to enter + prohibition + to stop

Normally, *tachiiri* would be written with okurigana, as 立ち入り. But people often omit okurigana in posters, so the four-kanji compound 立入禁止 tends to appear without kana.

Combinational Exceptions

Once, when a friend came over for dinner, he sported a T-shirt with sharp-looking kanji, and I couldn't rip my eyes away from the characters:

池袋
大勝軒

I knew 大勝 probably said *taishō*, combining "big" and "victory." And the top two kanji certainly looked familiar. But what did it all say? "'Best Ramen in Sapporo,' or something," said my friend, working from a three-year-old memory of the translation. Hmm . . . I couldn't quite see that, as "ramen" (ラーメン) was conspicuously absent. For "best," I would expect 一番, *ichiban*, but I figured *taishō* could do the job. While others busied themselves with dinner preparations, I sneaked off to look up the kanji, figuring it wouldn't take but a few minutes. Boy, was I wrong!

After considerable effort, I concluded that 大勝, *taishō*, did indeed mean "best." Well, actually, my dictionary defined the word as "great victory," but close enough. I got nowhere with the mysterious final character (because, as I later discovered, it had an extra artistic swoosh).

But I tore my hair out most over the initial compound, 池袋. I quickly located each kanji in a dictionary: 池 *(CHI, ike)* is "pond" or "reservoir" (as in 電池, *denchi*: battery), and 袋 *(TAI, fukuro)* is "bag." Pond bag? Going by the on-yomi, I figured that it should have been *chitai*. That's a word. In fact, there are several instances of *chitai* in Japanese, but none involve the kanji at hand. I also looked up *Sapporo:* 札幌. Nothing to do with that shirt.

For the rest of the evening, I obsessed over the mysterious kanji. Soon, though, I had an opportunity to ask the Japanese guy who had helped my friend buy the shirt. And his answers made me want to tear my hair out all over again. The final kanji, 軒, often appears in the names of ramen restaurants, though there's no official reason for this. And the

The yomi is KEN. This kanji enables the Japanese to specify how many houses they're discussing. Just as we say a "flock of sheep" and a "gaggle of geese" in English, "2軒" refers to two houses in Japanese.

first compound, 池袋, is *Ikebukuro,* a section in Tokyo with great ramen. Sapporo has a branch of this chain restaurant. I couldn't have guessed any of that. But I should have at least considered the kun-kun combination in *Ikebukuro. Chitai,* my ass!

Kun-Kun Combos

Actually, I didn't know that most place names in Japan combine kun-yomi. This isn't obvious, as it's not true of *Nihon* (Japan), *Tōkyō, Kyōto,* or any of the major islands: *Hokkaidō, Honshū, Shikoku,* or *Kyūshū.* Those are some significant exceptions! However, the kun-kun rule does apply to these Japanese locales:

広島	Hiroshima	青森	Aomori
箱根	Hakone	宮島	Miyajima
長野	Nagano	長崎	Nagasaki
成田	Narita	高山	Takayama

In Exhibits 1 and 2, we saw four more place names that fit this kun-kun pattern: 秋田 (Akita), 沖縄 (Okinawa), 大阪 (Ōsaka), and 横浜 (Yokohama). Most prefecture names also match this pattern.

Place names aren't the only words that generally have kun-kun constructions. People's names do, too, particularly family names, such as 山田 (Yamada), 田中 (Tanaka), 鈴木 (Suzuki), and 高橋 (Takahashi). When I mistakenly read the last one as *kōkyō* in a reading comprehension class, it provoked laughter, especially because I'd overlooked the *-san* trailing after *Takahashi.* (As a sign of respect, the Japanese attach *-san* to given or family names when addressing or referring to someone.) Given names can contain kun-kun constructions, on-on constructions, and *nanori* (a type of ateji, as discussed in Exhibit 36).

Besides names, a random scattering of words contain kun-kun pairings. Again, these can frustrate kanji learners, because the brain wants to see on-yomi in these words and otherwise draws a blank:

建物	*tatemono:* building
若者	*wakamono:* young person
名前	*namae:* name
手紙	*tegami:* letter
切手	*kitte:* stamp

出会	dea•u: to encounter someone
出来る	dekiru: to be able to
苦手	nigate: to be bad at
生け花	ikebana: flower arranging
空手	karate
神風	kamikaze: "divine wind"
腹切り	harakiri: ritual disembowelment
長居	nagai: staying somewhere too long
合間	aima: interval
日傘	higasa: parasol
水引	mizuhiki: string for tying gifts
金持ち	kanemochi: rich person
閏年	urūdoshi: leap year

Jūbako-Yomi and Yutō-Yomi

Jūbako-yomi (重箱読み) and yutō-yomi (湯桶読み) are words that combine kun-yomi and on-yomi. Jūbako-yomi connect an initial on-yomi with a kun-yomi. The term jūbako itself is an example, breaking down as follows:

On + Kun Combination

jūbako: 重 (JŪ: nest of boxes) + 箱 (hako: box)

Meanwhile, yutō-yomi refers to words connecting an initial kun-yomi with an on-yomi. As it turns out, the word yutō fits the pattern:

Kun + On Combination

yutō: 湯 (yu: hot water) + 桶 (TŌ: bucket)

If you can figure out how a "nest of boxes" and a "bucket of hot water" relate to the matter at hand, you get a gold star (or a commemorative bucket of hot water).

Here are other examples of jūbako-yomi and yutō-yomi:

On + Kun

本屋	honya: bookshop
金色	kiniro: golden color
素顔	sugao: unmade-up face, true self
新型	shingata: new style

Kun + On

場所	basho: place
古本	furuhon: used book
切符	kippu: ticket
思惑	omowaku: thought, intention

Kun + On + On

合気道	aikidō: a martial art
車椅子	kurumaisu: wheelchair

A final note on jūbako-yomi and yutō-yomi: Compounds formed from certain kanji tend to have kun readings. That's true of 払 (to pay). Although it has an on-yomi of FUTSU, this kanji often goes by its kun reading of hara•u in compounds. That happens in sixty-three of the sixty-six 払 compounds listed in Spahn. Thus, we have the following examples:

Kun + Kun

人払い	hitobarai: clearing (the room) of people
前払い	maebarai: advance payment
売り払	urihara•u: to sell off, dispose of

On + Kun + On

支払金	shiharaikin: payment

The same kun-yomi tendency occurs with 掘 (to dig). Again, it has a perfectly good on-yomi, KUTSU, but often goes by ho•ru. Of the twenty-seven compounds listed in Spahn for 掘, twenty-one use the kun reading. Here are some such usages:

Kun + Kun

掘り下	horisa•geru: to dig down, delve into
掘り込	horiko•mu: to dig into
掘り出	horida•su: to dig out, unearth
金掘り	kanehori: miner

On + On + Kun

露天掘り	rotenbori: strip mining

Wago, Kango, and Kokugo

A Japanese-language teacher astonished me with his mental clarity when he drew a neat schematic:

```
KAN        JI
KOKU       GO
```

He said these combinations give you *kanji, kango, kokuji,* and *kokugo,* four categories that collectively account for most of the ways in which kanji singletons and compounds have come into existence in Japan. Feeling thick, I asked him to slow down and explain, which he kindly did.

Kan (漢) refers to China. *Koku* (国) means "nation," in this case Japan. *Ji* (字) is "character." And *go* (語) means "word" or "language." This yields the following:

kanji	漢字:	China + character
kokuji	国字:	nation (Japan) + character
kango	漢語:	China + word
kokugo	国語:	nation (Japan) + word

Exhibit 30, "Just the Facts: Classification of Characters," explained various types of character composition, presenting *kokuji* as the seventh kind. This whole book purports to investigate kanji. Therefore, we won't define *kokuji* or *kanji* here. Instead, we'll look now at the remaining items in the Big Four: *kango* and *kokugo,* plus a related concept, *wago.*

Wago: 和語

Wago (Japan + word) is the vocabulary that existed in Japan long before kanji arrived on its shores and expanded the lexicon. *Wago* is alive and well in Japan today. According to Yaeko Habein in *Decoding Kanji,* whenever you encounter *wago,* you're likely to have heard it from a female speaker, as opposed to a man or an official document. (Those two sources tend to produce *kango.*)

When Japanese words consist of only one kanji, the words have probably come from this native language. Consider, for example, 春 (*haru:* spring [the season]), 女 (*onna:* woman), and 出る (*deru:* to leave). And when okurigana trail behind kanji, as with the last example, the word is definitely *wago.*

Compounds using only kun-yomi have also most likely come from the spoken language that preexisted the written one. That's true of お手洗い (*otearai:* bathroom).

For a discussion of the sound of *wago,* see Exhibit 46, "Thematic Explorations: Syllabic Similarity."

Kango: 漢語

As we saw in Chapter 1, when kanji arrived in Japan, it sometimes did so in the form of *kango,* or whole compounds (e.g., the very words *kango* and *kanji*). The Japanese adopted the compounds more or less wholesale, using the shapes of the characters, retaining the meanings, and changing only the sounds to their own Chinese-inspired on-yomi. *Kango* compounds always combine on-yomi.

Educated Japanese people absorbed many *kango* by reading Chinese literature. Thus, a certain hoity-toitiness accompanies some such words. For instance, whereas the Japanese had merely spoken of "eating" (食べる, *taberu*), thanks to Chinese they acquired the concept of "dining" (食事する, *shokuji suru*). But not all *kango* emanate prestige. Scores of everyday words such as *gakkō* (学校: school), *sensei* (先生: teacher), and *jōhō* (情報: information) are *kango,* as well.

Kokugo: 国語

Upon importing kanji, the Japanese felt a need to distinguish Japanese creations from foreign ones. While continuing to use the word *wago* to refer to native vocabulary, they coined *kokugo.* Though these words are nearly synonymous, the 国 (*KOKU, kuni:* nation) in 国語 conveys a sense of national pride.

Kokugo also has a meaning apart from *wago.* Just as *kokuji* are kanji singletons invented in Japan from bits of Chinese characters, *kokugo* are compounds created in Japan from characters that had never before teamed up to form a compound. *Kokugo* almost always combine on-yomi, otherwise using kun-yomi or a hybrid of the two.

Let's look at one example. Possibly inspired by the Chinese characters for "absurd," 可笑的, the Japanese replaced this concoction with their own: 笑止 (*shōshi*). By combining "laugh" (*SHŌ, wara•u*) with "to stop" (*SHI, toma•ru*), they denoted something so ridiculous that one can't stop laughing at it. This process recalls the reform-minded thinking involved with *kokkun* (the fourth type of ateji described in Exhibit 36), wherein the Japanese assigned 森 the more logical meaning of "forest."

Common examples of *kokugo* include *kaisha* (会社: company), *ginkō* (銀行: bank), *mendō* (面倒: nuisance), and *fuben* (不便: inconvenient). Japanese contains far fewer *kokugo* than *kango*.

If the creation of *kokugo* compounds represented a psychological distancing from China, the development of abstract *kokugo* reflected increasing contact with the West. Japanese originally had few abstract words, according to Kindaichi. When Japan began westernizing during the Meiji era (from 1868 to 1912), the Japanese invented new compounds that could stand for abstract ideas, such as the following:

現象 (*genshō:* phenomenon)
= 現 (*GEN:* to appear) + 象 (*SHŌ:* phenomenon)

客観 (*kyakkan:* objectivity)
= 客 (*KYAKU:* object) + 観 (*KAN:* to view, observe)

Kindaichi notes that many *kokugo* imply "some sense of evaluation" (p. 179).

This image shows the evolution of eight characters from pictographs to the shapes people use today. From left to right for each line, here is the story behind each character, according to Kenneth Henshall in *A Guide to Remembering Japanese Characters:*

- 日 (*NICHI, hi:* sun, day): The original form showed the sun with a sunspot. People could see sunspots back then?!
- 山 (*SAN, yama:* mountain): The pictograph showed a mountain range with a prominent central peak.
- 土 (*DO, tsuchi:* soil): Henshall shows a different pictographic form as being the earliest. His image, an oval hovering above a straight line, represented a clod of earth on the ground.
- 雲 (*UN, kumo:* cloud): The curlicues in early pictographic forms represented billowing vapors. These eventually straightened out, becoming 云. But 云 later came to be an uncommon character meaning "to speak." At that time, the Chinese added 雨 (rain) to 云, making 雲 the new way of writing "cloud."
- 月 (*GETSU, GATSU, tsuki:* moon): The pictograph here depicted a crescent moon with a pitted surface. But that wasn't the earliest form. An earlier one had this moon tilted on its axis.
- 海 (*KAI, umi:* sea): The pictograph shown here seems to depict a fish swimming in a river (川) or perhaps beached on a sandbar. But Henshall and other sources don't agree with that as the origin of 海. Rather, according to them, 海 breaks down as "all" or "every" (毎) + water (氵), because "all water" flows to the sea. And as for 毎, that has evolved from a pitchfork shape (representing a blade of grass) combined with 母 (mother). That's a long way off from the fish in the river, but maybe the person who created this image figured, Why let facts get in the way of a good story?
- 木 (*MOKU, ki:* tree): The pictograph showed a tree with sweeping branches.
- 魚 (*GYO, sakana:* fish): The original form represented a fish—one with oversized, extra-detached gills . . . or perhaps with wings?!

日 SUN   山 MOUNTAIN   土 SOIL   雲 CLOUD

月 MOON   海 SEA   木 WOOD   魚 FISH

Multiple Readings of Certain Compounds

It can be puzzling to encounter a word such as 生物 that has two possible pronunciations, each with a different meaning:

seibutsu: living creature, life, biology (informally)
namamono: raw food

With interstitial okurigana (生き物), this compound gains yet another meaning:

ikimono: living creature, life

We can start to cut through the confusion by determining whether these words use on-yomi or kun-yomi. They break down as follows:

SEI + BUTSU   on + on
nama + mono   kun + kun
i·ki + mono   kun + kun

The differences in these 生物 readings have to do with *kango* and *kokugo* and certain decisions made when the Japanese imported kanji. Just as they had no problem switching between *kun* and *on* readings for each character, they were comfortable reading some imported compounds in two ways. They would see a compound both as on-on (making it *kango*) and as kun-kun (making it *kokugo*, even though *kokugo* words often contain on-on constructions). Therefore, the Japanese now read 生物 as *seibutsu* (which is *kango*) and as *namamono* (which is *kokugo*).

Some *kango* and *kokugo* readings of the same compound acquired different meanings (again, as with 生物). At other times, the meanings were interchangeable. In the lists below, Types 1 and 2 provide examples of both cases.

Invented *kokugo* compounds provided another route to multiple readings. When the Japanese attached a native word or a newly coined word to a compound of their own creation, that concocted compound may have combined on-yomi, kun-yomi, or a hybrid of the two. Ateji was also possible, as we've seen with 今日, initially read as *kyō* and later as *konnichi,* according to on-on readings. When we see hybrids (on-kun or kun-on), we know some meddling

occurred in Japan; the compound cannot be an intact *kango* import. You'll find some hybrids below.

Type 1: Different Readings, Different Meanings

In this group, the *kango* and *kokugo* words have different pronunciations *and* different meanings.

> At one point, both of these words meant the same thing—"market." But because all things Chinese seemed fashionable, the Japanese allowed their native word to take the "lesser" and more familiar meaning of local market, whereas the *kango* word came to mean something larger and more glamorous, a stock market.

> This is ateji, as neither 上 nor 手 correlates with the sound *umai.*

	On-On	**Kun-Kun**
市場	*shijō* stock market	*ichiba* food market
目下	*mokka* at present	*meshita* subordinates
一切	*issai* not at all	*hitoki·re* a piece
一寸	*issun* one inch	*chotto* a little
上手	*jōzu* skillful	*uwate, kamite* upper part
	uma·i skillful	
気配	*kehai* sign, indication	*kikuba·ri* attentiveness
一時	*ichiji* 1:00	*ittoki* brief
大方	*taihō* broad-minded	*ōkata* almost
月日	*tsukihi* months and days, time	*gappi* (on-kun) date

	On-On	**Kun-Kun**
初日	*shonichi* opening day	*hatsuhi* New Year's Day sunrise
前方	*zenpō* front	*maekata* before, immature
手練	*shuren* dexterity	*teren* (kun-on) coaxing, wiles

Type 2: Different Readings, Same Meanings

In this group, the readings differ, but the meanings are identical or very close. If I've presented the meaning just once, it's identical for the two readings.

	On-On	**Kun-Kun**
一度	*ichido* once, one time	*hitotabi*
夫婦	*fūfu* husband and wife	*meoto, myōto*
日中	*nitchū* during the day	*hinaka* broad daylight, daytime
日々	*nichi-nichi* daily, every day	*hibi* daily, days
晦日	*kaijitsu* the last day of the month	*misoka*
終日	*shūjitsu* all day long	*hinemosu*

年月	*nengetsu* months and years, time	*toshitsuki*
金山	*kinzan* gold mine	*kanayama* mine

Type 3: Multiple On-On Readings

十分	*jūbun* enough, ample
	juppun 10 minutes
安息日	*ansokujitsu* Christian sabbath
	ansokunichi Jewish sabbath

Type 4: Multiple Kun-Kun Readings

早生	*hayau•mare* Born between Jan. 1 and Apr. 1
	wase early-ripening (rice), precocious

This is ateji, as 終日 doesn't match the reading *hinemosu*.

Mizuho Fukushima (written on the card in larger characters as 福島　みずほ) is chief of the Social Democratic Party. This is her name card, which she uses when campaigning. The name Fukushima is an on-kun hybrid! There's only one way to read this compound, but in a sense it has two meanings; in addition to being a family name, Fukushima is a prefecture in northern Honshu. The rest of the card reads as follows:

- 今、政治を変える！ (*Ima, seiji o kaeru*! Now, to change government!)
- 愛と平和 (*ai to heiwa*: love and peace)
- 社民党 (*Shamintō*: Social Democratic Party), which appears twice on the card
- 党首 (*tōshu*: party chief)
- 参議院議員 (*sangiin giin*: member of the house of councilors), which has an intriguing repetition of sounds

Helping Hands

In *Decoding Kanji*, Yaeko Habein writes that of the 1,945 kanji then in the Jōyō set, 370 are used only in compounds, never alone. About 170 more are rarely used alone. Almost all these hangers-on function as prefixes (接頭辞, *settōji*, or "contact" + "head" + "word," because a prefix makes contact with the front of a word) and suffixes (接尾辞, *setsubiji*, in which the middle kanji means "tail"). However, just because a kanji can serve as a prefix or suffix, that doesn't mean that's its sole function. Most of the characters below can take any position in a word and may have different meanings than when serving as affixes (prefixes and suffixes collectively). For example, the suffix -家 indicates a specialist (e.g., 作家, *sakka:* writer), but 家 can also stand on its own as *ie* (home, house) or take other positions, as in 家庭 (*katei:* home).

Having taught students to understand these small parts of words, Timothy J. Vance believes that a "relatively small investment of time can yield surprisingly large dividends" in terms of comprehension. The information below largely comes from his *Building Word Power in Japanese: Using Kanji Prefixes and Suffixes*, which contains detailed information about various affixes and copious sample sentences.

Many of the affixes below originated in Chinese and are therefore on-yomi. This makes sense because their function is to bond to other kanji and form compounds. I've noted a few exceptions.

You'll find the affixes categorized in a way that I hope is useful. When surveying the items in each category, you'll realize how much they overlap and how careful you need to be when choosing an affix. Note that these lists are by no means complete.

Prefixes (接頭辞, *settōji*)

Quantitative and Qualitative Prefixes
These add-ons tell you how big and great something is and how many there are.

- 超- (*CHŌ-:* super, ultra)
超大国, *chōtaikoku:* superpower; 超能力, *chōnōryoku:* supernatural power

- 第- (*DAI-:* the -th)
第四回, *daiyonkai:* the fourth time

- 大- (*DAI-:* great)
大成功, *daiseikō:* great success; 大豊作, *daihōsaku:* extremely good harvest

- 各- (*KAKU-:* each)
各家庭, *kakukatei:* every household; 各段階, *kaku-dankai:* every stage

- 旧- (*KYŪ-:* former)
旧所有者, *kyūshoyūsha:* former owner; 旧制度, *kyūseido:* the old system
    Note: Don't see 旧 as I initially did—as "one" + "day," which I interpreted as some way of writing *tsuitachi*, "the first of the month"!

- 両- (*RYŌ-:* both)
両親, *ryōshin:* parents; 両方, *ryōhō:* both

- 再- (*SAI-:* re-, again)
再発見, *saihakken:* rediscovery; 再放送, *saihōsō:* rebroadcast

- 最- (*SAI-:* the most)
最初, *saisho:* the first; 最後, *saigo:* the last; 最高, *saikō:* the highest, the greatest

- 新- (*SHIN-:* new)
新幹線, *Shinkansen:* bullet train (lit., new trunk line); 新時代, *shinjidai:* new era

- 諸- (*SHO-:* several, various)
諸問題, *shomondai:* various problems; 諸外国, *shogaikoku:* foreign countries

- 総- (*SŌ-:* whole, total)
総人口, *sōjinkō:* total population; 総売上げ, *sō-uriage:* total sales

- 全- (*ZEN-:* all)
全部, *zenbu:* all; 全然, *zenzen:* entirely, (not) at all; 全体, *zentai:* the whole

Negating Prefixes
These prefixes give words negative meanings (e.g., not, no, un-, in-, mis-).

- 不- (*FU-:* not, lack of)
不正, *fusei:* injustice; 不足, *fusoku:* insufficiency; 不便, *fuben:* inconvenient

- 非- (*HI-*: not, mis-, non-, un-)
  非常, *hijō*: emergency, exceptional; 非行, *hikō*: misconduct

- 未- (*MI-*: not yet)
  未定, *mitei*: undecided, pending; 未婚, *mikon*: unmarried; 未来, *mirai*: future (lit., not yet come)

- 無- (*MU-*: not, lack of)
  無理, *muri*: impossible; 無言, *mugon*: silence; 無意味, *muimi*: meaningless

Suffixes (接尾辞, *setsubiji*)

People Suffixes

These suffixes differ, depending on the occupations with which they're associated.

- -員 (*-IN*: member, -er)
  銀行員, *ginkōin*: bank clerk; 販売員, *hanbaiin*: salesperson; 調査員, *chōsain*: survey taker

- -人 (*-JIN, -NIN*: person, inhabitant)
  一般人, *ippanjin*: ordinary person; 社会人, *shakaijin*: full member of society; 料理人, *ryōrinin*: cook

- -家 (*KA*: person, expert, -er, -ist)
  建築家, *kenchikuka*: architect; 専門家, *senmonka*: specialist; 画家, *gaka*: painter, artist

- -工 (*-KŌ*: worker, usually in a factory)
  配管工, *haikankō*: plumber; 熟練工, *jukurenkō*: skilled worker

- -生 (*-SEI*: student)
  卒業生, *sotsugyōsei*: a graduate; 同級生, *dōkyūsei*: classmate

- -者 (*-SHA, -JA, -mono*: person, -er, -ee)
  医者, *isha*: doctor; 患者, *kanja*: a patient; 筆者, *hissha*: author
  > Unlike most kanji in this exhibit, 者 cannot occupy the first position of a compound. It is unusual in often going by the kun-yomi *mono*, as in 独り者, *hitorimono*: unmarried person.

- -士 (*-SHI*: practitioner, -er)
  弁護士, *bengoshi*: lawyer; 飛行士, *hikōshi*: pilot

- 師 (*-SHI*: practitioner, -er)
  手品師, *tejinashi*: magician; 理容師, *riyōshi*: hairdresser

- 手 (*-SHU*: practitioner, -er)
  運転手, *untenshu*: driver; 歌手, *kashu*: singer; 選手, *senshu*: player

Group Suffixes

These suffixes denote groups of people.

- -部 (*-BU*: department, club, team)
  宣伝部, *sendenbu*: publicity department; 編集部, *henshūbu*: editorial department

- -団 (*-DAN*: group, team)
  訪米団, *hōbeidan*: delegation to the U.S.; 調査団, *chōsadan*: investigating commission

- -派 (*-HA*: group, faction, school)
  印象派, *inshōha*: Impressionists; 保守派, *hoshuha*: conservative faction

- -会 (*-KAI*: meeting, gathering, society, association)
  送別会, *sōbetsukai*: farewell party; 理事会, *rijikai*: board of directors

- -界 (*-KAI*: world, circles)
  世界, *sekai*: world; 経済界, *keizaikai*: economic circles; 文学界, *bungakukai*: literary world

- -層 (*-SŌ*: class, stratum)
  知識層, *chishikisō*: intelligentsia; 無関心層, *mukanshinsō*: those who are indifferent

- -隊 (*-TAI*: group, corps)
  警官隊, *keikantai*: police force; デモ隊, *demotai*: group of demonstrators

Place Suffixes

These suffixes point to regions, institutions, companies, buildings, rooms, and the like.

- -地 (*-CHI*: ground, land)
  住宅地, *jūtakuchi*: residential section

- -園 (*-EN*: garden)
  動物園, *dōbutsuen*: zoological garden; 植物園, *shokubutsuen*: botanical garden

- -所 (*-JO, -SHO*: place, facility)
  研究所, *kenkyūjo*: research institute; 事務所, *jimusho*: office

- -場 (*-JŌ, -ba*: place, facility)
  駐車場, *chūshajō*: parking lot; 運動場, *undōjō*: playground

Note: -場 is an unusual suffix in also having a kun-yomi form, *ba,* as in 売り場, *uriba:* shop counter.

- 館 (-*KAN:* hall, large building)
図書館, *toshokan:* library; 映画館, *eigakan:* movie theater

- 社 (-*SHA:* company)
会社, *kaisha:* company; 新聞社, *shinbunsha:* newspaper company

- 室 (-*SHITSU:* room)
教室, *kyōshitsu:* classroom

Space and Time Suffixes

These two suffixes use the same kanji but serve different functions and have different readings.

- 中 (-*CHŪ:* during, in the midst of)
工事中, *kōjichū:* under construction; 考慮中, *kōryochū:* under consideration

- 中 (-*JŪ:* entire, throughout)
日本中, *Nihonjū:* throughout Japan; 一日中, *ichinichijū:* all day

Abstraction Suffixes

In Exhibit 40, I mentioned that Japan lacked abstract terms before the Meiji era. You certainly wouldn't know it to look at this healthy crop of suffixes.

- 度 (-*DO:* degree, -ness)
完成度, *kanseido:* degree of perfection; 重要度, *jūyōdo:* degree of importance

- 上 (-*JŌ:* pertaining to, -al, -ally, -wise)
文法上, *bunpōjō:* grammatical; 学問上, *gakumonjō:* academic

- 化 (-*KA:* -ization, -ification)
民主化, *minshuka:* democratization; 近代化, *kindaika:* modernization

- 性 (-*SEI:* -ness, -ity, character)
可能性, *kanōsei:* possibility; 生産性, *seisansei:* productivity

- 的 (-*TEKI:* -tic, -al, -tive)
科学的, *kagakuteki:* scientific; 基本的, *kihonteki:* basic

Object Suffixes

Many words sporting this type of suffix are inanimate objects, though clearly that's not always true of -類 (-*RUI*).

- 物 (-*BUTSU,* -*mono:* thing, substance)
出版物, *shuppanbutsu:* a publication; 郵便物, *yūbinbutsu:* mail
Note: This suffix frequently goes by a kun-yomi, *mono,* as in 金物, *kanamono:* hardware.

- 品 (-*HIN:* article, object)
食品, *shokuhin:* food products; 輸入品, *yunyūhin:* imported items

- 類 (-*RUI:* class, items, kind, type, genus)
書類, *shorui:* document; 人類, *jinrui:* humankind; 食肉類, *shokunikurui:* carnivorous animals

Money Suffixes

When I complained to a native speaker about the amount of differentiation in Japanese, meaning the degree of hair-splitting between similar words (more on that in Exhibit 56, "Thematic Explorations: Shades of Meaning"), he protested that 料金 (*ryōkin*) translates to three different words in English: "fare," "charge," and "fee." Here's the comeback I should have used: At least four Japanese suffixes indicate that very concept! Of course, compared with the other affix categories, four is a rather low number!

- 代 (-*DAI:* charge, cost)
ホテル代, *hoterudai:* hotel charges; 昼食代, *chūshokudai:* cost of lunch

- 費 (-*HI:* cost, expense)
医療費, *iryōhi:* medical expenses; 交通費, *kōtsūhi:* transportation expenses

- 金 (-*KIN:* money)
入学金, *nyūgakukin:* enrollment fee

- 料 (-*RYŌ:* fee, charge)
授業料, *jugyōryō:* tuition; 保険料, *hokenryō:* insurance premium

Style Suffixes

In this category more than any other, the overlap between suffixes amazes me. Look at the last example in each line, plus the first one for -式 (-*SHIKI*). Shouldn't they all use the same suffix?! Apparently not!

- -調 (-CHŌ: style, character)
口語調, kōgochō: colloquial-style; ビクトリア調, Bikutoria-chō: Victorian-style

- -風 (-FŪ: -style, -like, -looking)
現代風, gendaifū: modern-style; 西洋風, seiyōfū: Western-style

- -流 (-RYŪ: -style, -like)
自己流, jikoryū: personal style; ヨーロッパ流, Yōroppa-ryū: European-style

- -式 (-SHIKI: -style, -type)
洋式, yōshiki: Western-style; 中国式, Chūgokushiki: Chinese-style

Emotional Suffixes

Kindaichi has noted "Japanese people's tendency to verbalize their various emotional states" (p. 179). Strangely, I've found just two suffixes for this purpose.

- -感 (-KAN: feeling, sense)
安定感, anteikan: feeling of stability; 一体感, ittai-kan: sense of unity

- -心 (-SHIN: spirit, sentiment)
冒険心, bōkenshin: spirit of adventure; 依頼心, iraishin: tendency to rely on others

Opinion and Viewpoint Suffixes

These suffixes indicate people's points of view or beliefs. Interestingly, English doesn't seem to have equivalent structures, except for -ism.

- -観 (-KAN: view of —)
人生観, jinseikan: view of life; 女性観, joseikan: view of women

- -論 (-RON: discussion, debate, opinion, theory)
理論, riron: theory; 進化論, shinkaron: the theory of evolution; 教育論, kyōikuron: a theory of education

- -説 (-SETSU: opinion, theory, doctrine)
ダーウィン説, Dāuin-setsu: Darwinian theory

- -視 (-SHI: seeing as, regarding as)
同一視, dōitsushi: regarding as identical; 楽観視, rakkanshi: regarding optimistically

Medical and Chemical Suffixes

Now, we do have this in English, -itis and -osis being the most obvious examples.

- -病 (-BYŌ: disease, illness)
ハンセン氏病, Hansenshi-byō: Hansen's disease (leprosy)

- -剤 (-ZAI: drug or chemical agent)
消化剤, shōkazai: aid to digestion; 刺激剤, shigekizai: stimulant

Suffixes of Influence

These suffixes indicate things that influence other things. If that seems vague, it's because this category is like that one table at a wedding reception where you seat all the misfits who don't belong at other tables.

- -別 (-BETSU: classified by, according to)
年齢別, nenreibetsu: by age; 科目別, kamokubetsu: by subject

- -法 (-HŌ: method, way, law)
発想法, hassōhō: way of conceiving of things; 表現法, hyōgenhō: method of expression

- -下 (-KA: under)
戒厳令下, kaigenreika: under martial law

- -圏 (-KEN: sphere, radius)
勢力圏, seiryokuken: sphere of influence; 爆撃圏, bakugekiken: bombing range

- -力 (-RYOKU: ability, capacity, power)
英語力, Eigoryoku: ability with English; 集中力, shūchūryoku: ability to concentrate

- -用 (-YŌ: use, for)
外人用, gaijinyō: for foreigners' use; 携帯用, kei-taiyō: portable

How Kanji Modify Each Other in Compounds

The ocean of kanji compounds seems nearly infinite, but one can group them into just a few categories, according to how their parts relate to each other. (This exhibit is therefore analogous to Exhibit 30, "Just the Facts: Classification of Characters," which categorized singletons according to the way their components relate to each other.) Experts don't always agree on categories of compounds. I've chosen categories that make most sense to me, with minimal hair-splitting.

My examples mainly come from *Let's Learn More Kanji* by Richard Glenn Covington, Joyce Yumi Mitamura, and Yasuko Kosaka Mitamura. This exhibit includes only compounds of two kanji, which is what you'll see most often. When compounds contain three kanji, the first or last is usually an affix, such as those listed in Exhibit 42. A four-kanji compound may contain an affix or might be a union of two compounds (e.g., 大学時代, *daigakujidai*: college days).

Yaeko Habein has written two books about compounds. She maintains that the most common ones fall into Types 2, 3, and 4 below.

Type 1: Duplication of a Single Kanji

This type always includes the duplication kanji 々, which makes nouns plural or otherwise intensifies the word at hand. For more on such repetition, see Exhibit 53, "Thematic Explorations: You Can Say That Again!"

人 (*JIN, hito*: person) x 2
= 人々 (*hitobito*: people)

時 (*JI, toki*: time) x 2
= 時々 (*tokidoki*: sometimes)

月 (*GATSU, tsuki*: month) x 2
= 月々 (*tsukizuki*: every month)

Type 2: Combination of Similar or Related Kanji

正 (*SEI, tada•shii*: correct) + 確 (*KAKU, tashi•ka*: certain)
= 正確 (*seikaku*: accurate)

永 (*EI, naga•i*: long time) + 久 (*KYŪ, hisa*: long time)
= 永久 (*eikyū*: forever)

道 (*DŌ, michi*: way, road) + 路 (*RO, ji*: route)
= 道路 (*dōro*: road)

生 (*SEI, i•kiru*: life) + 活 (*KATSU*: liveliness)
= 生活 (*seikatsu*: life)

姉 (*SHI, ane*: elder sister) + 妹 (*MAI, imōto*: younger sister)
= 姉妹 (*shimai*: sisters)

見 (*KEN, mi•ru*: to see) + 聞 (*BUN, ki•ku*: to hear)
= 見聞 (*kenbun*: information, experience)

Type 3: Combination of Opposite Kanji

多 (*TA, ō•i*: many) + 少 (*SHŌ, suku•nai*: few)
= 多少 (*tashō*: more or less)

長 (*naga•i*: long) + 短 (*miji•kai*: short)
= 長短 (*chōtan*: good and bad points)

上 (*JŌ, ue*: top) + 下 (*GE, shita*: bottom)
= 上下 (*jōge*: up and down)

有 (*YŪ, U, a•ru*: to have, exist) + 無 (*MU*: not, none, to cease to be)
= 有無 (*umu*: yes or no, existence or nonexistence)

Type 4: The First Kanji Modifies the Second One, a Noun

The initial kanji can be a noun or adjective.

外 (*GAI, soto*: outside) + 国 (*KOKU, kuni*: country)
= 外国 (*gaikoku*: foreign countries)

白 (*HAKU, shiro•i*: white) + 紙 (*SHI, kami*: paper)
= 白紙 (*hakushi*: blank paper)

夕 (*SEKI, yū*: evening) + 日 (*NICHI, hi*: sun)
= 夕日 (*yūhi*: setting sun)

Type 5: The First Kanji Is a Verb, the Second One Its Object

失 (*SHITSU, ushina•u*: to lose) + 業 (*GYŌ*: job)
= 失業 (*shitsugyō*: losing a job, unemployed)

作 (*SAKU, tsuku•ru*: to make) + 文 (*BUN*: sentence)
= 作文 (*sakubun*: essay)

投 (*TŌ, nage•ru:* to throw) + 球 (*KYŪ, nama:* ball)
= 投球 (*tōkyū:* throwing or pitching a ball)

Type 6: The First Kanji Is the Subject, the Second One Its Verb or Adjective

地 (*JI, CHI:* ground) + 震 (*SHIN, furu•eru:* to shake)
= 地震 (*jishin:* earthquake)

氷 (*HYŌ:* ice) + 解 (*KAI:* to dissolve)
= 氷解 (*hyōkai:* thawing)

骨 (*KOTSU, hone:* bone) + 折 (*SETSU, o•ru:* to bend, break)
= 骨折 (*kossetsu:* bone fracture)

年 (*NEN, toshi:* year) + 少 (*SHŌ, suku•nai, suko•shi:* a little, few)
= 年少 (*nenshō:* youth)

Type 7: One Kanji Is an Affix

The second and third examples in each subcategory introduce affixes that Exhibit 42 did not include. These and other unexplored affixes come from *The Complete Guide to Everyday Kanji* by Yaeko Habein and Gerald Mathias.

Prefixes

不- (*FU-:* not) + 安 (*AN:* peacefulness)
= 不安 (*fuan:* insecure)

以- (*I-:* than, from) + 下 (*KA, shita:* below)
= 以下 (*ika:* less than)

予- (*YO-:* beforehand) + 定 (*TEI, sada•meru:* to fix, establish)
= 予定 (*yotei:* plan)

Suffixes

法 (*HŌ:* law) + -的 (*-TEKI:* -ic)
= 法的 (*hōteki:* legal)

突 (*TOTSU, tsu•ku:* abruptly) + -然 (*-ZEN:* state of things)
= 突然 (*totsuzen:* suddenly)

帽 (*BŌ:* cap) + -子 (*-SHI, -SU:* thing)
= 帽子 (*bōshi:* hat)

Type 8: The Compound Abbreviates a Longer One

国際 (*kokusai:* international) + 連合 (*rengō:* union)
= 国連 (*kokuren:* United Nations)

東京 (*Tōkyō:* Tokyo) + 大学 (*daigaku:* university)
= 東大 (*Tōdai:* Tokyo University)

原子 (*genshi:* atom) + 爆弾 (*bakudan:* bomb)
= 原爆 (*genbaku:* atomic bomb)

日本 (*Nihon:* Japan) + 航空 (*kōkū:* aviation)
= 日航 (*Nikkō:* Japan Airlines)

The kanji on these candles are 福 (*FUKU:* blessing, fortune, wealth) and 愛 (*ai:* love). These are written in grass script, *sōsho* (more on that in Exhibit 57, "Just the Facts: Typefaces"), so they're very hard for non-native speakers to interpret. It may be tempting to read this pair of kanji candles as forming a compound, but they don't.

Will the Real Compound Please Stand Up?

Kanji compounds are such a delight with their neat, witty, and poetic constructions that one could fall into a trap. Maybe any two kanji that seem like they could go together *do* go together. Ah, not so. Your task is to figure out which of the following compounds are real words. Don't search for errors in the definitions or in the on-yomi of individual kanji; in all cases, the correct meanings and readings appear. The question is whether these combinations actually exist. Write T (true) or F (false) in the spaces provided. You'll find answers in the Answer Key. *Ganbatte kudasai!*

1. Compounds with 幸 (KŌ, shiawa•se, sachi: good fortune, happiness)

幸福	happiness + good fortune *kōfuku:* happy	___
幸不幸	happiness + not + happiness *kōfukō:* happiness or misery	___
幸運	good fortune + luck *kōun:* good fortune	___
薄幸	thin, weak + happiness *hakkō:* ill-fated	___
言幸	to say + good fortune *genkō:* fortune teller	___
幸日	good fortune + day *kōbi:* lucky day	___
山の幸	mountain + good fortune *yama no sachi:* mtn. food products	___
幸当たる	good fortune + to win a lottery *kōataru:* to win at gambling	___

2. Compounds with 激 (GEKI, hage•shii: violent, severe, sudden)

激血	violent + blood *gekiketsu:* violent crime	___
激化する	severe + to change *gekika suru:* to intensify	___
急激	sudden + sudden *kyūgeki:* abrupt	___
激運動	severe + to move + to move *gekiundō:* extreme sports	___
激臭	severe + odor *gekishū:* strong odor	___
激変	sudden + to change *gekihen:* to change radically	___
過激	to exceed + severe *kageki:* extreme	___
激心	severe + heart *gekishin:* change of heart	___
激怒	violent + anger *kegido:* wild rage	___

3. Compounds with 能 (NŌ: ability, function; yo•ku: skillfully)

無能	no + ability *munō:* incompetent	___
不可能	not + possible + ability *fukanō:* impossible	___
喜劇無能	comedy (1st 2 chars.) + no + ability *kigeki munō:* comedy of errors	___
欠能体	lack + ability + body *ketsunōtai:* physical disability	___
全知全能	all + to know + all + ability *zenchi zennō:* all-knowing and all-powerful	___
万能	myriad + ability *bannō:* omnipotence	___
効能	effect + ability *kōnō:* efficacy	___
本能	inherent + ability *honnō:* instinct	___
性能	nature + function *seinō:* performance, efficiency	___

生能	birth + ability *seinō:* innate ___	
能書	ability + writing, drawing *nōsho:* calligraphy ___	
能動	ability + to move *nōdō:* activity ___	

4. Compounds with 軽 (*KEI, karu•i, karo•yaka:* light; *karo•njiru:* to make light of, to slight)

軽食	light + to eat, meal *keishoku:* light meal ___
軽点	light + focus *keiten:* to relax, unwind ___
軽蔑	to slight + to despise *keibetsu:* contempt, disdain ___
軽石	light + stone *karuishi:* pumice stone ___
軽人	light + person *keijin:* thin person ___
軽薄	light + frivolous *keihaku:* insincere ___
軽快	light + fast *keikai:* light, nimble ___
軽々しい	light + light *karugarushii:* frivolous, rash ___
軽心	light + heart *keishin:* to unburden oneself emotionally ___
口軽	mouth + light *kuchigaru:* loose-lipped ___

気軽	spirit + light *kigaru:* lighthearted, ready ___

5. Compounds with 力 (*RYOKU, RIKI, chikara:* power, force, strength, energy)

引力	to pull + force *inryoku:* gravitation, attraction ___
人力車	person + power + car *jinrikisha:* rickshaw ___
過力	to pass by + power *kariki:* power of past events over an individual or society ___
力士	power + samurai, warrior *rikishi:* sumo wrestler ___
出力	to go out + power *shutsuryoku:* output ___
報道力	public news (1st 2 chars.) + power *hōdōryoku:* power of the press ___
力落とし	energy + to fall *chikaraotoshi:* discouragement ___
力行	power + to act *rikkō:* exertion ___
脱力	to remove + power *datsuryoku:* drained of strength ___
感力する	to feel deeply + power *kanryoku suru:* to be overcome with emotion ___
怪力	mysterious + power *kairiki:* superhuman strength ___
発言力	to issue + word + power *hatsugenryoku:* a voice, a say ___

Homonyms and Near Homonyms

There's something odd about corpses and homonyms in Japanese. A profusion of corpse-related homonyms sets people right up for misunderstandings and jokes. Consider these confusing pairs:

kojin	故人	(dead person)
kojin	個人	(individual)

itai	遺体	(corpse)
itai	痛い	(painful)

shitai	死体	(corpse)
shitai	肢体	(limbs)

shinin	死人	(dead person)
shin'in	真因	(true cause)

Fortunately, kanji clarifies these types of mix-ups, allowing you to show that when you call someone *chijin,* you mean "acquaintance" (知人), not "idiot" (痴人). Similarly, kanji makes it clear whether, when you say *jiko,* you're talking about yourself (自己) or an accident (事故).

In the list of corpse homonyms above, *shinin* and *shin'in* (the last pair) are near homonyms, rather than the actual thing. By "near homonym," I mean one of several types of situations:

- Pairs that sound identical except for a slight difference in how the *n* sound relates to surrounding vowels. (*Shinin* is しにん, whereas *shin'in* is しんいん.) This difference affects pronunciation and meaning, as we saw in Exhibit 16, "Just the Facts: The Japanese Syllables," with *kin'en* (禁煙, きんえん: no smoking) and *kinen* (記念, きねん: anniversary, memorial). Here's another example:

tani	谷	(たに: valley)
tan'i	単位	(たんい: academic unit)

- Pairs such as *kyō* (今日, きょう: today) and *kiyō* (器用, きよう: dexterous, clever). In these pairs, one word contains a consonant (*k,* in this case) followed by a small *ya* (や), *yu* (ゆ), or *yo* (よ), creating a diphthong such as *kya* (きゃ), *kyu* (きゅ), or *kyo* (きょ).

The other word contains the same consonant but is followed by a full-sized や, ゆ, or よ. Here's another example featuring a *b* instead of a *k:*

byōin	病院	(びょういん: hospital)
biyōin	美容院	(びよういん: hair salon)

- Words that are identical, except for short versus long vowels:

hoshi	星	(star)
hōshi	奉仕	(service)
hoshii	欲しい	(to want, yearn for)

- Pairs in which multiple syllables have this kind of short-long vowel discrepancy:

yume	夢	(dream)
yūmei	有名	(famous)

- Pairs whose consonants sound slightly different (often voiced):

hanasu	話す	(to talk)
hanatsu	放つ	(to release)

senshū	先週	(last week)
zenshū	禅宗	(Zen religion)

daiyō	代用	(substitute)
taiyō	太陽	(sun) or 大洋 (ocean)

- Pairs in which native speakers place different emphasis on otherwise identical syllables:

haSHI	橋	(bridge)
HAshi	箸	(chopsticks)

KIkan	機関	(engine)
kiKAN	気管	(trachea)

NIji	二時	(2:00)
niJI	虹	(rainbow)

Similar-sounding Japanese words obviously provide many opportunities for confusion! As Haruhiko Kindaichi wrote in *The Japanese Language,* "The lack of syllabic variety in Japanese has produced many words that are pronounced alike or nearly alike. The other day when I switched on the radio, I heard the words:

shikai shikai shikai. I wondered what it meant and later learned that the correct form was *shika-ishi-kai shikai* (chairmanship of the dentists' conference)" (p. 111). He then mentioned that there are about thirty words pronounced *kōshō.*

Thirty is unusually high, but it's certainly not uncommon to have three or four words that are exact homonyms. During dictionary searches, it often seems that more words are homonyms than not. In fact, homonyms account for the majority of words on page 206 of my Random House Japanese-English dictionary. Of the 61 entries, 31 are homonyms or near homonyms, and 30 are not. Out of the 31 homophonous words, only 4 are near homonyms; the rest are perfect matches.

Here's a rare but particularly confusing situation: Some homonym pairs have the opposite meaning! That's true of these:

好天	*kōten:*	good weather
荒天	*kōten:*	rough weather

This reminds me of how one word in Urdu, the national language of Pakistan, means both "yesterday" and "tomorrow"! The verb tense allows Pakistanis to grasp the meaning.

Some Japanese homonyms have entirely different kanji, which helps. That's true in this group of *yōshi* homonyms:

用紙	*yōshi:*	blank page
要旨	*yōshi:*	gist, main idea
容姿	*yōshi:*	looks
養子	*yōshi:*	adopted child

However, many homonym pairs share a kanji, so you need to be particularly careful with those. Consider, for instance, these homonyms or near homonyms:

機会	*kikai:*	chance
機械	*kikai:*	machine
書店	*shoten:*	bookstore
商店	*shōten:*	store
書名	*shomei:*	book title
署名	*shomei:*	signature
国家	*kokka:*	nation
国歌	*kokka:*	national anthem
不通	*futsū:*	interruption of transportation service
普通	*futsū:*	usual
会員	*kaiin:*	member of an organization
海員	*kaiin:*	sailor

Game: *Homonym Match-Up*

Kana Needed: N / Kanji Level: 2 / Difficulty Level: 2

Below, you'll find groups of homonyms. Match compounds to definitions, filling in blanks with the appropriate letters. Answers appear in the Answer Key. *Ganbatte kudasai!*

A. *shinchō*
   1. 慎重 _____   a. Person's height
   2. 身長 _____   b. Cautious, prudent

B. *shinchū*
   1. 心中 _____   a. Occupation, stationing
   2. 進駐 _____   b. Innermost thoughts
   3. 真鍮 _____   c. Brass

C. *shindo* (3 instances) and *shindō* (1 instance)
   1. 震度 _____   a. Quaking, oscillation, trembling
   2. 深度 _____   b. Progress
   3. 進度 _____   c. Magnitude of an earthquake (Japanese scale)
   4. 震動 _____   d. Depth of water

D. *shingai*
   1. 侵害 _____   a. Violation, infringement
   2. 心外 _____   b. Unexpected, regrettable

E. *shingaku*
   1. 進学 _____   a. Theology
   2. 神学 _____   b. Entrance into school of a higher level (e.g., university from high school)

F. *shingi*
1. 審議 ＿＿＿ a. Truth
2. 信義 ＿＿＿ b. Faith, fidelity, loyalty
3. 真偽 ＿＿＿ c. Discussion, scrutiny

G. *shingo* and *shingō*
1. 新語 ＿＿＿ a. Newly coined word
2. 信号 ＿＿＿ b. Traffic light, signal

H. *shinjin*
1. 新人 ＿＿＿ a. Religious belief
2. 信心 ＿＿＿ b. Newcomer

I. *shinju* and *shinjū*
1. 真珠 ＿＿＿ a. Pearl
2. 心中 ＿＿＿ b. Double suicide

J. *shinka*
1. 深化 ＿＿＿ a. True value
2. 進化 ＿＿＿ b. Fire of anger or jealousy
3. 心火 ＿＿＿ c. Deepening
4. 真価 ＿＿＿ d. Evolution

K. *shinken*
1. 真剣 ＿＿＿ a. Parental authority
2. 親権 ＿＿＿ b. Earnest, sincere

L. *shinkō*
1. 進行 ＿＿＿ a. Belief, religion
2. 親交 ＿＿＿ b. Progress
3. 信仰 ＿＿＿ c. Friendship

M. *shinkoku*
1. 申告 ＿＿＿ a. Report
2. 深刻 ＿＿＿ b. Serious, grave

This kanji means "dragon" (龍, *RYŪ*, *tatsu*). Speaking of homonyms, there's a plethora of kanji with the on-yomi of *RYŪ*, and quite a few kanji have the kun-yomi of *tatsu*. There's even one other kanji with both of those yomi and with the meaning of "dragon"—namely, 竜. This is a newer version of 龍, which now appears mainly in people's names. That's a shame, because although 龍 has evolved considerably from the pictograph that originally showed a dragon's pointy body parts, it's easier to see an animal form in 龍 than in the simplified 竜.

Syllabic Similarity

Once when I emailed a friend about a Japanese company, I remembered the name wrong and typed the second word in rōmaji as *Hanbei* (anti-American), rather than *Hanbai* (sales). My friend must have been puzzled about just what kind of company this was! If I'd taken a moment to consider the kanji (反米, *hanbei*, which is "to oppose" + "America," versus 販売, *hanbai,* which is "to sell" + "to sell"), I most likely wouldn't have made this error. But the problem doesn't just exist on my end. Throughout Japanese, similar-sounding words form traps for unsuspecting Joes and Janes.

In Exhibit 45, we saw how homonyms and near homonyms create difficulties. Above and beyond that, countless words differ by only a single rōmaji letter. I've just turned to my Random House dictionary, hoping to tell you about *kōka, kokka, koko,* and *kōkō.* And I see that the problem is far worse than I imagined. Just look at all these similar or identical words:

kōka	硬貨:	coin
kōka	効果:	effect
kōka	工科:	engineering department
kōka	高価:	expensive
kōkai	航海:	sailing
kōkai	公海:	open sea
kōkai	後悔:	regret
kōkai	公開:	open to the public
kōkaidō	公会堂:	public hall
kōkan	好感:	good impression
kōkan	交換:	exchange
kōkatsu	狡猾:	cunning

I haven't even made it out of the *kōka* . . . range! To reach *koko* (here) and *kōkō* (high school), I'd have to wade through seven more sets of similar-sounding words.

Despite slight variations in spelling and large variations in meaning, these words have one important commonality. All are kanji compounds. That is, they're formed entirely from on-yomi. And on-yomi tend to sound alike. As I've come to understand, that's at the root of the problem.

I'd like to walk you through my thinking, even the wrong turns, because I hope this analysis can do for you what it did for me. Getting a handle on the sounds of on- and kun-yomi has changed the whole way I think about Japanese words.

Once, after a day of doing kanji research, I plopped down in front of the World Baseball Classic, which my husband was watching on TV. Too tired to complain about how boring baseball is, I shut my eyes and melted into the couch. But I couldn't sleep, because I kept hearing Japanese names (since Japan was playing South Korea): *Aoki, Nishioka, Fujikawa, Kawasaki, Matsuzaka.* I tried to shut it all out, but my brain kept screaming, "Kun-kun constructions! These are kun-kun constructions!" I knew that partly because the names resonated with simple vocabulary: "green," "tree," "west," "hill," "river," "pine forest." But even more than that, all the sounds had the same rhythm. No long vowels, no doubled consonants, no *kya*-type contractions. I thought of all the Japanese people I knew and considered their names: *Nagamatsu, Nakashima, Yamada, Shiraishi.* . . . Yes, kun-kun combinations every time. But what about *Yū Gōji,* the name of the guy who has helped me immeasurably with this book? I opened my eyes and thought, "That name is all on-yomi! I know that without having the slightest idea what it looks like in kanji." I tuned back into the game: *Shimizu, Aikawa, Suzuki.* Kun-yomi galore! Never before had baseball seemed so interesting!

I wasn't thinking anywhere along these lines when I first contemplated the homonym problem. Instead, I initially wondered whether many words sound alike simply because the Japanese lexicon is large. Japan already had its own native vocabulary *(wago)* before absorbing thousands of words from Chinese *(kango).* That's why there are at least two ways to say just about anything in Japanese—even the numbers from one to ten! The profusion of synonyms is undeniable, but still I sensed that that didn't explain all or even much of the problem at hand.

More likely, I thought, the issue had something to do with the syllabary. There are only five vowel sounds in Japanese, whereas English has three ways of pronouncing just *a.* Then, too, the Japanese syllabary has just nine main consonants: *k, s, t, n, h, m, y, r,* and *w.* But none of this holds much water for a variety of reasons.

When you take into account contracted syllables (that is, *kya, kyu, kyo,* and so on), you add 21 syllables to the list. And when you consider voiced syllables (that is, *ga, ba, pa, bya, pya,* and so on), you find 36 more. The total, then, is 108 syllables.

A word can start with any syllable but ん *(n)*. Subsequent positions in a word can take all syllables. I don't advise losing yourself in calculations of factorials, as I did! Let's just ignore ん. Doing so still leaves 107 syllables that end in vowel sounds and that can therefore combine smoothly. This should allow for considerable variety. Theoretically, you could string together any of the 107 syllables and produce readable words, such as the following constructions, which I have invented:

ta + ka + zu + ro + mi
se + no + ra + ki
kya + mo + ri

If you tried this experiment with English letters (the building blocks of English words), you'd end up with things like "xlgf," more often than not.

Ah, but here's the complicating factor—and the key to the issue, I believe. As you know, Japanese consists of two types of words, *kango* and *wago.* Of these, only *wago* words sound like strings of syllables. In fact, that's exactly how the native vocabulary sounds:

kanarazu   without fail
mezurashii   rare
Hajimemashite   How do you do?

Imagine for a moment the ancient Japanese stringing together many small syllables as if they were dainty pearls on a necklace. That's *wago.* In sharp contrast, picture laborers laying two large rocks side by side. That's closer to the construction of *kango,* which use on-yomi as building blocks.

From Haruhiko Kindaichi in *The Japanese Language* and Yaeko Habein in *The History of the Japanese Written Language,* I gather that indigenous Japanese lacked contracted syllables (such as *kya*), long vowels, and doubled consonants. And, I realize, these are the three sources of syncopated rhythms in *kango* words (e.g., 薬局, *yakkyoku:* pharmacy; and 歩道橋, *hodōkyō:* footbridge).

Wago therefore has fewer "ingredients," but the words tend to be long, which produces more differentiation between words. It would be hard to hear *mezurashii* as *atarashii* (new) or *kanashii* (sad), even though they share an ending.

The opposite is true of on-yomi. They fall into patterns based on Chinese sounds, patterns that are quite limited and repetitive in Japanese. (The same problem doesn't exist in Chinese, because tones differentiate words that would otherwise be homophones. But Japanese essentially lacks tones, so such distinctions disappear.) There are eighteen kanji called *cho* and seventy types of *chō*. Thus, you have *chōshoku* (朝食: breakfast), *chōjo* (長女: eldest daughter), and *chōsa* (調査: investigation)—all formed with different *chō*'s. These eighty-eight *cho/chō* syllables help to form innumerable compounds. It's inevitable that many sound similar.

How inevitable? I wanted to assess the matter systematically, so I consulted the rōmaji readings index in Spahn and counted the two types of yomi from *A* through *C.* On the first page (all *A* words), I saw only three on-yomi—and eighty-five kun-yomi! Then again, *A* is prevalent in native Japanese, according to Kindaichi.

Patterns among on-yomi soon emerged, particularly with *C* yomi:

CHA	CHAKU	CHI	CHIKU	CHIN	CHITSU
CHO	CHŌ	CHOKU	CHU	CHŪ	CHUTSU

These yomi all start off sounding similar (with roots of *cha, chi, cho,* or *chu*). If they continue from there, they include long vowels or else they have add-ons such as *ku* and *tsu* or, less frequently, *n* and *i*. And that's it! The same patterns over and over again!

Knowing that *A–C* might not be representative letters, I then sought letters with the most on-yomi. The winners:

SA, SAI, SAKU, SAN, SATSU, SE, SECHI, SEI, SEKI, SEN, SETSU, SHA, SHAKU, SHI, SHICHI, SHII, SHIKI, SHIN, SHITSU, SHO, SHŌ, SHOKU, SHU, SHŪ, SHUKU, SHUN, SHUTSU, SO, SŌ, SOKU, SON, SOTSU, SU, SŪ, SUI (35 on-yomi)

KA, KAI, KAKU, KAN, KATSU, KE, KECHI, KEI, KEKI, KEN, KETSU, KI, KICHI, KIKU, KIN, KITSU, KO, KŌ, KOKU, KON, KOTSU, KU, KŪ, KUN, KUTSU, KYA, KYAKU, KYO, KYŌ, KYOKU, KYŪ (31)

RA, RACHI, RAI, RAKU, RAN, RATSU, REI, REKI, REN, RETSU, RI, RICHI, RIKI, RIKU, RIN, RITSU, RO, RŌ, ROKU, RON, RU, RUI, RYAKU, RYO, RYŌ, RYOKU, RYŪ (27)

GA, GAI, GAKU, GAN, GATSU, GE, GEKI, GEN, GETSU, GI, GIN, GO, GŌ, GOKU, GON, GOTSU, GU, GŪ, GUN, GYAKU, GYO, GYŌ, GYOKU, GYŪ (24)

Again, the same patterns jumped out, including the four common add-ons, plus two more: *ki* and *chi*. It also became apparent that on-yomi consist of the following:

1 consonant + 1 vowel or contracted vowel (+ one of 6 common endings)

This simple recipe accounts for yomi as disparate as *SAI, KYAKU,* and *RETSU.* The similarity in patterns becomes especially obvious when you consider rhymes that cut across the four lists:

KA, SA, RA, GA
KAI, SAI, RAI, GAI

KAKU, SAKU, RAKU, GAKU

KAN, SAN, RAN, GAN

KATSU, SATSU, RATSU, GATSU

KEKI, SEKI, REKI, GEKI

KEN, SEN, REN, GEN

KETSU, SETSU, RETSU, GETSU

KI, SHI, RI, GI

KIN, SHIN, RIN, GIN

KO, KŌ, SHO, SHŌ, SO, SŌ, RO, RŌ, GO, GŌ

KOKU, SHOKU, ROKU, GOKU

KON, SON, RON, GON

KU, SHU, SU, RU, GU

KYAKU, SHAKU, RYAKU, GYAKU

It's no wonder so many compounds sound alike. And Japanese vocabulary stands a chance of going further in that direction. As Kindaichi pointed out about 50 years ago, on-yomi building blocks offer the possibility of creating innumerable new words, ones that native speakers understand just from seeing the kanji.

If syllables in Japan can seem similar, so can banners at the temple Sugimoto-dera in Kamakura. The kanji on the left-hand side are the mirror image of those on the right-hand side, because we're most likely seeing the left-hand banners from behind; they're facing the correct direction for those descending the steps after visiting the shrine. The vertical kanji refer to the name of the temple (Sugimoto) and to 十一面観音 (Jūichimen Kannon), the eleven-faced Goddess of Mercy:

• 十一面 (eleven faces)
• 杉本 (Sugimoto)
• 観音 (Kannon, the Buddhist deity of mercy)

The topmost kanji, 納奉 *(hōnō),* mean "to dedicate, offer." On the margins, other kanji give dates and donors' names.

Look-Alikes in Compounds

Words composed of look-alike characters can make you do a double-take. Check these out:

大丈夫	*daijōbu:* all right
大木	*taiboku:* large tree
大夫	*taifu:* high steward
本体	*hontai:* main body of machine, console
未来	*mirai:* future
本来	*honrai:* naturally
失笑	*shisshō:* sarcastic laughter
肺肝	*haikan:* lungs and liver
矢先	*yasaki:* arrowhead
賃貸し	*chingashi:* lease, rent
臣民	*shinmin:* royal subject
画面	*gamen:* screen
命令	*meirei:* decree, order
存在	*sonzai:* existence, being

In the following compound, the first character seems to have been flipped upside down to form the second one:

豊富	*hōfu:* plentiful

The next group prompts a different sort of double-take, because components repeat within each compound:

車庫	*shako:* garage
車輪	*sharin:* car wheel
囚人	*shūjin:* prisoner
火炎	*kaen:* flame
労力	*rōryoku:* trouble, effort, labor
協力	*kyōryoku:* cooperation
身贔屓	*mibiiki:* nepotism

And here are some look-alike compounds, whole words that look like each other:

本当	*hontō:* really
体当たり	*taiatari:* body blow

認定	*nintei:* authorization, acknowledgment
設定	*settei:* establishment, creation

地図	*chizu:* map
地区	*chiku:* district

If look-alike compounds make you do a double-take, how many times would you need to look at a sign like this to figure out what it says? The sign is at Hiyoshi Shrine in Yamaguchi City, which is in Yamaguchi Prefecture on the western tip of Honshu. The text on the sign explains the history of the shrine. "Hiyoshi" is 日吉, and "shrine" is 神社 (*jinja*). You can see 日吉 神社 a little left of center, near the bottom.

Wonderful Words

One fantastic part about learning other languages is finding words for concepts that don't exist in one's native tongue. Japanese is full of such surprises. Take, for example, these great words:

冷静 (*reisei:* one who is calm and thus makes good decisions) = cool + calm

花恥ずかしい (*hanahazukashii:* so beautiful as to put a flower to shame) = flower + shame

首っ引き (*kubippiki:* constantly referring to a dictionary) = neck + to pull

虻蜂取らず (*abuhachi torazu:* trying to catch both a fly and a bee in one swoop of the hand and failing to catch either; attempting two tasks simultaneously and accomplishing neither) = horsefly + bee + to take

昼行灯 (*hiru andon:* [as useless as] a lantern in broad daylight; slow-witted person; daydreamer) = daytime + to carry with + lamp

祭り込む (*matsurikomu:* to place an obnoxious person in an out-of-the-way post to be rid of him or her) = to enshrine + to put in

魚道 (*gyodō:* path regularly taken by a school of fish; fishway) = fish + path

蛍雪 (*keisetsu:* diligent study, implicitly by the light of fireflies and the reflection from snow) = firefly + snow

竹の子 (*take no ko:* bamboo shoot) = bamboo + child
A bamboo shoot is the child of bamboo!

畑水練 (*hatake suiren:* like learning swimming on dry land—useless book learning as opposed to life experience) = field + water + practice

畳水練 (*tatami suiren:* like practicing swimming on a tatami) = tatami mat + water + practice

点検商法 (*tenkenshōhō:* unscrupulously making sales by posing as an inspector and declaring the need to replace items) = spot + inspection + merchant + system

置き薬 (*okigusuri:* household medicines left behind by door-to-door salesmen who later collect money for the used portion) = to leave behind + medicine

置き傘 (*okigasa:* spare umbrella kept at one's workplace) = to leave behind + umbrella

若年寄 (*wakadoshiyori:* young person who looks or acts old) = young + age + to draw near

Looking at Clouds (and Flowers) from Both Sides Now

One can easily lose oneself in the cloud and flower sections of a kanji dictionary, looking at all the wonderful compounds:

雲海 (*unkai:* sea of clouds) = cloud + sea

紫雲 (*shiun:* auspicious purple clouds) = purple + cloud

戦雲 (*sen'un:* clouds of war) = war + cloud

片雲 (*katagumo:* clouds on only one side of the sky) = one-sided + cloud

行雲流水 (*kōun ryūsui:* floating clouds and flowing water, which is to say taking life easy) = to travel + cloud + to flow + water

花盗人 (*hananusubito:* one who steals flowers or cherry-blossom branches) = flower + to steal + person

花守 (*hanamori:* one who guards flowers or cherry blossoms against theft) = flower + keeper

花便り (*hanadayori:* news of how the flowers are blooming) = flower + news
Kashin (花信) means the same thing, so the Japanese must be serious about getting this news!

花明かり (*hanaakari:* soft brightness at evening due to an abundance of white cherry blossoms) = flower + bright

両手に花 (*ryōte ni hana:* flowers in both hands—having a double advantage or sitting between pretty women) = both + hand + flower

Funny-Sounding Words

These expressions are a joy to hear and say because of internal rhymes or near rhymes:

秋学期	*akigakki:* fall semester
自棄酒	*yakezake:* drowning one's cares in sake
記憶力	*kiokuryoku:* ability to remember
自殺説	*jisatsusetsu:* rumor about a suicide
主我主義	*shuga shugi:* egoism, love of self
歩道橋	*hodōkyō:* footbridge
働かなきゃ	*hatarakanakya:* you must work
進む	*susumu:* to advance, make progress
包む	*tsutsumu:* to wrap
続く	*tsuzuku:* to continue
移る	*utsuru:* to change, move
映す	*utsusu:* to reflect

祝福	*shukufuku:* blessing
消防署	*shōbōsho:* fire station
生き字引	*ikijibiki:* walking dictionary

Try saying this last one ten times fast!

A few more words sound funny for different reasons:

- Alternating rhymes:

掛けさせられる	*kakesaserareru:* to be made to sit down

- These words practically travel down lines in the syllabary:

機械工	*kikaikō:* mechanic
主唱者	*shushōsha:* advocate

If you want to record wonderful words, this notebook with *washi* (和紙, Japanese paper) glued to the front is the ideal place for that. The kanji are in seal style. (For more on that, see Exhibit 57, "Just the Facts: Typefaces.")

WHAT KANJI SAY ABOUT JAPAN

4

Language is a cultural mirror, one that reflects how its native speakers view the world. What concepts have they represented linguistically? Do they speak directly or indirectly? With what imagery do they create analogies? Bringing these questions down to the scale of this book, what do kanji reflect about Japan?

Exhibit 49, "Spectacular Shapes: Gates, Birds, and Thread," puts kanji under the microscope, scrutinizing three frequently used components. This, by the way, is a most un-Japanese way of viewing kanji. Native speakers look at kanji holistically and quickly, gleaning whatever they need and moving on with their business. But as newcomers with boundless curiosity, we can take time to stop and analyze the roses—or the metals, as in Exhibit 50, "Thematic Explorations: Metals." The gold or metal component 金 appears so often in characters that it's worth peeking into the realm of Japanese metallurgy. And now that you have a handle on how kanji don't always mean what they seem to, have a go at Exhibit 51, "Game: What's the Meaning of This?!"

Another set of characters prompts wonderment, as well as occasional confusion. If 日 stands for Japan, the land of the rising sun, does that make America (米) the land of rising rice? What about Egypt (埃) as mere dust, France (仏) as a Buddhist stronghold, Germany (独) as a bunch of lonely hearts, and Malaysia (馬) as home to the horsey set? Exhibit 52, "Just the Facts: Country Kanji," enters the wonderful world of kanji abbreviations for country names. The first part provides information that you'll use in the next part, "Game: International Intrigue."

Playfulness permeates the Japanese language. Take, for example, words such as *baibai* (売買: buying and selling), *tsurutsuru* (slippery), *zukazuka* (making a rude entrance), and *wazawaza* (purposely). Exhibit 53, "Thematic Explorations: You Can Say That Again!" presents other words with internal repetition.

Japanese playfulness extends to compounds with double meanings. Take, for instance, 蛍火 (*hotarubi*: firefly + fire). On a literal level, this means "light of a firefly." But it also refers metaphorically to the glowing embers of a fire. The Japanese love fireflies, so this metaphor seems affectionate, poetic, and clever all at once. For more such wordplay, see Exhibit 54, "Thematic Explorations: Double Meanings." As you read it, consider whether the Japanese still hear the metaphors as metaphors or whether they've become so much a part of the language as to have lost that sense. For example, when people speak of "surfing" the Web, I sometimes picture a surfboard on waves. But when I hear references to cruising the streets (for late-night entertainment) or cruising furniture (as babies do), water rarely comes to mind. "Cruise" in these senses has split off from its nautical roots; its metaphorical status has withered.

Similarly, proverbs often drift from their original contexts. When people use such language nowadays, they don't really hear what they're saying. The expression "I'm in the same boat" doesn't make us visualize a boat at all, much less the original one. And what *was* the original vessel? The Titanic? Noah's Ark? Hard to know. Many Japanese people have the same disconnect when they refer to, say, *goetsu dōshū,* 呉越同舟, which means "bitter enemies stuck in the same boat by chance" or "antagonists joining together for a common purpose." Again, what boat? Is this proverb simply a reappropriation of a Western one? (That sometimes happens, though Japanese people don't always recognize the import for what it is.) Fortunately, the kanji in 呉越同舟 give us an inkling of its origin. The last two characters are "same" + "boat." And the first two kanji, *Wu* and *Yue,* refer to two rival states in ancient China (called *Go* and *Etsu* in Japanese). So the proverb must be an Asian product after all. Maybe the English version is, too!

If both English and Japanese speakers tend to miss the references in proverbs, they're also deaf to the original tone much of the time. It would be more than bizarre if Valley Girls were truly beseeching the Lord whenever they said, "Oh my God!" The tone and intent of this phrase have evolved over the centuries, even though the wording hasn't. The current mismatch between the wording and the meaning renders it an idiomatic expression, an ateji of sorts. Like an archaeological relic, this phrase points to an ardent religious feeling from the past. In the same vein, Exhibit 55, "Thematic Explorations: Hyperbolic Humility," presents Japanese idioms whose anachronistic content and tone allow us to see the culture as it once was.

This issue of what people say versus what they hear is of particular interest when it comes to kanji, because certain characters communicate concepts more efficiently than spoken words can. When someone says *moto,* another person can understand it as something like "base," "root," or "origin." That general sense suffices for conversational purposes. But the written version of *moto* conveys much more, because five characters, all pronounced *moto,* represent various aspects of this one idea:

下	below, down, low
元	beginning, origin
本	root, bottom
素	elementary, principle
基	fundamentals

Exhibit 56, "Thematic Explorations: Shades of Meaning," explores shades of meaning as represented by homophonous kanji. The exhibit also looks at the idea that when a language splits hairs in this way, it shows what people in that culture care deeply about and feel a need to specify. For most languages this assumption holds true. But in Japanese it's trickier to draw this conclusion, because Chinese has left a great imprint on the language, primarily through kanji.

So there you have it: Kanji components, wordplay, metaphors, and differentiated characters, all reflecting the Japan of yesterday and today. And what have we learned from this reflection? Well, we know about the industries, religions, and aspects of the natural world that have shaped the Japanese mind. We also know that the Japanese have a great sense of humor, twisting the language to clever effect. But they're just as likely to be serious, producing a moralistic phrase about hard work, loyalty, or humility. We can see, above all, that because the culture has blended so many influences, it can be difficult to pinpoint the origins of words or ideas. So if kanji sometimes proves to be a cloudy mirror, that's because it's reflecting something murky and impure—but always fascinating.

Gates, Birds, and Thread

Certain components appear again and again inside kanji, especially gates, birds, and thread. What does this say about Japanese culture or about the ancient Chinese culture in which these components emerged? Let's take them one by one and explore the question.

Gates: 門 (*MON*, *kado: gate*)

The profusion of gates in kanji makes sense. Gateways catch the eye in Asia, especially the *torii* outside Shinto shrines. (Incidentally, the kanji for *torii*, 鳥居, breaks down as "bird" + "to exist." A *torii* is meant to be a resting place for birds, the messengers of Shinto gods.) In the 2003 South Korean movie *Spring, Summer, Fall, Winter... and Spring,* a gate serves as a prominent symbol, separating the busy, modern world from a tranquil, isolated Buddhist monastery. As the gate doors swing open, connecting the two realms, there's a sense of possibility, of freedom and spaciousness. When they close, one feels locked into the circumscribed world of the monastery. Fortunately, the kanji gates below tend to be fairly harmless.

Some of them are also quite logical. In the first, 間, one can easily imagine the sun (日) as it peeps through the doors of a gate. In the next character, 問, a mouth (口) appears at the gate to ask a question. In the third, 聞, someone presses her ear (耳) to the gate, awaiting an answer to the question she has just asked. After those three examples, logic deteriorates a bit. In 闇, for instance, a sound (音) inside a gate somehow leads to darkness.

間	*KAN, aida:* between
問	*MON, to•u:* to ask
聞	*MON, ki•ku:* to listen, ask
開	*KAI, a•keru:* to open
閉	*HEI, shi•maru:* to close
関	*KAN, seki:* barrier, connection
闇	*AN, yami:* darkness
闘	*TŌ, tataka•u:* to fight, struggle

Strange Things to Find Inside Your Gate

a horse	闖	(*CHIN:* to inquire about, sudden entry)
life	闊	(*KATSU:* wide, broad-minded)
a tree	閑	(*KAN:* leisure)
a mountain	閊	(*tsuka•eru:* to be obstructed or clogged, get stuck)
a heart	悶	(*MON, moda•eru:* to be in agony)

Compounds with Multiple Gates

閘門	*kōmon:* locking a gate
関門	*kanmon:* gateway, barrier
開門	*kaimon:* opening a gate
開閉	*kaihei:* opening and closing
欄間	*ranma:* transom
間間	*mama:* often, occasionally
閨閥	*keibatsu:* family groupings through marriage
門閥	*monbatsu:* lineage, pedigree
開闢	*kaibyaku:* (since) the creation
闇闇	*yamiyami:* without one's knowledge, suddenly, easily

Birds: 隹 (*SUI: short-tailed bird*)

The kanji for "bird," 鳥 (*CHŌ, tori*), serves as a radical in many bird-related characters. These include 鶴 (*KAKU, tsuru:* crane), 鳩 (*KYŪ, hato:* "dove" or "pigeon," the bird that replaces the cuckoo in Japanese clocks, which are called 鳩時計, *hatodokei*), and 鶏 (*KEI, niwatori:* "chicken," "hen," or "rooster," whose kun-yomi translates as "garden bird"). I'm sure 鳥 makes the Japanese think of a bird, but they might not see anything avian in 隹, which can stand alone or serve as a component. You'll find 隹 in these kanji with unbirdlike meanings:

曜	*YŌ:* day of week
離	*RI, hana•reru:* to separate, leave
集	*SHŪ, atsu•meru:* to gather, collect
雑	*ZATSU, ZŌ, ma•zeru:* miscellaneous
難	*NAN, muzuka•shii:* difficult

Why are there so many birds in characters, particularly ones as common as weekday names? Perhaps the Japanese (and originally the Chinese) have had a special attachment to birds. Haruhiko Kindaichi argues that the nature-loving Japanese are so familiar with various birds that *wago* (the native Japanese lexicon) is rich in bird names. He notes, too, that "Japanese differentiates between the cries of birds: *saezuru* for small birds, *tsugeru* (to inform) for chickens, *nanoru* (to call oneself) for cuckoos and skylarks, *tataku* (to tap) for water rails, and *kyō o yomu* (to read a sutra) for nightingales" (p. 168). Be that as it may, it's awfully hard to see the bird connection in the following compounds:

隻手	*sekishu:*	one-armed = one of a pair + hand
雀斑	*sobakasu:*	freckles = sparrow + spots
雄弁	*yūben:*	eloquence = male, brave, great + speech
焦点	*shōten:*	focal point = to scorch + point
雌熊	*meguma:*	female bear = female + bear
雑婚	*zakkon:*	intermarriage = mixed + marriage
難破	*nanpa:*	shipwreck = difficult + to break
離婚	*rikon:*	divorce = to separate from + marriage

Thread: 糸 (SHI, *ito*: thread)

I once watched a Japanese kanji expert struggle to write 綺麗 (*kirei*: beautiful). Although he normally would have drawn the characters from left to right, he wasn't sure how they should look, so he started with what he knew—the complicated second kanji. To my amazement, he zipped through it perfectly. Then he returned to 綺. Blanking out on its left-hand side, he again went with what he knew, rendering the right-hand side just fine. Finally, it came time to draw the left-hand side. After hesitating, he placed a mountain (山) where there should have been thread (糸). He had confused 綺 with a different character: 崎 (*saki, misaki*: cape, promontory). "Wow," I thought, "it's hard for him, too! Even experts forget the thread." Whenever I blank out about the left-hand side of a character, it's bound to be the thread component. (And thread around the finger is supposed to help you remember things!) Somehow, one never thinks of thread as part of a character. Trees, yes. Hands, sure. Water, definitely. But not thread. It rarely "ties" in to the meaning. Few of the kanji below have anything to do with thread.

Nevertheless, thread is a common kanji component because of its significance in Chinese history. The Chinese were the first to produce raw silk from silkworms. This practice had definitely started by 3000

BCE, possibly even three thousand years earlier! In other countries, demand for Chinese silk reached such heights that the famed Silk Road opened in the second century BCE, enabling silk-based trade with distant locales. The kanji 糸 is a pictograph of two silkworm cocoons (幺) with a little (小) thread unwinding below.

Kanji Featuring the Thread Component

紙	SHI, *kami*: paper
線	SEN: line
終	SHŪ, *o•waru*: to finish
練	REN, *ne•ru*: to knead, to train
約	YAKU: to promise
純	JUN: pure
細	SAI, *hoso•i*: thin, narrow
組	SO, *kumi*: group, set
結	KETSU, *musu•bu*: to tie, bind
経	KEI, *he•ru*: to pass
絡	RAKU, *kara•mu*: to get entangled
絵	KAI, E: picture
続	ZOKU, *tsuzu•ku*: to continue
緒	SHO, *itoguchi*: beginning
縮	SHUKU, *chiji•maru*: to shrink
縞	KŌ, *shima*: stripe
系	KEI: system, lineage
係	KEI, *kakari*: person in charge
機	KI, *hata*: device
幾	KI, *iku-*: how many

Thread Kanji Representing Colors

Several kanji with thread components represent colors. Originally, these meant "green thread," "purple thread," and so on. The first five are much more common than the last two.

緑	RYOKU, *midori*: green
紫	SHI, *murasaki*: purple
紅	KŌ, *kurenai*: red
緋	HI: scarlet
紺	KON: dark blue
縹	HYŌ, *hanada*: light blue
緇	SHI: black

Compounds with Multiple Pieces of Thread

紡糸	*bōshi*: spinning, yarn
細糸	*hosoito*: fine thread
紡織	*bōshoku*: spinning and weaving

紛糾　*funkyū:* complication, entanglement
纏綿　*tenmen:* entanglement
系統　*keitō:* system, lineage
純系　*junkei:* (genetically) pure line
終結　*shūketsu:* conclusion
締約　*teiyaku:* to sign a treaty
続編　*zokuhen:* sequel
絶縁　*zetsuen:* breaking off a relationship
縁結び　*enmusubi:* marriage
緯線　*isen:* latitude
経線　*keisen:* longitude

Compounds with Three Threaded Kanji

結合組織 *ketsugō soshiki:* connective tissue
紡績糸　*bōsekiito:* yarn
線維素　*sen'iso:* roughage, fiber, cellulose

A Bird Inside a Gate Secured with Thread

Now for the ultimate challenge—identifying compounds combining gates, birds, and thread! So far, I've found words including just two of the three:

離間　*rikan:* estrangement
離縁　*rien:* divorce, disowning
集約　*shūyaku:* intensive
結集　*kesshū:* to concentrate, marshal together
緑門　*ryokumon:* arch of greenery
権門　*kenmon:* powerful person
総門　*sōmon:* main gate

The English word "gate" suggests something impassable, something that says "Keep Out!" A *torii* couldn't be more different. It has no doors and instead seems to have an ethereal openness, as one can see even in 門, the "gate" kanji. Whereas most gates create a sense of rigid separation between "inside" and "outside," the *torii* creates the feeling of a passage, of a smooth, gentle transition between the two. In fact, people are required to pass under certain *torii* gates. Historically, that was true of the one in the photo; commoners were permitted to come to the holy island of Itsukushima (popularly called Miyajima) only if they approached by boat, passing through this gate in the water. This *torii* is part of Itsukushima Shrine, a Shinto shrine dating back to the 6th century CE. The current gate dates back to 1875, but the original one went up in 1168. Constructed on piers, the gate is about 16 meters (52 feet) high.

Metals

Before I supply any information about metals, here's a quiz! Match items on the left with those on the right. The right-hand descriptions reflect how the Japanese (and perhaps originally the Chinese) have seen these metals (according to the kanji, anyway) and may differ from your view. In some cases, more than one metal matches a description.

1. Copper ___   a. White metal
2. Platinum ___   b. Red metal
3. Gold ___   c. Black metal
4. Iron ___   d. Yellow metal
5. Lead ___
6. Silver ___

The results in the Answer Key might surprise you! You'll find explanations below.

After encountering words such as *kurogane, shirogane,* and *akagane,* which respectively mean "black metal," "white metal," and "red metal," I became intrigued by these colorful terms. As kun-kun combinations, they must be quite old. And yet I've never associated Old Japan with mining or metals but rather with softer materials, such as bamboo and wood. I wondered whether Japan's mountains contained pay dirt.

I discovered that around 300 BCE, Kyushu residents began using iron tools, having borrowed knowledge from China. These tools increased farming productivity and helped the Japanese establish an agricultural economy that replaced hunter-gatherer ways.

The problem lay in procuring metal, given the few mining resources in Japan. Coal deposits exist in inland Hokkaido and Kyushu. Iron comes from Hokkaido and northern Honshu. Modest amounts of gold and copper exist in Hokkaido, Honshu, and Karafuto. Other mineral resources include lead, zinc, and silver.

Mining in Japan continues today but rapidly declined in the 1980s. By contrast, imports of natural resources have grown significantly. In particular, Japan imports considerable amounts of coal (to produce electricity) and metals. In 2001, Japan spent $102.9 billion on minerals, accounting for almost 30 percent of all imports. One source called Japan the world's lead-ing consumer of nickel (especially from Indonesia).

It makes sense that any industrial nation requires metals, particularly one producing as many vehicles and electronic goods as Japan does. Unfortunately, none of this information sheds much light on the development of words such as *kurogane.* But here's what we do know about the kanji:

Yellow Metal: Gold

金 (KIN, *kane:* gold, metal, money)
The character 金 emphasizes gold as a mineral. This kanji also means "money" and appears in compounds such as 料金 (*ryōkin:* fare, fee).

黄金 (*kogane* or *ōgon:* gold) = yellow + metal
As the breakdown shows, this compound literally means "yellow metal." *Kogane* is a less common way of saying "gold" and indicates the preciousness of this metal.

White Metal: Silver, Platinum, and . . . Lead?!

銀 (GIN, *shirogane:* silver)
Shiro means "white," so the kun-yomi, *shirogane,* means "white metal." It makes some sense that ancient people saw silver as a white metal. But why did they attach this word to 銀? According to Kenneth Henshall in *A Guide to Remembering Japanese Characters,* the right-hand side, 艮, means "to stop" and expresses "white" phonetically but also suggests "to take a second look" or "to scrutinize." Because silver resembles less precious metals, it warrants careful examination.

白金 (*hakkin:* platinum) = white + metal
This compound contains two kanji that I would have read collectively as *shirogane.* Instead, we use two on-yomi to read this compound.

鉛 (EN, *namari:* lead)
Of all the "white metals," this singleton presents the greatest surprise. How can lead be white?! Henshall says the right-hand side of 鉛 phonetically expresses "white" but also means "hollowed out," combining

口 (source, opening) with 八 (out of) to convey "extraction." Speaking of extractions, Henshall squeezes one more interpretation out of the phonetic in 鉛. He notes that some scholars see this "white" as referring to cosmetics, because facial powder is white and because *shiro* is the Japanese word for both "whiteness" and "cosmetics." He adds that many ancient cosmetics were lead-based.

Black Metal: Iron

鉄 (*TETSU, kurogane*: iron)
As I mentioned, *kuroi* means "black," so the kun-yomi of 鉄, *kurogane,* means "black metal." That's a good fit for "iron." In 鉄, according to Henshall, the right-hand side acts phonetically to express "black," perhaps also lending the sense of "big." This phonetic refers to iron and by extension to steel, he says.

Red Metal: Copper

銅 (*DŌ, akagane*: copper)
When I hear *akagane,* I think "red metal." Copper is indeed a red metal; so far so good. Then I would expect to see 赤 (*aka•i*: red) somewhere in the kanji for "copper." Instead, the kanji is 銅! I figure that when it came time to represent this *wago* word, the Japanese couldn't find a kanji combining 金 and 赤. Instead, they chose 銅. Although 同 means "same," phonetically it expresses "red," says Henshall.

Other Metals and Minerals

Several related terms don't correlate to the "color + metal" schematic:

Tin: 錫 (*SEKI, SHAKU, suzu*)
The right-hand side is *yasashii,* "easy," because tin is very malleable.

Steel: 鋼 (*hagane*)
The right-hand side is *oka,* meaning "hill," in this case a towering and formidable hill, says Henshall. This phonetic also expresses "strong," he says, giving a composite meaning of a "strong" or "formidable metal."

Zinc: 亜鉛 (*aen*) = subordinate + lead
The first kanji means "next," "sub," or "Asia," followed by the character for "lead." Zinc is the next lead? Zinc is inferior to lead? Zinc is Asian lead? Beats me. But in the *Kodansha Kanji Learner's Dictionary,* Jack Halpern indicates that 亜 functions here to mean "subordinate."

The next compounds seem self-explanatory:

Bronze: 唐金 (*karakane*) = China, foreign + metal

Ore: 粗金 (*aragane*) = coarse, rough + metal

Mercury: 水銀 (*suigin*) = water + silver

Coal: 石炭 (*sekitan*) = stone + charcoal, coal

Mine: 鉱山 (*kōzan*) = ore + mountain

Some terms are in katakana, reinforcing the sense that Japan imports these metals:

Nickel: ニッケル (*nikkeru*)

Aluminum: アルミニウム (*aruminiumu*), abbreviated as アルミ (*arumi*)

We've seen that "black metal" means iron in 鉄 (*kurogane*), but here's a whole new take on black metal. In Hannō City in Saitama Prefecture, just north of Tokyo, a liquor store owner has used two oil drums as containers for sorted broken glass. He labeled one drum 黒 (*kuro*: black) for dark glass and the other one 白 (*shiro*: white) for clear glass . The white paint with which he drew the kanji oxidized to a bright orange when the metal drum rusted.

Kana Needed: N / Kanji Level: 0 / Difficulty Level: 1

What's the Meaning of This?!

Choosing from the options, pick the correct definition. Two answers may be right. (Note: Just for fun, I've presented the characters in Part I as simple sums of meanings. But don't take this too seriously. These kanji may not be *kaiimoji* at all. That is, a component may give a character its sound, contributing nothing to its meaning. For now, put these scholarly concerns aside and enjoy the game!) More than one answer may be right. Answers appear in the Answer Key.

Part 1

1. 軟 (car + lack)
    a. Environmentally friendly
    b. Underprivileged
    c. Soft

2. 湖 (water + old + moon, flesh)
    a. Lake
    b. Swamp
    c. Sewage

3. 患 (to pierce + heart)
    a. Broken heart
    b. To be sick
    c. Grilled beef heart

4. 煙 (fire + west + earth)
    a. Smoke
    b. Jet engine
    c. Hell

5. 袖 (clothing + reason)
    a. Shame
    b. Goosebumps
    c. Sleeve

6. 妙 (woman + few, a little)
    a. Scarce
    b. Odd
    c. Exquisite

7. 裕 (clothing + valley)
    a. Surplus
    b. Shopping center
    c. Closet

Part 2

1. 非常口 (not + normal + opening)
    a. Malocclusion
    b. Emergency exit
    c. Mick Jagger's mouth

2. 回復 (to turn + to return to)
    a. Doing something repeatedly
    b. Getting lost
    c. Recovering from an illness

3. 口座 (opening + place)
    a. Face
    b. Dentist
    c. Bank account

4. 改札口 (to reform + paper money + opening)
    a. Turnstile
    b. Change in interest rates
    c. Stock market

5. 木羽 (wood + wings)
    a. Angel
    b. Shingles on building
    c. Statue

6. 牛歩 (cow + to walk)
    a. Herding cattle
    b. Pasture
    c. Snail's pace

7. 化生 (to change + life)
    a. Menopause
    b. Metamorphosis
    c. Midlife crisis

8. 出所 (to leave + place)
    a. Departure in a vehicle
    b. Release from prison
    c. Nostalgia

9. お見舞い (honorific *o* + to see + dance)
    a. To attend a ballet
    b. To commit a crime
    c. To visit a sick person

Country Kanji

Japanese is wordy, and its words tend to be long. According to linguist Haruhiko Kindaichi in *The Japanese Language,* performing plays translated into Japanese takes twice as long as in the original language. Kindaichi's book fills one volume in English, two in Japanese. Perhaps for this reason Japanese newspapers and magazines often use abbreviations, particularly for country names. The first kanji in a country's name usually stands for the whole. Hence, 日, *NICHI* or *NI,* represents 日本, *Nihon* (Japan).

Country-name kanji can be tricky. Many are compounds of obsolete kanji originally chosen for their phonetic value. If they no longer have that pronunciation, the thread is hard to trace. For instance, 白耳義 stands for *Berugī* (Belgium). Using current on-yomi, you would read this as *hakujigi.* As we saw in Exhibit 36, "Just the Facts: Doesn't Sound the Way It's Spelled," this mismatch is ateji; the sounds of the individual kanji don't correspond to the sounds of the whole word. (The meanings of the characters don't match the meaning of the whole word, either. If these meanings did match, the individual kanji would make you think that 白耳義 referred to the "significance of white ears.") Although 白耳義 does not sound the way it's spelled, 白 does have the usual on-yomi *(HAKU)* when functioning as an abbreviation of the full country name. That is, 日白 is read as *Nichihaku* and refers to Japan-Belgium relations.

In pairings of country kanji, the more "important" country usually appears first. Hence, 日 precedes in 日中, *Nitchū* (Japan-China); 日米, *Nichibei* (Japan-United States); and 日韓, *Nikkan* (Japan–South Korea). Similarly, 米 (the United States) would come first in an article about United States–Mexico relations.

In the table on page 119, the second column displays kanji for the full names of countries and conti-

nents, as well as regions that were once independent entities, such as Manchuria, Mongolia, and Prussia. The third column shows kanji abbreviations for places, as well as pronunciations of those single kanji. The last column supplies other meanings and readings for the kanji singletons. The alternate meanings and readings are irrelevant here, but I've presented them just to satisfy curiosity.

Nowadays, it's common to represent country names and their abbreviations with katakana, especially newer names (e.g., イスラエル, *Isuraeru:* Israel). If a place name has no kanji, only katakana, it doesn't appear below. When both kanji and katakana abbreviations exist for a place, the third column presents those (e.g., 阿 and ア for Africa, in the first row).

A few more items of note:

- Certain kanji appear repeatedly in the full names of countries (e.g., 利 for the sound *ri*).
- Holland goes by the second kanji in its name, maybe because the first kanji represents "Africa."
- Sweden and Switzerland have the same abbreviation.
- The United States is formally called アメリカ合衆国, *Amerika Gasshūkoku,* but embassies usually refer to the United States as 米国, *Beikoku,* which means "rice country"! The 米 comes from 亜米利加, *Amerika.* Although 米 now has the on-yomi of *BEI,* it was also read as *ME* in the past.
- Vietnam's full name means "far south," the reference point being China. As a mnemonic, you could remember the compound for Vietnam as "Southern Cross" (the small, cross-shaped constellation over the South Pole to which Crosby, Stills, & Nash referred in their eponymous song), because 越南 breaks down as "cross" + "south."

Game: *International Intrigue*

You've traveled back in time to an era of worldwide war. (Actually, you've arrived in a time warp, as Prussia and Manchuria somehow coexist with Myanmar.) And you've discovered a box of notes about the warring countries. Japanese spies wrote these notes. To conceal their meaning, they used a code, substituting homonyms for country kanji. For instance, when they meant 墨 (*BOKU:* Mexico), they instead wrote 僕 (*boku:* I, used by males). But in no time flat, you decipher their vocabulary and record your findings.

Now you're ready to interpret the spies' text. In each sentence below, the spies discuss four or five countries. List the countries under discussion. (Hint: Look at the kanji in the sentences and figure out which ones appear in the Abbreviation column on the facing page. Whenever you find one that does, you've found an answer.) Answers appear in the Answer Key. *Ganbatte kudasai!*

1. 馬から葡萄と白い蘭がかかっています。
   Uma kara budō to shiroi ran ga kakatte imasu.
   Grapes and white orchids hang from the horse.

   _____

   _____

   _____

   _____

2. 仏教では蒙昧は瑞気じゃありません。
   Bukkyō de wa mōmai wa zuiki ja arimasen.
   In Buddhism, ignorance is not a good omen.

   _____

   _____

   _____

3. 伯父さんは英才ですが、独りぼっちのときは、馬を希います。
   Ojisan wa eisai desu ga, hitoribotchi no toki wa, uma o koinegaimasu.
   My uncle is talented, but when he's all alone, he desires horses.

   _____

   _____

   _____

   _____

4. 115丁目の西側には、土と言っては埃しかありません。
   115-chōme no nishigawa ni wa, tsuchi to itte wa hokori shika arimasen.
   On the west side of that city block, the soil is nothing but dust.

   _____

   _____

   _____

5. 豪を買うことを承諾したとき、印と墨汁をつかいました。
   Hori o kau koto o shōdaku shita toki, in to bokujū o tsukaimashita.
   When (he) agreed to buy the moat, (he) used (his) seal and India ink.

   _____

   _____

   _____

Country	Country-Name Kanji	Abbreviation	Yomi and Meaning
Africa	阿弗利加: *Afurika*	阿 *(A)*; ア	*A, O, omone•ru:* to be obsequious
Asia	亜細亜: *Ajia*	亜 *(A)*	*A:* to rank next, come after
Australia	豪州: *Gōshū*; 濠太剌利: *Ōsutoraria*	豪 *(GŌ)*	*GŌ, hori:* moat
Austria	墺太利: *Ōsutoria*	墺 *(Ō)*	*Ō:* land, shore
Belgium	白耳義: *Berugī*	白 *(HAKU)*; ベ	*HAKU, shiro•i:* white
Brazil	伯剌西爾: *Burajiru*	伯 *(HAKU)*; ブ	*HAKU:* eldest brother, uncle
Canada	加奈陀: *Kanada*	加 *(KA)*	*KA, kuwa•eru:* to add
China	中国: *Chūgoku*	中 *(CHŪ)*	*CHŪ, naka:* middle
Denmark	丁抹: *Denmāku*	丁 *(TEI)*; デ	*CHŌ:* city block; *TEI:* 4th in a series
Egypt	埃及: *Ejiputo*	埃 *(AI)*; エジプト	*AI, hokori:* dust
Europe	欧州: *Ōshū*; 欧羅巴: *Yōroppa*	欧 *(Ō)*	*Ō:* Europe
France	仏蘭西: *Furansu*	仏 *(FUTSU)*	*BUTSU, hotoke:* Buddhism
Germany	独逸: *Doitsu*	独 *(DOKU)*	*DOKU, hito•ri:* alone
Great Britain	英国: *Eikoku*; 英吉利: *Igirisu*	英 *(EI)*	*EI:* brilliant, talented
Greece	希臘: *Girishia*	希 *(GI)*	*KI, koinega•u:* to desire
Holland	阿蘭陀: *Oranda*	蘭 *(RAN)*	*RAN:* orchid
Hungary	洪牙利: *Hangarī*	洪 *(KŌ)*; ハンガリー	*KŌ:* flood, vast
India	印度: *Indo*	印 *(IN)*	*IN, shirushi:* seal, sign
Italy	伊太利: *Itaria*	伊 *(I)*	*I:* that one
Japan	日本: *Nihon*	日 *(NICHI, NI)*	*NICHI, NI, hi:* sun, day
Korea, North	北朝鮮: *Kita Chōsen*	朝 *(CHŌ)*	*CHŌ, asa:* morning
Korea, South	韓国: *Kankoku*	韓 *(KAN)*	*KAN, kara:* well hedge
Malaysia	馬來西亜: *Marēshia*	馬 *(MA)*; マ	*BA, uma:* horse
Manchuria	満州: *Manshū*	満 *(MAN)*	*MAN, mi•chiru:* to be full
Mexico	墨西哥: *Mekishiko*	墨 *(BOKU)*	*BOKU, MOKU, sumi:* India ink
Mongolia	蒙古: *Mōko*	蒙 *(MŌ)*	*MŌ:* Spanish moss, ignorance
Myanmar	緬甸: *Myanmā*	緬 *(BEN)*; ミャ	*MEN:* fine thread
Norway	諾威: *Noruuei*	諾 *(DAKU)*	*DAKU, ubena•u:* to agree to
Philippines	比島: *Hitō, Firipin*	比 *(HI)*	*HI, kura•beru:* to compare
Poland	波蘭: *Pōrando*	波 *(HA)*; ポ	*HA, nami:* wave
Portugal	葡萄牙: *Porutogaru*	葡 *(PO)*	*BU, HO:* grape
Prussia	普魯西: *Purosha*	普 *(FU)*	*FU, amane•ku:* general, wide
Russia	露西亜: *Roshia*	露 *(RO)*	*RO, RŌ, ara•wa:* in the open
Spain	西班牙: *Supein*	西 *(SEI)*	*SEI, SAI, nishi:* west
Sweden	瑞典: *Suēden*	瑞 *(ZUI)*	*ZUI, mizu:* good omen
Switzerland	瑞西: *Suisu*	瑞 *(ZUI)*	*ZUI, mizu:* good omen
Taiwan	台湾: *Taiwan*	台 *(TAI)*	*DAI, TAI:* platform
Thailand	泰: *Tai*	泰 *(TAI)*; タイ	*TAI:* calm, large
Turkey	土耳古: *Toruko*	土 *(TO)*; ト	*DO, TO, tsuchi:* earth, soil
United States	米国: *Beikoku*; 亜米利加: *Amerika*	米 *(BEI)*	*BEI, kome, yone:* rice
Vatican	教皇庁: *Kyōkōchō*	教 *(KYŌ)*; バチカン	*KYŌ, oshi•eru:* to teach, religion
Vietnam	越南: *Etsunan, Betonamu*	越 *(ETSU)*	*ETSU, ko•su:* to cross, exceed

Chōsen is another way to say "Korea."

You Can Say That Again!

A young woman calls a friend from a hospital, using words with a curious rhythm:

"Moshimoshi, Kan-san desu ka? Suzuki Mizuki desu. Ima, byōin kara desu. Kyō no gogo wa mō mecha-kucha de, watashi wa otaota shite imasu. Sakki, kyū ni, chichi no mimi kara byōbyō to chi ga dete kite, botabota to nagare ochite kitandesu. Chichi wa 'zuki-zuki piripiri shite, kurakura suru' to iimashita. Sono chi ga totemo kimochi warukatta node, watashi mo sukoshi mune ga mukamuka shite kimashita. Chichi no kao ga nakanaka itsumono ikiiki to shita kao ni modoranai node, watashitachi wa chichi o kono byōin ni tsurete kimashita. Koko no machiaishitsu ni wa takusan no hitobito ga imasu. Watashitachi wa tada daradara to matte iru dake desu. Haha wa shinpai de, hoho ga shōshō aoi desu. Haha wa piripiri mo shite ite, shinpai de mō yoreyore ni natte imasu. Watashi wa onaka ga pekopeko desu. Chichi no yōtai ga kono mama zuruzuru to susumu yori, chikajika gen'in ga wakaru to ii to omoimasu."

Here's what she said:

"Hi, Kan? It's Mizuki Suzuki. This afternoon has been horrible. I'm at the hospital right now, and I don't know what to do. Earlier, endless amounts of blood suddenly started flowing from my father's ear. My dad said he felt a throbbing pain, stinging, and dizziness. It was so disgusting that I felt nauseated. My father wasn't looking well at all, so we brought him to the hospital. There are lots of people in the waiting room. The wait is incredibly boring. My mother is so anxious that her cheeks are pale. And she's worn out from being on edge. I'm starving. This unbearable experience drags on and on. I hope we find the cause of the illness soon."

Did you notice that, in the English version, the only rhyme (Mizuki Suzuki) came from Japanese? Aside from "so-so," "boogie-woogie," words from other languages (e.g., "couscous" and "mahimahi"), and baby talk, English offers few expressions with internal repetition. By contrast, Japanese offers thousands of repeating words, particularly *giseigo* (擬声語: to mimic + voice + word), which are onomatopoetic, and *gitaigo*

(擬態語: to mimic + appearance + word), which describe psychological states and other non-auditory phenomena. Beyond these, scads of ordinary Japanese words such as *kōkō* (高校: high school) contain internal repetition.

The Japanese adore this kind of repetition. It amuses them to no end to roll such rhymes off their tongues. For some native speakers, this quirk of the language even inspires national pride. In *Japanese Beyond Words: How to Walk and Talk Like a Native Speaker*, Andrew Horvat quotes illustrator Gomi Tarō as saying that when it comes to *gitaigo*, "I suddenly become very proud and boastful and have a burning desire to introduce them and get people to understand them" (p. 154). Gomi illustrated many *gitaigo* in *An Illustrated Dictionary of Japanese Onomatopoeic Expressions*.

Perhaps it's no surprise that the Japanese have devised a repetition kanji, 々. Known as both *odoriji* (踊り字: literally, a character that jumps, dances, leaps, or skips!) and *kurikaeshi kigō* (繰り返し符号: repetition sign), this symbol pretty much says, "Once more, same as before." Not all repetitive words have kanji; the Japanese write many in hiragana or katakana. Here's how they might choose to represent the ones from the above passage:

Kanji

gogo	午後	(afternoon)
mechakucha	滅茶苦茶	(ruined)
chichi	父	(my father)
mimi	耳	(ear)
byōbyō	眇々	(boundless)
nakanaka	中々	(by no means)
ikiiki	生き生き	(lively)
hitobito	人々	(people)
haha	母	(my mother)
hoho	頬	(cheek)
shōshō	少々	(a little)
chikajika	近々	(the near future)

Kana

moshimoshi	hello
otaota	shocked, not knowing what to do

botabota	large amount of liquid
zukizuki	throbbing pain
piripiri	stinging
kurakura	dizziness
mukamuka	nausea
koko	here
daradara	boring, going on and on
piripiri	on edge
yoreyore	worn out
pekopeko	starving
mama	as is
zuruzuru	untenable situation that drags on inconclusively

When a word repeats, it might simply become plural, as when 人 (*hito*: person, people) turns into 人々 (*hitobito*: people). But oftentimes the meaning changes, as in the following examples. Note the voicing in *kuniguni* and *tokidoki*:

国	*kuni*: country
国々	*kuniguni*: various countries
時	*toki*: hour
時々	*tokidoki*: sometimes
色	*iro*: color
色々	*iroiro*: various
昔	*mukashi*: old times
昔々	*mukashi mukashi*: once upon a time

Here are other common words with repetitive forms:

元	*moto*: origin
元々	*motomoto*: originally, from the outset
赤	*aka•i*: red
赤々	*akaaka*: brightly
若	*waka•i*: young
若々	*wakawaka•shii*: youthful
久	*hisa*: long time
久々	*hisabisa*: for the first time in a long time
上	*JŌ*: up
上々	*jōjō*: the very best
女	*me*: woman
女々	*meme•shii*: effeminate, unmanly

山	*yama*: mountain
山々	*yamayama*: mountains, very much
区	*KU*: division
区々	*kuku*: various, diverse, mixed, petty
直	*JIKI*: direct
直々	*jikijiki*: direct
快	*Ō*: dissatisfaction
快々	*ōō*: despondent, in low spirits
伸	*no•biru*: to stretch
伸び伸び	*nobinobi*: to feel at ease, refreshed

A few kanji repeat in AABB patterns. Take, for example, 三々五々 (*sansan-gogo*: in small groups, by twos and threes). Oddly, the compound involves threes (三) and fives (五), not twos and threes! Here are other AABB words:

侃々諤々	*kankan-gakugaku*: outspoken
侃	*KAN*: moral strength or integrity
諤	*GAKU*: speaking the truth
明々白々	*meimei-hakuhaku*: perfectly evident
明	*MEI*: clear
白	*HAKU*: white
伸び伸び延々	*nobinobi-en'en*: repeatedly postponed
伸	*no•biru*: to stretch
延	*EN*: to prolong, stretch
平々凡々	*heihei-bonbon*: ordinary to an extreme, very ordinary
平	*HEI*: even, flat
凡	*BON*: mediocre

Sometimes the yomi changes from *kun* to *on* when the word acquires a repetition:

続	*tsuzu•ku*: to continue
続々	*zokuzoku*: one after another
年	*toshi*: year
年々	*nennen*: year by year
近	*chika•i*: near
近々	*kinkin*: in the near future (though this is more commonly read as *chikajika*)

Double Meanings

To gain insight into the mind-set of a certain culture, examine its metaphors, its framework for comparisons. Do the people often draw analogies to nature? To war? Perhaps they give equal weight to both, as American anthropologist Ruth Benedict discovered about the Japanese, therefore naming her 1944 study of Japan *The Chrysanthemum and the Sword*. Figurative language hints at a country's history, its values, and its fears. Jokes and euphemisms point to particular areas of discomfort (concerning death, sex, moral transgressions, and the like).

We can scrutinize Japanese this way and learn a lot, but kanji provides a special prism with which to view the issue. Certain characters and compounds have double meanings, often revealing a great deal about Japanese beliefs and priorities. For instance, *kirei*, 綺麗, means both "beautiful" and "clean," indicating that the two traits are closely related in the Japanese mind.

When characters and compounds have double meanings, it's either because the Japanese see conceptual connections between them or because they treat one term as a metaphorical spinoff of the other. The word *aoi*, 青い, provides examples of both phenomena. Literally, it means both "blue" and "green"; the Japanese view these as interchangeable. Figuratively, *aoi* means "fresh," "young," and "immature." English has the same metaphor, as when we deem an inexperienced person "green."

This exhibit doesn't include examples such as *aoi*, because that double meaning doesn't tell us much about Japan and its culture. We'll only concern ourselves with the terms that reveal most about Japan—and in some cases about China, where these characters originated. There's much that we don't know about the etymology of these singletons and compounds, so my explanations often include fanciful speculation.

Imperial Majesty

One can surmise from the next two compounds that the Japanese viewed the imperial family and court in a godlike way, as though they lived in the heavens.

雲上 *(unjō)* = cloud + above
1. above the clouds
2. the imperial court

雲井 *(kumoi)* = cloud + well (for water)
1. the sky
2. palace
3. the imperial court

竹の園生 *(take no sonō)* = bamboo + garden (combining "garden" and "life")
1. bamboo garden
2. imperial family

The bamboo garden provides a more down-to-earth image than the heavens, but given the importance accorded to bamboo in Japan (as an integral part of religious ceremonies, art, music, buildings, and everyday objects), the analogy still implies great reverence.

Livelihoods and Money

釣り *(tsuri)*
1. fish
2. change or coins (returned after a large bill payment)

One could define the components of 釣 in multiple ways, most logically as "metal" + "hook" (that is, a metal fishhook). But 金 also means "gold" and "money," so I wonder whether there's a monetary association here, too. In ancient times, perhaps fishermen equated fish with money. Later on, it must have been no great stretch to associate the character with change or coins, referred to now with the honorific *o*, making the word *otsuri*.

績 *(SEKI)*
1. silk spinning (as in 紡績, *bōseki*: spinning)
2. achievement (as in 成績, *seiseki*: performance)

One can imagine that spinning was once a measure of achievement, especially in China, where this character originated and where sericulture (silkworm production) was a huge industry.

米櫃 *(komebitsu)* = rice + chest, coffer, tub
1. rice bin

2. breadwinner
3. means of livelihood

Here we have a triple, all pointing to rice production as a major means of subsistence.

雲水 (*unsui*) = cloud + water
1. itinerant priest
2. beggar

These meanings have a conceptual link, rather than a metaphorical one. Buddha required his followers to detach from the material life. Instead of holding down jobs, they were expected to wander and beg. It's hard to figure out how clouds and water combined to create a wandering priest, except for the formlessness of these on-the-move entities.

The Natural World

離山 (*rizan*) = to separate + mountain
1. isolated mountain
2. departure from a temple

I initially thought the temple in question stood on an isolated mountain. But now I wonder whether the mountain symbolizes a temple cut off from the bustling world. Leaving the temple would mean heading down the mountain and joining society.

優曇華 (*udonge*) = to excel + cloudy weather + flower
1. the mythical udumbara plant of India, also known as "plantain flower"
2. something very rare (from the legend that the udumbara plant flowers once in three thousand years)
3. insect eggs laid by a lacewing in a flowerlike pattern whose shape portends good or ill fortune

Perhaps to prevent this rarely used compound from growing musty, the Japanese gave it the third meaning—insect eggs.

咲
1. *wara•u*: to laugh
2. *sa•ku*: to bloom

In China, this character originally meant "to laugh" and "to smile." So did 笑. When these kanji arrived in Japan, the Japanese assigned both characters the kun-yomi *wara•u*, as this meant "to smile" and "to laugh." At some point the two characters began evolving in different directions, and 咲 received an added mean-

ing, "to bloom." This change meant taking a metaphorical leap; the Japanese viewed a blooming flower as if it were laughing happily. In Japan, 咲 has now all but lost its association with laughter.

Sex (in Both Senses of the Word)

Japanese has so many metaphors pertaining to sexuality and gender that I've divided them into subcategories. Again, this wealth of figurative language shows the Japanese need to speak of such matters indirectly, because they're simply too charged to mention by name.

Women as Flowers

Because of Japan's long agricultural tradition, plants often serve as the basis for metaphors, especially flowers, which can represent female sexuality. That explains the following two expressions:

花柳 (*karyū*) = flower + willow
1. blossoms and willows
2. red-light district

両手に花 (*ryōte ni hana*) = both + hand + flower
1. to have a double advantage
2. to sit between two pretty women

Menstruation

The vast numbers of euphemisms for menstruation—for which the formal word is *gekkei,* 月経 (month + passage of time)—indicate that many Japanese feel deep embarrassment about this topic, as well as disgust. In *Womansword*, Cherry Kittredge writes, "There is no question that menstruation came to be viewed as pollution. Menstruation is said to be *kegarawashii*, or filthy, disgusting, obscene" (p. 19). All the terms below refer figuratively to menstruation and literally to something else.

旗日 (*hatabi*) = flag + day: flag day

With a red circle on a white background, the Japanese flag could be said to resemble menstrual staining. According to Kittredge, the same thinking produced the now-outdated bit of slang 日の丸, *hinomaru*. Breaking down as "sun" + "full," this alludes to the "rising sun." Kittredge writes of both terms, "It took a satirical wit to link menstruation with the patriotic symbol; prior to World War II, nationalism was almost synonymous with state Shinto, a religion that included the concept of menstruation as contamination" (p. 19).

月の障り *(tsuki no sawari)* = moon + hindrance: cloud over the moon
When you translate this term as "monthly obstacle," you can see the link to menstruation.

生理 *(seiri)* = life + basic principles: physiology
The breakdown here is more matter-of-fact, and "physiology" and "menstruation" both have anatomical bases, so it's easier to make the leap from this vague euphemism to the implied meaning.

Female Genitalia

English speakers certainly have euphemisms for female genitalia. The vague reference to "down there" equates to the Japanese *are* (that far-away thing). But the Japanese also represent vaginas with shellfish! Kanji students learn that 貝 has monetary connotations (e.g., 買, *ka•u:* to buy), but teachers give short shrift to its sexual aspect!

貝 *(kai)*
1. shellfish
2. women's genitalia
Kittredge says that abalone, spraying surf clam, corbicula, sea anemone, and herring roe have all been used to represent vaginas. She mentions a springtime fertility festival in Inuyama, Aichi Prefecture, in which "a huge model clamshell is carried through the streets, opening and closing gently in the breeze. . . . The sexy shellfish is supposed to grant marital bliss, babies, cures for sexual diseases, and bounteous crops" (p. 111).

As for other key parts of female genitalia, Donald Richie (a longtime observer of Japanese culture) imparts some fascinating information in his *Japan Journals* while describing a party he attended. The centerpiece of the table, a "structure of chestnuts," prompted a discussion of the word *kuri* (栗: chestnut). The conversation drifted to *risu* (栗鼠: squirrel). Richie doesn't say how that happened, but I note that the two terms share a kanji. The guests then fit the words together: *kuri to risu,* "chestnut and squirrel." As he points out, this is Japanese for "clitoris": クリトリス,

kuritorisu. "Wordplay is always popular at parties, and this was an enormous hit" (p. 225), says Richie. He doesn't analyze the significance of the imagery, but if you imagine a chestnut and a squirrel's tail, the wordplay becomes clearer.

Gender Roles, Marriage, and Divorce

Countless words point to the exalted status of the male and the diminished role of the female in traditional Japanese society. For this reason, many women chafe at two common words that mean "wife." Both depict women as inhabiting the interior of the house: 奥さん, *okusan,* "wife" (奥 means "interior" but truly refers to the depths of a building), and 家内, *kanai,* "my wife" (house + inside). The double meanings of several words similarly illuminate gender roles in Japan:

雄 *(YŪ, osu)*
1. male
2. brave, great
This character isn't for humans but rather for other creatures. Still, the double meaning makes it quite clear how males stack up in the Japanese mind!

傷物 *(kizumono)* = defect + things
1. damaged goods (unsold, substandard goods)
2. an unmarried woman who has lost her virginity

売れ残り *(urenokori)* = to sell + remainder
1. unsold merchandise
2. older unmarried woman

山の神 *(yamanokami)* = mountain + god
1. god of a mountain
2. one's wife
Now, this one I like!

行き戻り *(yukimodori)* = to go + to return
1. round trip
2. divorced woman
Traditionally, when a woman married, she moved from her parents' home to her husband's home. And if the marriage ended, she had no choice but to move back in with her parents. Having figuratively made a round trip, this divorced woman acquired the label *yukimodori* or the similar disparaging term *demodori,* 出戻り (to leave + to return), a "returnee."

三行半 = three + lines of text + half
1. *mikudarihan:* letter of divorce
2. *sangyōhan:* three-and-a-half lines of text

The compound prompts two possible yomi, but they're closer in meaning than you might think. As Kittredge tells us, a woman couldn't request a divorce until the nineteenth century. But during the Edo era, a man could do so by leaving his wife a note saying that he wanted to separate. Kittredge observes, "The divorce letters were so short that they came to be called 'three-and-a-half lines' (mikudarihan). Women who saw the ominous notes understood instantly, even if they were illiterate" (p. 57).

War and Aggression

戦
1. *SEN, ikusa:* war; *tataka•u:* to wage war, fight
2. *onono•ku:* to shudder, tremble

This pairing implies that war can inspire a "fight" or "flight" response.

征 *(SEI, iku)*
1. to subjugate
2. to attack the rebellious
3. to collect taxes

This kanji has the sense of going afar to fight the good fight. But the third meaning makes it clear that some of the most difficult battles are internal (as in Internal Revenue Service).

Feelings

自戒 *(jikai)* = self + to admonish
1. self-discipline
2. admonishing oneself

To English speakers, these meanings seem fairly far apart. After all, hard work, exercise, and healthy eating fall under the rubric of self-discipline. We admonish ourselves if we fail to meet those standards. But self-discipline needn't involve self-laceration, and discipline isn't the primary agenda anyway; results are. By contrast, self-discipline is a crucial part of Japanese culture and of character building, spawning such sayings as "Self-discipline polishes away the rust of the body." Devoting a whole chapter to self-discipline,

Benedict wrote of the "Japanese assumption" that all people need self-training. In his 1978 work *The Japanese,* Robert Ozaki emphasized the masochistic aspects of this approach. "The Japanese always talk about the importance of suppressing and controlling 'self'" (p. 240), he said. "Historically, Japanese books on moral improvement and how-to-live methods . . . went so far as to expound an aesthetics of unhappiness that borders on masochism. It was held that hardship tempers one's heart. Unhappiness strengthens the psyche. . . . One should be grateful for . . . any hardship encountered in life" (p. 246). Given this mentality, the two readings of 自戒 seem a bit closer.

自慰 *(jii)* = self + consolation, amusement, seduction
1. self-consolation
2. masturbation

No explanation needed here!

会心 *(kaishin)* = to meet + heart
1. congeniality
2. satisfaction

If you have an open heart when you meet someone, you will be congenial. And if your heart feels full after you've met someone, you can consider yourself satisfied.

腹の虫 *(haranomushi)* = intestines + worm
1. intestinal worms
2. one's heart, anger

In English, we speak of being so angry that it "eats you up inside." The Japanese appear to have imagined this more graphically!

憤死 *(funshi)* = to be indignant + to die
1. to die in a fit of anger
2. to get an "out" in baseball (with men on base)

The first meaning includes suicides caused by indignation. The second applies this idea to baseball!

Unnatural Death

生還 *(seikan)* = life + to return
1. to come back alive
2. to cross home plate

If you equate an "out" in baseball with death, it makes sense that the converse is true; if you come back "alive" from your trip around the bases, you're eligible to cross home plate.

首実検 *(kubi jikken)* = neck + truth + examination
1. identification of a severed head
2. identification of a suspect
I can't explain this pair but included them for fun.

生害 *(shōgai)* = life + harm
1. to be killed
2. to commit suicide
The end result is the same, but the means are very different! Perhaps the Japanese imagine that those who commit suicide were killed by depression and such.

Insults

鴨 *(ō, kamo)*
1. duck
2. easily deceived person
In English, a "sitting duck" is an easy target for attacks, criticism, or unscrupulous dealings. In Japanese, it seems that any duck is at risk for deception!

大根 *(daikon)* = big + root
1. type of radish
2. a woman's fat legs
Oh, dear. This makes many of us sitting ducks! (And if we weren't sitting, perhaps we'd have thinner thighs!)

毛唐人 *(ketōjin)* = hair + China + person
1. hairy barbarian
2. foreigner, abbreviated as *ketō*
The middle kanji refers to Tang-dynasty China. The perception of the Chinese as hairy seems more than a little distorted! But most likely the Japanese first used 唐人 to mean "Chinese people" and then "foreigner." After meeting Westerners (such as the Portuguese), the Japanese probably tacked 毛 onto the front of the word, creating the greatest of insults: "hairy foreigner."

蛸入道 *(takonyūdō)* = octopus + to enter + way
1. octopus
2. bald man
A similar term, 大入道 *(tōnyūdō)*, means "large bald-shaven monster."

In the bathroom of a business hotel in Kobe, the thoughtful hosts have spared nothing when it comes to anticipating guests' needs and questions about how to use the facilities. The kanji break down as follows:

LEFT SIDE
- 男子 *(danshi*: male)
- 小用 *(shōyō*: urination)
- 便座をあげて陶器面を出して使用して下さい。
  Benza o agete tōkimen o dashite shiyō shite kudasai.
  Please use by lifting the seat and exposing the rim of the toilet bowl.

RIGHT SIDE
- 大便 *(daiben*: feces)
- 及び *(oyobi*: and)
- 女子 *(joshi*: female)
- 小用 *(shōyō*: urination)
  (that is, Defecation and Female Urination)
- 陶器面に便座をのせて後向きになり、腰かけて使用して下さい。
  Tōkimen ni benza o nosete ushiro muki ni nari, koshikakete shiyō shite kudasai.
  Put the seat down on the rim of the toilet bowl and turn around, then sit to use.

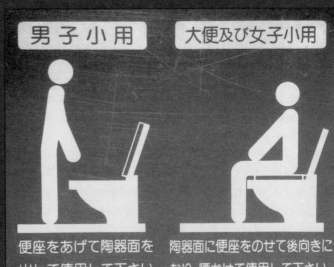

男子小用　　大便及び女子小用

便座をあげて陶器面を　　陶器面に便座をのせて後向きに
出して使用して下さい　　なり、腰かけて使用して下さい

Hyperbolic Humility

Driving along one day, I mused about how extreme the Japanese can be with hyperbole. To me, the best example is 一生懸命, *isshōkenmei,* which means "to do one's best" but literally says "to do it as if your life depended on it." Another hyperbolic word is 首切り, *kubikiri,* "dismissal from a job," or literally "decapitation"! Then I switched on the radio and heard lyrics in one song after another as if for the first time: "I would die for you. I would bleed myself dry for you. I can't go on living without you." Perhaps native English speakers are extreme, too—but apparently love brings out the hyperbole in us, not work.

Americans also tend to exaggerate when giving compliments. So says Sanae Tsuda of Tokaigakuen Women's College in her 1992 paper, "Contrasting Attitudes in Compliments: Humility in Japanese and Hyperbole in English." Compliments such as "You make the best soup in the world, Lisa!" strike Tsuda as borderline "tall tales." She argues that English speakers enlarge facts hyperbolically to create a "friendly feeling."

By contrast, the Japanese make others feel good by diminishing themselves and those closely associated with them. In Japan, Tsuda received such compliments as "Your daughter is really good at school. Compared to her, my daughter is no good at all." Tsuda points out that the allegedly no-good daughter had far better grades than Tsuda's kid did. The Japanese don't accept such compliments but swiftly respond with claims of inferiority. One shouldn't take this self-deprecation at face value, Tsuda asserts, any more than one would look to Lisa for the world's best soup. Japanese humility serves an important function, says Tsuda—it reinforces the hierarchical social structure.

This sense that hierarchies hold a society together comes straight out of Confucianism, the ideals of a Chinese thinker who lived in the fifth century BCE. According to Confucian values, if people know their place, acting with loyalty to family, employers, and the state, then society can function harmoniously.

These values bring to mind the samurai belief system, as a samurai was required to die for his lord at a moment's notice. It may seem strange to spot Confu-cian influences on the samurai belief system, given that Zen Buddhist thinking shaped the samurai world. But Japanese religion is one big salad, as someone put it, tossing together Shinto, Buddhism, Taoism, and Confucianism. Many Japanese cheerfully blur the distinctions.

Intrigued by notions of Japanese hyperbole and humility, I looked at Japanese proverbs (*kotowaza,* 諺) on a website created by Kanji Haitani (who has a fortuitous given name!). His site, http://home.earthlink.net/~4jword/index3.htm, offers 3,400 proverbs! I figured that timeworn sayings represent the collective beliefs of a culture, especially since the Japanese tend to cite proverbs frequently and enthusiastically. In fact, the sayings listed below reflect several influences. Many compounds originated in classical Chinese literature. Others derive from Buddhist scriptures. And some were made in Japan.

Most of the proverbs contain four characters, a requirement for so-called *yojijukugo,* 四字熟語 (four-character compounds). Old Chinese poems told stories in four lines or four stanzas. The first served as an introduction, the second developed the premise, the third produced a climax or an unexpected change, and the fourth brought the story to a conclusion. The four characters in *yojijukugo* now represent those tales in a pithy way.

These compounds are considered idiomatic because the whole says something different from the sum of its parts. (I would say the whole is "greater" than the sum, but that doesn't sound appropriate when speaking of Japanese humility.) Therefore, a breakdown of the compound may not capture the meaning of any given saying. It's more satisfying to focus on the hyperbolic humility within, as well as the staggering number of ways in which the Japanese (and in some cases the Chinese) have admonished themselves to be humble, loyal, disciplined workers.

Hard Work and Achievement

切磋琢磨 (*sessa takuma:* having a rival is a great motivator) = to cut + to polish + to polish + to polish

臥薪嘗胆 (*gashin shōtan:* going through unspeakable

hardships and privations to attain one's objective) = to lie prostrate + firewood + to burn up + courage

捨万求一 (*shaban kyūitsu:* pursuing one overriding objective while forsaking all the others, or literally, "to forsake ten thousand and seek one") = to discard + ten thousand + to pursue + one

刻苦精進 (*kokku shōjin:* to be arduous, work diligently enduring hardships, make a strenuous effort) = to carve + hardship + meticulous + to advance

刻苦精励 (*kokku seirei:* to be arduous, work diligently enduring hardships, make a strenuous effort) = to carve + hardship + meticulous + to be diligent

刻苦勉励 (*kokku benrei:* to be arduous, work diligently enduring hardships, make a strenuous effort) = to carve + hardship + efforts + to be diligent

勤倹力行 (*kinken rikkō:* to work hard and practice frugality) = diligence + frugal + efforts + journey

Discipline and Abstinence

鯨飲馬食 (*geiin bashoku:* drinking like a fish and eating like a horse, drinking oceans of liquor and eating mountains of food) = whale + to drink + horse + to eat

禁欲生活 (*kin'yoku seikatsu:* an ascetic existence, abstinence) = prohibition + desire + life + living

克己精進 (*kokki shōjin:* self-control and close application, self-denial and diligent devotion) = to overcome + self + excellence + to advance

克己復礼 (*kokki fukurei:* exercising self-restraint and conforming to the rules of etiquette and formality) = to overcome + self + to restore + propriety

自己抑制 (*jiko yokusei:* self-restraint, self-control, self-repression, abstinence, self-inhibition) = self + self + to repress + rule

Arrogance

自画自賛 (*jigajisan:* singing one's own praises, blowing one's own horn, self-admiration, though this literally means "a painting with an inscription or poem written by the artist") = self + painting + self + praise, inscription

横行闊歩 (*ōkō kappo:* swaggering walk, stalking about with a haughty air, roaming at will, walking around as if one owned the place) = sideways + to go + wide + to walk

大風呂敷 (*ōburoshiki:* big talk, vain boasting, blowing one's own trumpet, though this literally means "large *furoshiki*," which is a cloth used for wrapping things) = big + wind + backbone + to spread (although this is ateji, so the breakdown means little)

紙屑同然 (*kamikuzu dōzen:* arrogantly seeing others as no better than a scrap of paper) = paper + trash + same + sort of thing

驕兵必敗 (*kyōhei hippai:* defeat is inevitable for an arrogant army) = pride + army + inevitable + defeat

傲岸不遜 (*gōgan fuson:* arrogant and presumptuous, intolerable insolence) = to be proud + beach + not + modest

傲岸無礼 (*gōgan burei:* arrogant and rude) = to be proud + beach + not + propriety

傲慢不遜 (*gōman fuson:* haughty, arrogant, overbearing, intolerable insolence) = to be proud + ridicule + not + modest

傲慢無礼 (*gōman burei:* arrogant and insolent, haughty and contemptuous) = to be proud + ridicule + not + propriety

自己顕示 (*jiko kenji:* making oneself conspicuous, an ego trip, exhibitionism) = self + self + to appear + display

自己肥大 (*jiko hidai:* self-aggrandizement, self-glorification, something becoming large by feeding upon itself) = self + self + to get fat + big

自己満悦 (*jiko man'etsu:* self-congratulation) = self + self + pride + ecstasy

自己満足 (*jiko manzoku:* self-satisfaction, complacency) = self + self + pride + sufficient

Loyalty and Obedience

赤烏帽子 (*aka eboshi:* a piece of headgear, ordinarily black but red in this case, worn by Japanese men before and during the Edo period; metaphorically, *aka eboshi* means that family members should fall in line with the head of the family, despite odd behavior on his part, such as wearing a red *eboshi*) = red + crow, raven + hat + object

一死報国 (*isshi hōkoku:* dying for one's country) = one + to die + to reward + country

自決 (*jiketsu:* self-determination, resignation [from a post], suicide) = self + to decide

御役御免 (*oyaku gomen:* dismissal, firing, retirement, being relieved of one's post) = honorable + office + honorable + dismissal

殉死 (*junshi:* to kill oneself upon the death of one's lord, a term now used when someone devoted to a job dies in the line of duty [e.g., firefighters]) = martyrdom + death

御目見得 (*omemie:* the privilege of having an audience [with one's lord, a dignitary, a superior, etc.], a term that also refers to one's debut appearance or the debut of a product, a work of art, etc.) = honorable + eye + to be seen + to get

Honor and Name

顔負け (*kaomake:* to be put to shame, be outdone, or literally, "to lose face") = face + to lose

顔汚し (*kaoyogoshi:* disgrace, discredit) = face + to dishonor

汚名 (*omei:* blot on one's name, stigma, dishonor) = to dishonor + name

汚名返上 (*omei henjō:* to clear one's name, redeem oneself, save one's reputation) = to dishonor + name + to return + up

玉砕主義 (*gyokusai shugi:* the principle of honorable death and no surrender) = gem + to be crushed + main thing + honor. The "gem" here is a metaphor for one's life. So the idiom says, "Even if they crush the life out of me, I'd rather die than surrender."

Life-and-Death Situations

活殺自在 (*kassatsu jizai:* having absolute power over a person; power of life or death) = life + to kill + self + to exist

起死回生 (*kishi kaisei:* revival of the dead, recovering from a hopeless situation, pulling something back from the brink of defeat) = to wake up + death + times + life

九死一生 (*kyūshi isshō:* narrow escape from the jaws of death) = nine + deaths + one + life

再起不能 (*saiki funō:* to have no hope of recovery) = second time + to wake up + no + capacity

死活問題 (*shikatsu mondai:* matter of life or death, vital question) = death + living + question + topic

On this Tokyo tombstone, the two characters on the left, 施主 (*seshu*), mean "the one who built the tomb." The other two columns are the posthumous names of the two people, probably a couple, who are "sleeping" there for eternity. When Japanese people die, they acquire names different from the ones they had while living. People like to represent these names with older forms of kanji.

Shades of Meaning

When you translate words from one language into another, there's rarely a 1:1 fit. If too many words from the first language meet too few from the other, the first language appears to split hairs, and the second seems woefully inarticulate.

When you ask a Spanish speaker for a lemon in either English or Spanish, you might receive a lime, as these concepts are interchangeable in Spanish. If you feel there are times when a lime simply won't do, this can be frustrating. But having too many choices is also problematic. In Japanese, I can barely utter two words without hearing something like, "No, no, no. We don't pour *mizu* over tea leaves. *Mizu* means 'cold water.' *Oyu* is the water used in tea and in baths."

This kind of differentiation is endemic in Japanese, partly because of cultural priorities. As the Japanese value rice, they distinguish between many rice terms. They plant *momi* (籾: unhulled rice) in a seed bed, where it becomes *sanae,* a young plant (早苗) and then *nae* (苗) when it's ever so slightly older. By the time it becomes *ine* (稲: a rice plant), it's ready to be replanted in a muddy field, where it turns into *inaho* (稲穂: ear of rice). You buy it as *kome* (米: uncooked rice), and when you serve it, you call it *meshi* (飯, also read as *han,* as in *gohan*), which refers literally to cooked rice but figuratively to the whole meal.

The Japanese similarly differentiate terms relating to sea creatures. There are separate words for "herring roe" *(kazunoko)* and "salmon roe" *(sujiko* or *ikura)*. One type of fish, the gray mullet, acquires new names as it progresses through the life cycle: *oboko,* then *subashiri,* then *ina,* then *bora,* and finally *todo.*

These subtleties disappear in translation. Our word "sincerity" lacks the distinctions that one can make with three Japanese words:

真 *(SHIN, makoto)*	truth and sincerity in the most general sense
信 *(SHIN, makoto)*	honesty learned over a lifetime as one chooses not to lie
実 *(JITSU, makoto)*	natural honesty, reflecting Confucian beliefs that people are innately good

I'm impressed that the Japanese can express such shades of meaning. And I empathize with any aggravation they must feel when trying to make "sincerity" meet their needs. But obviously the problem doesn't occur only when Japanese people speak English. They struggle to make these distinctions in their own spoken language, too. All three words are pronounced *makoto,* and two even share the on-yomi of *SHIN.*

Ironically, this problem developed because Japanese is even less differentiated than Chinese in some ways! When the Japanese brought kanji into their language, it was as if male parts on a Chinese plug met with too few female Japanese receptors. For all the ways in which the Chinese differentiated concepts of honesty and sincerity, the Japanese could offer just one sound, *makoto.* However, they let the shades of meaning show through in the written language. In such cases, the kanji says more than spoken words.

This creates confusion, as when a teacher instructs children to work in a *sōzōryoku* way on an essay. Confusion ensues. Did she mean 想像力, "imaginative" in the sense of something unrealistic? Or did she mean just the opposite—創造力, "creative" in the sense of something achievable? To clarify her intent, she may write the word on the board in kanji.

But writing presents further difficulties with words such as *moto* (base), which, as we've seen, has five possible kanji. In three of the cases, the meanings are quite close. Native speakers don't always know which kanji to use, so they disguise their confusion by using hiragana. They may not even realize that various kanji exist for a single spoken word, as with these extremely individuated compounds:

obasan	伯母	(aunt older than one's parent)
	叔母	(aunt younger than one's parent)
ojisan	伯父	(uncle older than one's parent)
	叔父	(uncle younger than one's parent)

Again, most Japanese use hiragana for these words.

On the next page, I present a smattering of words that sound alike and mean almost exactly the same thing but have different kanji. I don't explain the differences, as that's beyond the scope of this exhibit. I simply want to give you a heads-up about this potential challenge.

SAME SOUNDS, SLIGHTLY DIFFERENT MEANINGS

Noun	Meaning	Possible Kanji				
guai	conditions	具合	工合			
haji•me	beginning	始	初			
kata	type, model, shape	形	型			
kawa	skin, leather	皮	革			
machi	town	町	街			
michi	way, road	路	道	途	迪	廸
nakami	contents	中	身	中	味	
sore	that one	其	夫			

Verb	Meaning	Possible Kanji			
arawa•su	to express	表	現	著	
a•u	to meet	会	遭		
haka•ru	to measure	測	量	計	図
ita•mu	to ache	痛	傷		
kakawaru	to be connected with	関わる	係る		
kawa•ru	to change, exchange	変	代	替	換
ki•ku	to be effective	効	利		
kota•eru	to answer	答	応		
mawa•su	to turn around	回	廻		
mi•ru	to see	見	視	観	
na•ku	to cry	鳴	泣		
ne•ru	to refine	練	錬		
nobo•ru	to rise, climb	上	昇	登	
o•kuru	to send	送	贈		
omo•u	to think	思	想		
sato•ru	to realize	悟	覚		
to•maru	to stop, stay	止	泊	留	
to•ru	to take	取	撮	捕	盗
tsuto•meru	to work	勤	努	請	
u•keru	to receive	受	請		

Adjective	Meaning	Possible Kanji		
atata•kai	warm	暖	温	
atsu•i	hot	暑	熱	
kata•i	hard, inflexible	固	堅	硬
kuwa•shii	detailed, full	委	詳	精
maru•i	round	円	丸	
yawa•rakai	soft	柔	軟	

手水の つかいかた

まず 左手を 洗います。

つぎに 右手を 洗います。

おわりに 左手に 水を うけて 口を そそぎます。

Before entering a shrine, visitors should wash their hands and even their mouths according to a set procedure. Using few kanji, several furigana, and spaces between words, this sign at a Tokyo shrine makes the instructions for ritual cleansing very clear for Japanese children:

- 手水の　つかいかた
  Temizu no tsukaikata
  How to do a ritual cleansing
- まず　左手を　洗います。
  Mazu hidarite o araimasu.
  First, wash your left hand.
- つぎに　右手を　洗います。
  Tsugini, migite o araimasu.
  Next, wash your right hand.
- おわりに　左手に　水を　うけて 口を　そそぎます。
  Owarini hidarite ni mizu o ukete kuchi o sosogimasu.
  Last, take water in your left hand and rinse your mouth.

JAPANESE FEELINGS ABOUT KANJI

5

Here's a quick quiz. Match the following fonts with the places you'd be most likely to see them in Japan:

1. Road sign __   a. 書道

2. Shop sign __   b. 書道

3. Sumo poster __   c. 書道

4. Chinese restaurant sign __   d. 書道

5. Newspaper text __   e. 書道

The Answer Key has the solution. In all cases, the kanji says *shodō* (calligraphy), but most of these characters are a far cry from the traditional brush-strokes expected in a *shodō* class. Typefaces, which can dramatically change the look of kanji, serve a variety of functions in Japan and tend to appear in specific places. For more information about type-faces and their purposes, see Exhibit 57, "Just the Facts: Typefaces."

For Japanese people, fonts can evoke particular associations and feelings. In *A Lateral View*, Donald Richie says that when signs display *gyōsho* (the semicursive style in which most Japanese write) or *sōsho* (a loosely flowing cursive that's hard even for natives to read), they bring to mind "the old capital, Kyoto, and its softer, mellower moods. A shop sign in gyosho indicates a degree of refinement, a kind of delicacy that could be feminine. Sosho . . . can also indicate self-conscious elegance—perhaps something with an artistic flavor" (p. 90).

Of course, our fonts also create certain feelings. We have multiple typefaces for that reason. **This** makes a bold, contemporary statement, and `this` reminds you of a newspaper, whereas **that** sets a businesslike tone, and *that* feels warm and cheerful, as a friend's handwriting does.

But there's a double effect for the Japanese. While a font tugs on them in a certain way, each character also elicits strong responses. The Japanese may feel excited to see the kanji 酒 (*sake:* alcohol) with its implied conviviality but sobered by 院 (*IN:* institution) with its links to hospitals and graduate schools.

This isn't impossible for Westerners to relate to; we cringe at hearing words we despise—so much so that on the TV show *Inside the Actors Studio,* host James Lipton asks actor-guests for their least favorite words. "Smegma" was one memorable answer—a word that certainly assaults the ears. But if we see "smegma" in written form, I think it loses some punch. The alphabet is ordinary to us, with the same simple shapes used again and again. In and of themselves, the circles and lines don't prompt visceral reactions.

By contrast, the shapes of kanji can cause written Japanese to prompt visceral responses. An economics professor from Japan (a longtime resident of the United States) told me that kanji stir up a lifetime of associations and subtle feelings, whereas kana do nothing for him. Rōmaji do even less and are harder to read than English.

In Robert Trumbull's 1965 *New York Times* article, "How to Write in Japanese," famed novelist Yukio Mishima made similar comments: "'Romaji is awful,' Mr. Mishima said flatly. 'The visual effect of a Chinese character is very important.' He slashed out the rounded, multistemmed character for 'rose,' and looked at it admiringly. 'See how the rose appears physically in the shape of the Kanji,' he said. 'A writer loves to give such an effect to his readers.'"

In Japan, where one encounters thousands of kanji each day, it's hard to imagine that people take in many characters in a highly conscious way. When walking through the forest, one can't observe every tree or leaf. The same is true of kanji, particularly in Tokyo, a sign-saturated environment with visual stimuli in all directions, including upward, as neon pulses from the uppermost stories of tall buildings. A typical Tokyo resident browses the morning paper, passes billboards and storefront signs, hurries past the copious signage in subway tunnels, spaces out in front of the ubiquitous ads plastered inside trains, and reads documents at work, all without once noticing the shapes of kanji or observing any strong responses to them. And yet, at some level, reactions clearly occur. That's the strange thing about nuances and associations; they happen unconsciously. So we have a paradox; Japanese people can be at once utterly unaware of kanji and yet keenly responsive to the fonts and strokes of characters.

This paradox plays nicely into the hands of advertisers, who exploit the way people take in information subliminally. To stimulate desires for products, savvy marketers toy with images. And what is a kanji character but another image to manipulate in a fashion-conscious society awash in carefully crafted images?

This needn't be a sinister, paranoid idea. Advertising efforts might simply involve signs with typefaces that make people want to enter a store. *Yosemoji* (寄席文字: to gather people + characters), a typeface with thick strokes, actually means "letters to draw in customers."

Entrepreneurs also capture people's attention by using kanji in unorthodox ways. A difficult character might appear in a store's sign just to make people stop and puzzle it out. Or kanji may have been altered, as in this ad for a course to help people pass exams: 严験. This would ordinarily say 受験 (*juken:* taking an exam), combining 受 (*JU, uke•ru:* to take [an exam]) and 験 (*KEN:* test). But someone cleverly removed the 又 (*mata:* again) from the 受, implying that after taking the preparatory course, you won't have to take exams "again." (Matt Treyvaud was smart enough to notice and explain this pun, as well as the next one, in his blog No-sword at http://no-sword.jp/blog.)

Another poster for the same course presents a made-up character, 勐, combining 身 (*mi:* body, person) and 力 (*chikara:* power, ability). A sentence on the poster explains the pun: 力が身につく, *Chikara ga mi ni tsuku,* which means, "Power will stick to you." This common Japanese expression has to do with mastering skills or learning things comprehensively. The people who created the poster mimicked this concept by showing how the 力 sticks to the 身 component in 勐.

This is how one writes "rose," read as *bara:* 薔薇. I wonder if Mishima drew something else, because I certainly don't see anything "rounded" in these characters.

The prevalence of Japanese homonyms creates further opportunities for attention-getting plays on words, including using the wrong kanji on purpose. For instance, one contest challenges participants to think of the most creative ad possible, and the contest logo contains the made-up compound 考告, rather than 広告, "advertisement." The reading of both compounds is *kōkoku,* making readers' minds flit to advertising. But with the use of 考 (*kanga•eru:* to think), the first compound implicitly encourages people to think creatively.

If these instances appeal to the intellect, other displays of kanji simply please the eye, such as *hana-moji* (花文字), flowers planted in the shape of kanji. At times, people also use characters with a celebratory spirit, giving them starring roles in bonfires and in fireworks shows. To learn about this, see Exhibit 58, "Just the Facts: Kanji Ablaze." And for more fun with kanji, try your hand at a kanji version of *sūdoku* in Exhibit 59, "Game: Weekday *Sūdoku.*"

Longtime Associations with Beauty and Art

Kanji have long been important visual stimuli in Japan. For centuries, calligraphy and Japanese paintings have gone hand in hand. When poetry wraps around painted images, it provides a visual and verbal counterpoint. This occurred to striking effect when renowned calligrapher Hon'ami Kōetsu (1558–1637) teamed up with famed painter Tawaraya Sōtatsu (d. 1643?) on a series of scrolls. First Sōtatsu would paint an image (of, say, lotus blossoms). Kōetsu would then fill the empty spaces with famous *waka* (和歌) poems (thirty-one syllables in five lines) from the Heian (794–1185) and Kamakura (1185–1333) periods. Writing of this fruitful collaboration in *How to Look at Japanese Art,* Stephen Addiss observes, "Chinese poets had often added poems over paintings, but the two were not visually intertwined. The full artistic connections of calligraphy and painting were particularly enjoyed and developed by the Japanese, and these scrolls are among the masterworks of the genre" (p. 85).

Japanese calligraphy isn't merely pretty handwriting but rather is an art form unto itself. In the dramatic, free-form works of Shiryū Morita, a leading avant-garde calligrapher in the twentieth century, kanji ceased to be recognizable after he transformed them "almost to the point of abstraction" (p. 91), as Addiss puts it. In "Dragon Knows Dragon," Morita made the character for "dragon" (龍, *ryū*) resemble that mythical creature (or so says Addiss, who also believes that this kanji retains its pictographic shape, though I can't see that at all).

Japanese calligraphy can also have a spiritual component. Some people ritually copy Buddhist sutras to clear their minds. For more on this, see Exhibit 60, "Just the Facts: Kanji Meditation."

In both religious and secular realms, many Japanese believe that, as Addiss writes, "Any kind of brushwork reveals the personality of the artist, and that calligraphy in particular shows each person's individual character clearly. . . . People can hold back or disguise their nature in person, but not in their calligraphy" (p. 83). Exhibit 61, "Thematic Explorations: Calligraphy and Clarity of Mind," explores this idea from the perspective of H. E. Davey, an expert on *shodō* (the way of the brush). He maintains that learning the "way" of the brush instills a certain mind-set, thereby giving you a leg up with other Japanese "ways," such as *aikidō, kendō,* and *kadō.* To see the kanji for these and other cultural arts, check out Exhibit 62, "Thematic Explorations: The Way of Culture and the Arts." And to learn about the role of kanji in another art form, see Exhibit 63, "Just the Facts: Kanji Sound Effects in Manga."

The Younger Generation and Kanji

As kanji has ties to Old Japan and its traditions, one might conclude that trendsetting young people in Japan would want little to do with it. There's a lot of truth in this notion. Many young people find kanji to be torture. (For a light look at kanji and torture, see Exhibit 64, "Spectacular Shapes: Kanji Sandwiches." And for a reminder of how much fun kanji can be, try your hand at Exhibit 65, "Game: Kanji Word Find.")

For Japanese children, mastering kanji can feel like climbing Mount Fuji day after day, year after year. Because of the complexity of kanji, students undergo constant, repetitive drills. Perhaps because there's so much material to cover, schools insist on a strict adherence to rules, often at the expense of creative, original thought. Two exhibits look at rules taught in schools. Exhibit 66, "Just the Facts: *Genkōyōshi,*" discusses the gridlike paper on which students must write essays. And Exhibit 67, "Just the Facts: Don't Use These Kanji!" presents characters that students should know *not* to write.

Partly because kanji study takes so much time, daytime schooling isn't enough for Japanese youngsters. Roughly half the students from grades 1 through 12 attend nighttime cram schools (*juku*, 塾), where they have a whole new curriculum and a separate set of friends. At *juku*, students prepare for entrance exams that will allow them to attend almost all high schools and universities. High suicide rates for Japanese students are legendary, in large part because of enormous performance pressure in a society that leaves little room for failure.

Despite all this hard work, the inherent difficulty of kanji means that students continue to make writing mistakes and will only ever master a fraction of the characters that exist. Many Japanese associate kanji with chronic frustration and resent it as a nuisance.

Most of my younger Japanese-language teachers (native speakers in their twenties and thirties) have seemed afraid of kanji, an unpredictable behemoth that could expose gaps in their knowledge. Drawing blanks about the shapes of certain characters, they often laughed with embarrassment while consulting dictionaries. One instructor always implored us not to rat on her to the director of the school, and she wasn't entirely joking.

Despite the blitz of kanji instruction in schools, young people have a shaky knowledge of the characters, and the problem is only increasing. One reason is that young Japanese people are reading fewer books than ever, reaching far more eagerly for manga. Younger Japanese people also use computers extensively, which involves lots of reading, as well as writing, in the case of email. But sending email means typing Japanese, rather than writing it by hand. Many people see typing as the major reason that youngsters have such a weak grasp of characters. For more on old and new ways of typing kanji, see Exhibit 68, "Just the Facts: Typing Kanji."

Furthermore, according to a 2005 *Japan Times* column by kanji specialist Mary Sisk Noguchi, "Some observers trace the decline of the Japanese language to recent government education reforms. In 2002, the Japanese government revamped the school system. Its pet name for the project? 'Relaxed education.' Ever since, many parents have been shocked to note that their kids have trouble writing *kanji* at grade level. A number of these same moms and dads, increasingly reliant on Japanese word processing software, admit they are hard-pressed to handwrite the same *kanji* they expect their children to master."

Noguchi notes a flood of new TV programs on major networks, all the shows aiming to remediate native speakers' use of the language, both spoken and written. She says that in one episode of *Quiz! Nihongo-O!*, only seventeen of thirty contestants could write the kanji for

"nose" (鼻, *hana*), which third graders learn. Moreover, only four of the thirty could write 相撲 *(sumō)*, the characters for the national sport. Another 2005 article, a *Japan Today* piece about writing Japanese captions for foreign films, mentioned that these captions now include more easy-to-read kanji, as well as copious katakana, because the younger set has such weak reading skills.

This crisis even prompted the Lower House of the Diet to pass a bill in July 2005 to shore up *gengoryoku* (言語力: language ability). The new law enabled local governments all over Japan to spend more money on improving school instruction and upgrading libraries.

Kanji Now and Forever

Some Western scholars of Asian languages argue vehemently for script reform, by which they mean ditching kanji altogether in favor of romanization, thus relieving native speakers of a heavy burden. In *The Fifth Generation Fallacy*, linguist J. Marshall Unger makes a provocative point to this effect. He quotes the well-known philosopher and educator Inazō Nitobe as saying that because blind Japanese children read Braille via kana, rather than kanji, they gain a broad knowledge of all subjects, such as history, geography, literature. By contrast, sighted students spend equivalent amounts of time simply slaving over kanji acquisition.

Arguing that "some of Japan's best minds" agreed with him on the need for script reform before World War II but have now mostly lost interest in the topic, Unger lists people's usual justifications for retaining kanji: "The language contains too many homonyms to be written phonetically. The native vocabulary, after centuries of erosion by Chinese, is too impoverished to meet the needs of a modern society. Japanese ways of thinking depend on schooling in kanji." He cites further timeworn defenses of kanji, including, "the ways in which they save space on paper," their "semantic transparency," and the "wholesome effects of practicing calligraphy." Unger responds with a forceful blast: "All such statements . . . are simply false. Why do the Japanese keep repeating them?" He then answers his own question—it's merely to "sanctify the status quo." That is, retaining kanji fortifies a sense of group identity by excluding most foreigners.

William C. Hannas, a Georgetown University professor of Chinese and Korean who is also an expert in Japanese and Vietnamese, expresses similar thoughts. In his 1997 book *Asia's Orthographic Dilemma*, he proclaims, "Instead of using language to learn, East Asians are wasting their youth and resources learning about language" (p. 125). A forceful indictment indeed! Fortunately, he becomes sunnier when he says, "It is clear that Chinese characters are on their last legs" (p. 299). In fact, Hannas notes, "Change is already happening, and in the long run it makes no difference how much traditionalists whine about it" (p. 298).

If these gleeful pronouncements make you think you've missed a sea change in the use of kanji, consider another argument of his that points to the opposite conclusion. Hannas observes that in East Asia in general, and Japan in particular, people "tolerate the inefficiency of character-based writing until a foreign threat causes them to take stock . . ." (p. 46). For instance, when the Meiji era spurred on a Japanese panic to catch up to Westerners, calls for writing reform abounded. But the militarism of the early twentieth century brought a "false confidence," causing concerns about writing re-

form to disappear. Then, he says, they blossomed again "when Japan lost faith in its institutions through defeat in war" (p. 47). According to this logic, then, kanji will endure in Japan as long as Toyota, Sony, Nintendo, and other companies maintain their hold on Western consumers.

Hannas and Unger do make some good points, but these are complicated issues involving highly charged matters of literacy (and how you measure it) and the comparative educational systems of various countries, among other things. These matters fall way outside the scope of the discussion here.

Thank goodness for that. I'm happy to steer far away from proposals that exude such cold rationality. They plunge a knife into the heart of all those who love kanji. Script reform may be sensible, but it's blind and deaf to kanji sensibilities, the deep, soulful associations that enable a mere font or the strokes in a kanji rose to set people aquiver.

Baseball also sets people aquiver in Japan. This Tokyo Dome scoreboard shows the names of the players (listed in one column as Tigers and in another as Giants). To the right of the time, in the middle of the scoreboard, there are three compounds containing 打 (u•tsu: to hit):

- 打率, *daritsu*: batting average, which is .249
- 本塁打, *honruida*: number of homeruns, which is 9
- 打点, *daten*: runs batted in (RBI), which is 34

All these numbers apply to Andy Sheets (シーツ in the Tigers column of the scoreboard), who is the next to bat. "PL" refers to "home plate," and "1B," "2B," and "3B" refer to the bases. The characters to the right of that column are the names of the umpires monitoring each position.

An ad on the left is for the newspaper *Yomiuri Shinbun* (読売新聞). The Sapporo Beer ad across the bottom features the kanji 生 *(nama)*, which means "draft (beer)" in this context.

Typefaces

Much of the information in this exhibit came from www.sljfaq.org/afaq/shotai.html.

If you find it hard to read characters that you actually know, someone has likely presented them in an unfamiliar script or typeface. The three main calligraphic scripts are *kaisho* (楷書), the semi-cursive *gyōsho* (行書), and the ultra-cursive *sōsho* (草書). Look how the character becomes less legible as you read from left to right:

Kaisho　　*Gyōsho*　　*Sōsho*

Sōsho is one case in which messiness and imprecision are considered beautiful! Collectively called *kaigyōsōsho-tai* (楷行草書体), these three brush styles were created in China during the Age of the Three Kingdoms (220 CE–280 CE). Here's some information about all three styles, as well as less common ones. The character 書 (*SHO, ka•ku:* to write) appears in each style.

The compound 書体 (*shotai*) breaks down as "calligraphy" + "style" and means "calligraphic style" or "typeface." These styles are often referred to without the suffix *-tai*.

 kaishotai (楷書体) = square-style + calligraphy + style
The most traditional square style. Horizontal lines slant up from left to right. People mostly use this style for handwriting.

 gyōshotai (行書体) = line + calligraphy + style
Semicursive style that requires considerable practice to master.

Variation: shingyōshotai (新行書体) = new + line + calligraphy + style
More modern version of *gyōshotai*.

 sōshotai (草書体) = grass + calligraphy + style
Fully cursive style. The quickly drawn lines become nearly vertical. Primarily used for artistic expression and considered the most "abstract" form of the characters, *sōsho* is hard to read without special training. As we saw in Exhibit 22, "Just the Facts: Kana from Kanji," this style served as the basis for hiragana.

 tenshotai (篆書体) = seal-style characters + calligraphy + style
Used for making personal seals (*hanko,* 判子, or *inkan,* 印鑑) with which the Japanese "sign" documents to make them legally binding.

 reishotai (隷書体) = servant, clerk + calligraphy + style
Square clerical script. This is a simplified and more practical version of *tenshotai*.

Printed Styles

Whereas the preceding list presented handwritten styles, the next list names typefaces.

 minchōtai (明朝体) = Ming + dynasty + style
Style most commonly used in printed text. *Minchō* was originally used in woodblock carvings. This is the style used in the main chapter text of this book.

 goshikkutai (ゴシック体) = Gothic + style
Sans-serif typeface. In English, "Gothic typeface" once meant this, too, but no longer. This style appears throughout the exhibits in this book.

 Variation: *marugoshikkutai* (丸ゴシック体) = "round" *goshikkutai*
Used in road signs, this features the *goshikku* typeface with rounded corners.

kyōkashotai (教科書体) = textbook + style
Often used in textbooks, particularly in elementary school. This variant of the *kaisho* style resembles handwritten characters.

sōchōtai (宋朝体) = Sung + dynasty + style
Closely resembling the *kaisho* style, this was originally used in woodblock carvings.

kointai (古印体) = old + seal + style
Still used in seals, this style was invented in Japan.

Edomoji

Edomoji (江戸文字) refers to various lettering styles invented during the Edo period (1603–1867), mainly for advertising purposes.

kanteiryū (勘亭流) = *kantei* + style
Typeface associated with arts such as *kabuki* and *rakugo* (落語: storytelling). The word *kantei* derives from the nickname of Yakanroku Okazaki, who invented this typeface.

yosemoji (寄席文字) = to gather people + characters
Thick letters on posters and flyers intended to draw in customers. *Yosemoji* derives partly from *kanteiryū*.

kagomoji (篭文字) = cage + characters
Font with thick, square characters, often used in outline form.

higemoji (髭文字) = whiskers + characters
Characters with small "whiskers." That is, you can see individual bristle strokes, all created in specified patterns.

sumōmoji (相撲文字) = sumo + characters
Font used for sumo-wrestling posters and programs.

Movie Caption Fonts

To provide captions for movies, "title writers" use a special style of kanji. Because of space restrictions, the characters must be less than one millimeter tall! These are the various styles of captions:

eishotai (映書体) = projection + typeface
sukurīnmoji (スクリーン文字) = screen + characters
shinemashotai (シネマ書体) = cinema + typeface
eigamoji (映画文字) = movie + characters

Here is an example of *shinemashotai*:

シネマ書体

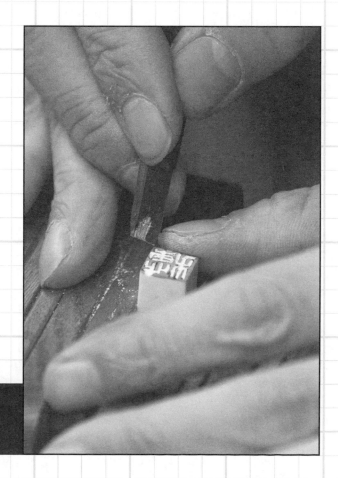

People in Japan usually sign documents with a *hanko* (判子), a stamp or seal bearing their name kanji. Most seal carvers develop distinctive styles. Here, a man is carving a *hanko*, and you can see just how small it is! How can anyone be that coordinated?!

Kanji Ablaze

Sometimes the copious strokes of kanji are too small and crammed together to distinguish. Well, perhaps it would be easier if the characters were enormous, distant, and ablaze!

Every August 16 (Ancestral Remembrance Day) in Kyoto, massive kanji burn on the sides of mountains. This event is known as 大文字五山送り火, *Daimonji Gozan Okuribi*. The kanji translate as follows:

大文字 (*daimonji*): 大 (*DAI*) means "big," and 文字 (*MONJI*) means "character."

五山 (*gozan*): 五 (*go*) is "five," and 山 (*yama* or *SAN* but voiced here to become *ZAN*) means "mountain." The bonfires burn on five mountainsides.

送り火 (*okuribi*): 送 (*oku•ru*) means "to see someone off," and 火 (*KA, hi*) means "fire," voiced here to become *bi*. These bonfires are built to see someone off, the "someone" being ancestral spirits.

This Buddhist tradition from the seventh century occurs at the end of Obon (お盆), an annual summer festival in which the Japanese honor ancestral spirits. It is believed that these spirits return to their family homes on Earth during the festival. On the final night, the spirits head back to heaven, assisted by people who light the way for them with bonfires.

Two bonfires take the shape of 大 (*DAI*: big). A third bonfire says 妙法 (*myōhō*) or "Marvelous Law of Buddha." A fourth depicts a ship. And the fifth is a *torii* (鳥居), the gate to a Shinto shrine.

The bonfires last about a half hour, though they're massive. The larger 大 is about as wide as a football field, connecting seventy-five piles of pine kindling. According to a blog on http://japundit.com, it makes sense culturally to put enormous amounts of work into building something that will flame out in thirty minutes: "This is another example of the Japanese appreciation for fleeting beauty—the peak time for cherry blossom viewing in the spring is also very short, for example. They consider this combination of beauty and brevity to be a metaphor for human life itself."

The theme of temporality also underlies the July fireworks show that has been held over Tokyo's Sumida River for hundreds of years. Some fireworks take the shape of kanji. In 1997, *Architronic: The Electronic Journal of Architecture* ran an essay by Jilly Traganou, who argued that life in Edo (江戸, the name of Tokyo from 1603 to 1867) centered around ephemeral pleasures, including "praying-paying-and-playing." Traganou writes, "The urban activities of Edo are strongly associated with temporal events (festivals, fireworks, etc.) and natural phenomena (views of cherry blossom, full moon, etc.)." Edo architecture reflected this transience, with small, informal, impermanent structures spontaneously arising along the river and in alleys, including tent theaters, teahouses, and whatever buildings one would need in a red-light district.

Accidental fires (known as 江戸の花, *Edo no hana*: literally, flowers of Edo) were common, adding to the impermanence of structures. Hard as it is to believe, Edo residents took pride in their accidental fires, extending that pride to fireworks shows, which "celebrated the temporal pleasures of Edo," Traganou says.

Fireworks came to Japan in the late sixteenth century. Initially, only the ruling class enjoyed these displays, but by the eighteenth century they had become popular throughout Japan. From 1773 through the 1940s, an annual fireworks show occurred at Ryōgokubashi, the largest bridge spanning the Sumida. Known as 川開き (*kawabiraki*: literally, the opening of the river), this festival and the cooling river breezes attracted so many people that boats almost entirely covered the surface of the river.

Clara Whitney was an American who arrived in Japan in 1875 at age fifteen and stayed for twenty-four years, chronicling significant events. In writing of the fireworks show, she described the river as "alive with lanterns of every color and shape, and musical with the notes of the shamisen." She mentioned fireworks that depicted "Fuji, a lady, umbrellas, dogs, men, some (kanji) characters, and other things, which I could not make out."

Imagine making fireworks in the shape of kanji! And imagine reading them! If it's tricky to suss them out when they're tiny but stable on the page, how skillful do you have to be to make them out when they're shooting through the air, soon to vanish?!

Kana Needed: N / Kanji Level: 0 / Difficulty Level: 1

Weekday *Sūdoku*

Sūdoku (数独), an addictive number-placement game, has amused the Japanese for twenty years but only recently became popular elsewhere. The kanji for *sūdoku* breaks down as follows: 数独 (*SŪ:* number) + (*DOKU:* alone), or "single number."

The modified *sūdoku* presented here contains weekday kanji, not numbers. All the weekday kanji represent important natural elements.

Below, each kanji should appear once in every row and once in every column. Use logic to fill in the missing kanji. Answers appear in the Answer Key. *Ganbatte kudasai!*

Sunday	Monday	Tuesday	Wednesday	Thursday	Friday	Saturday
日	月	火	水	木	金	土
NICHI sun	*GETSU* moon	*KA* fire	*SUI* water	*MOKU* tree	*KIN* gold	*DO* earth

土		月		木		金
	木	日		月	土	
月			土		金	
日		火				土
水	土				火	
	月		火	金		日
	水					火

Kanji Meditation

Absurdly easy to forget, dynamic to a fault, and far too similar looking, kanji can drive people over the edge. But the characters are also legendary for their calming properties. In fact, a meditation method known as *shakyō* (写経: to copy + sutra) involves repeatedly copying Buddhist sutras written in kanji. One proponent of this method, Rev. Kanto Tsukamoto, maintains (in a document at http://www.nichiren-shu.org) that when you focus on copying the Lotus Sutra, banishing any other thoughts from your mind and releasing yourself from all attachments, "Time stops and you can reach a deep, peaceful state of mind." Other adherents observe that sutra copying has achieved what no amount of meditative sitting, chanting, or walking has done for them.

A sutra is a teaching of Buddha. The kanji for "sutra," 経, combines "thread" and another part derived from thread on a loom. For that reason, I'm determined to see the English word "sutra" as the root of "suture," even though dictionaries say otherwise!

It doesn't seem to matter which sutra you choose to copy. Some people write the Heart Sutra (*Hannya Shingyō,* 般若心経). With its teachings on emptiness, this constitutes "the essence of the Buddhist Dharma," says Nadja Van Ghelue, an artist who sells her Heart Sutra calligraphy on the Internet. She says the sutra contains 276 kanji, depending on which version you select. It takes her thirty to sixty minutes to pass through it once. Each time she does, she gains new insights into the meanings of the words. Moreover, she feels at one with Buddha as his ideas flow through her.

Meanwhile, the Nichiren branch of Buddhism focuses on the Lotus Sutra (*Odaimoku,* お題目). Adherents copy just the seven characters in the title, 南無 妙法蓮華経, *Namu Myōhō Renge Kyō,* and because it's so short, they can write them again and again in one sitting. The sutra expounds on the merits of copying sutras, its title translating as "Glory to the Sutra" or "Hail, Lotus Sutra" and breaking down as follows:

南無	*namu:* amen
南	*NA:* south
無	*MU:* not, no

妙法	*myōhō:* excellent methods, Marvelous Law of Buddha
妙	*MYŌ:* mystery, excellent
法	*HŌ:* law
蓮華経	*rengekyō:* lotus flower sutra
蓮	*REN:* lotus
華	*KE (GE):* variant of 花 (flower)
経	*KYŌ:* sutra, Buddhist scripture

Tsukamoto says that copying these seven characters is equivalent to copying the entire sutra. He notes, too, that these characters "possess wonderful power to save people." Copying them allows you to "experience this wonderful power" and affords the "opportunity to be awakened to your Buddha nature." In fact, the founder of the Nichiren sect posited long ago that this one sutra reveals all of Buddha's achievements, good deeds, and virtues.

Copying sutras is a ritual, so you have to go about it in a certain way each time, first washing your hands and even rinsing your mouth. Some recommend a sitting meditation of seven to ten minutes before the *shakyō.* You might chant the sutra with your hands pressed together. Then, if you're not using a pen, you need to grind an ink stick on an inkstone. Far from being just the "daily grind," this aspect also proves meditative, at least for Van Ghelue, who says, "It calms your thoughts before writing, it warms up your arm and hand and the room fills with the wonderful smell of the resins in the ink stick." People draw the characters on *washi* (Japanese paper), rice paper, or onionskin. Afterward, they often dedicate their work to the hope that all sentient beings will achieve Enlightenment through the way of Buddha. There are also prescriptions for what to do with the calligraphy after that point: Store it carefully, burn it, or, if you're in Japan, present the finished sutra to the temple, where the pieces will be offered before an image of Buddha.

Partaking in this ritual may make you feel connected to people who lived as long ago as the first century BCE, when those in central Asia and elsewhere copied sutras onto bark, leaves, and cloth. Back in the days before photocopiers, copying served a practical purpose, allowing people to disseminate sutras.

Calligraphy and Clarity of Mind

If you thought you simply needed neat handwriting to draw attractive kanji, you're missing a key ingredient. So says H. E. Davey, who has devoted a whole book (and the majority of his life) to contemplating this issue. All ideas and quotations below come from Davey's *Brush Meditation: A Japanese Way to Mind & Body Harmony*.

The Japanese classical arts and "ways" all require complete harmony between mind and body. In *shodō* (書道: calligraphy or "the way of the brush"), the mind and body must work in unison to move the brush. Otherwise, the calligraphy becomes rough and unbalanced. A wavering brush reflects a wavering mind. But just as *shodō* can reveal a lack of mind-body unity, regular calligraphy practice can help cultivate that state.

Ideally, when drawing kanji calligraphy, you concentrate completely, existing only in the moment, rather than drifting to the past or future. Decisiveness is also essential; "in Japanese calligraphic art, as in living your life, you cannot go back . . ." (p. 45). The *shodō* expert combines precision and calmness: "Every stroke must be delivered like the slice of a razor-sharp samurai sword, yet the brush must be handled in a serene manner" (p. 45).

If all goes well, your kanji will reflect not only calmness but also movement. The characters "must seem as though they are in motion. This is *dochu no sei* (stillness in motion), which is frequently alluded to in esoteric manuals of Japanese philosophy and religion" (p. 84). You also need to show "motion in stillness," because *shodō* is "moving meditation, and as such it acknowledges that we are repeatedly in motion in daily activities" (p. 84). The more you practice *shodō*, the more you'll learn the rhythms with which to paint each character, and this will align you with nature's rhythms.

As you can see, the goal of *shodō* extends far beyond the product on the page or the development of skills. Instead, the process teaches you the "way." If you practice drawing kanji without attention to the "way," however, you're only engaging in *shūji*, 習字. As the kanji (to learn + character) reveal, this term refers to handwriting practice without the attendant spiritual mind-set.

To practice her calligraphy, a Japanese woman has copied characters from a book of kanji drawn in the popular style known as 楷書 (*kaisho*). Typically, Japanese calligraphy teachers require students to imitate the teacher's work exactly. From top to bottom, and right to left, the characters appear to be as follows:

- 靚 (*TO, mi•ru:* to see)
- 在 (*ZAI, a•ru:* to exist)
- 智 (*CHI:* wisdom)
- 猶 (*YŪ, nao:* to delay, furthermore)
- 迷 (*mayo•u:* to be perplexed, get lost)
- 況 (*KYŌ:* conditions)

The Way of Culture and the Arts

When read as *michi,* 道 means "road" or "way," in the mundane sense of asphalt and directions. By contrast, when you read this character as *DŌ,* it may retain that ordinary sense of "road," or it may refer to a spiritual path, the "way" of the universe. Japanese culture abounds in 道 compounds that translate as "the way of flowers," "the way of tea," "the way of empty hands," and so forth.

The on-yomi *DŌ* is the Japanese pronunciation of the Chinese word *Tao,* a philosophy that encourages going with the flow of nature. In Japan, the Taoist concept morphed long ago into ideas about performing native arts, crafts, and sports with a certain mind-set. That is, to excel in 道-related pursuits, one must unite body and mind, focusing both on the task at hand. As H. E. Davey writes in *Living the Japanese Arts & Ways: 45 Paths to Meditation & Beauty,* "The body reflects the mind, and so any art can function as a visible representation of our spiritual condition" (p. 93).

Davey says much more about "the way" in his four books on Japanese classical arts, so I recommend those for information about Japanese "ways." Lacking space here, I won't attempt detailed definitions of any of these philosophies or cultural products. Instead, I'll simply present the kanji for many cultural pursuits and related terms (some with 道, some without), as well as the breakdowns of the kanji.

Religion

Taoism	道教	*dōkyō:* way + suffix for name of religion
Confucianism	儒道	*judō:* "the way of Confucius"
Shinto	神道	*shintō:* "the way of the gods"
Buddhism	仏道	*butsudō:* "the way of Buddha"
Zen	禅	*zen*
koan (paradox on which monks meditate)	公案	*kōan:* public + proposition

Samurai, Martial Arts, and Other Sports

samurai	侍	*samurai*
military or martial arts	武道	*budō:* military + way
samurai code of chivalry	武士道	*bushidō:* military + samurai + way
judo	柔道	*jūdō:* "the gentle way"
jujitsu	柔術	*jūjutsu:* gentleness + skill
aikido	合気道	*aikidō:* "the way of the harmony of the spirit"
karate	空手道	*karatedō:* "the way of empty hands"
kendo (Japanese fencing)	剣道	*kendō:* "the way of the sword"
kyudo (Japanese archery)	弓道	*kyūdō:* "the way of the bow"
dojo (school for martial arts)	道場	*dōjō:* the way + place
sumo (Japanese wrestling)	相撲	*sumō:* each other + to bump

Decorative Arts and Crafts

ikebana (flower arranging)	生け花	*ikebana:* flower arranging, or 花道 (*kadō:* "the way of flower arranging")
bonsai (dwarf trees in pots)	盆栽	*bonsai:* basin + planting

calligraphy	書道	*shodō:* "the way of writing"
woodblock prints	浮世絵	*ukiyoe:* floating + world + painting
origami	折り紙	*origami:* to fold + paper
Japanese paper	和紙	*washi:* Japan + paper
lacquerware	漆器	*shikki:* lacquer + container, apparatus
Japanese pottery making	陶芸	*tōgei:* pottery + art
Japanese pottery	焼き物	*yakimono:* to bake + thing
raku pottery	楽焼き	*rakuyaki:* enjoyment, ease + to bake

Massage and Healing Arts

shiatsu (a type of massage)	指圧	*shiatsu:* finger + pressure
reiki (a healing modality)	霊気	*reiki:* spirit, universal + life energy
Japanese yoga	心身統一	*shinshin tōitsu:* mind + body + relationship + one, or "mind-body unification"

Stylish Objects and Design Terms

folding fan	扇	*ōgi*
paper lantern	提灯	*chōchin:* to carry in hand + lamp
tatami (straw floor mat)	畳	*tatami*
shoji (paper sliding door)	障子	*shōji:* to hinder + thing
tansu (chest of drawers)	箪笥	*tansu:* bamboo rice basket + clothes chest
wabi-sabi	詫び寂び	*wabi-sabi:* simplicity + rusticity, combining to mean "humble simplicity" or "rustic beauty"
mono no aware	物の哀れ	*mono no aware:* "sensitivity to things," especially to the sad beauty of impermanence
shibumi (n.)	渋み	*shibumi:* restrained elegance
shibui (adj.)	渋い	*shibui:* elegant

Theater and Literature

Noh (old-style theater)	能	*nō*
Bunraku (puppet theater)	文楽	*bunraku:* figures + music, enjoyment
Kabuki (traditional drama)	歌舞伎	*kabuki:* song + dance + skill
haiku	俳句	*haiku:* haiku + haiku

Music and Instruments

taiko (drum)	太鼓	*taiko:* big + drum
shamisen (three-stringed guitarlike instrument)	三味線	*shamisen:* three + flavor + line
shakuhachi (flute)	尺八	*shakuhachi:* Japanese foot + eight, or the length of the flute in old Japanese measurements
koto (stringed instrument that one plucks)	琴	*koto:* harp
karaoke	空オケ	*karaoke:* empty + orchestra (from English); usually written カラオケ

Visual Arts

| manga | 漫画 | *manga:* cartoon + picture |
| film | 映画 | *eiga:* reflection + picture |

> Anime and manga are close cousins. But *anime* is not here, as it has no kanji. It's written アニメ, short for アニメーション, "animation."

Tea

tea	お茶	*ocha:* any kind of tea
tea ceremony	茶道	*chadō* or *sadō:* "the way of tea"
teapot	急須	*kyūsu:* to hurry + necessarily
tea bowl (ceremonial)	茶碗	*chawan:* tea + bowl
teacup (regular)	湯飲み	*yunomi:* hot water + drink

Types of Tea

genmaicha	玄米茶	*genmaicha:* black, mysterious + rice + tea
matcha	抹茶	*matcha:* to grind into powder + tea
hojicha	焙じ茶	*hōjicha:* to roast + tea
sencha	煎茶	*sencha:* to roast, boil + tea
bancha	番茶	*bancha:* number in a series + tea
English tea or black tea	紅茶	*kōcha:* red + tea, because the Japanese see "black" tea as red

If you love Kit Kats, and if you love green tea, how about combining the two?! Green tea Kit Kats contain white chocolate subtly flavored with Uji matcha (宇治抹茶), as we see in the rightmost column. Uji is a city near Kyoto known for high-quality green tea. The second column from the right says 香り豊かな深い味わい (*Kaori yutakana fukai ajiwai:* Deep taste with abundant fragrance). The arc of gold on the lower left corner says 期間限定 (*kikan gentei:* restricted period), which is to say, "Available for a limited time only."

Kanji Sound Effects in Manga

Manga (Japanese cartoons) are rich in sound effects. The Japanese have taken the art of onomatopoeia to such lengths that their manga represent the sounds of remorse *(acha)*, a tongue hanging out *(biron),* and internal or external warmth *(hoka hoka).* This puts manga light-years ahead of American comics with their rudimentary sounds of *Pow! Boom! Zap!*

Japanese sound effects are usually rendered in katakana. But what happens when you represent them in kanji, as Katsuya Terada has done in his graphic novel *The Monkey King?*

Take *Don!* (ドン**!**), the sound of punching someone hard. In katakana, a bold font and a large point size turn up the perceived volume. But if you replace ドン with 鈍 (also pronounced *DON*), it could create even more of an impact. Readers skilled at reading both kanji and manga will absorb the yomi *DON*, disregard the meaning (dull, slow, stupid), and take the twelve, intricate strokes as a sign of something big. And good readers will absorb all this information without consciously noticing the kanji. Whereas the character would send most kanji students scurrying to the dictionary, fluent readers won't be in the least confused by the irrelevant meaning of this subliminal symbol.

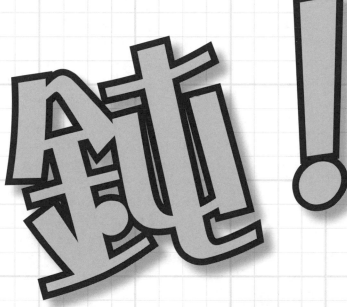

This bean-jam-filled wafer is called a *monaka* (最中: extreme + middle, which somehow means "the shape of the moon floating on a pond during the harvest festival"). The *monaka* in the picture is supposed to resemble a *hanko,* or personal name stamp. (See page 139 for a picture of a *hanko.*) The kanji in the left-hand column are 福富, Fukutomi, which must be the name of the manufacturer. The characters in the right-hand column are less clear. They appear to be 菓匠, which could break down as "cake" + "craftsman." If so, then one could interpret all the kanji as "Fukutomi Cakeworks." Or one could just enjoy the cookie along with some tea, accepting that it's probably not all that essential to know what the cookie says!

Kanji Sandwiches

It doesn't happen often, but twin components can sandwich another one. Let's see if the three kanji below have anything in common.

1. The first one, 嬲 *(JŌ, nabu•ru)* means "to ridicule." This *kaiimoji,* which originated in China, depicts two men who are bullying a woman. In the variant (i.e., the older) form, the inverse image appeared, with the two "women" sandwiching the "man." How seriously should we take this teasing or bullying? The only two 嬲 compounds Spahn provides are 嬲り物 *(naburimono:* laughingstock) and 嬲り殺し *(naburigoroshi:* to torture to death). That sounds serious indeed, even gruesome!

2. The second kanji, 辮, has just one yomi, *BEN,* and means "braid" or "pigtail." The character contains "thread" surrounded by two components that mean "sharp." Although 辛 *(kara•i)* now translates as "bitter," it originally represented a tattooist's needle. Back in China, where this kanji came into existence, the initial shape of 辮 contained just two instances of 辛, read as *HEN* and meaning "to knit." These components still lend sound and meaning to 辮, making it a *keiseimoji.* Spahn shows only one compound involving 辮—namely, 辮髪 *(benpatsu:* pigtail).

3. The third kanji, 斑, is the most frequently used, showing a king on either side of writing (although 文 also means "pattern," which is more relevant here). As *HAN,* 斑 means "spots." As *buchi, madara, hadara,* or *fu,* it means "spots," "patches," "streaks," and "speckled." By the time you reach the last reading, *mura,* the meaning has deteriorated to "unevenness," "blemishes," and "capriciousness." Oddly, this kanji originally looked much like 辮, which we just examined. Wherever we now see 王 in 斑, the Chinese initially had 辛, which again lent the sound *HEN* to this kanji. The sound has now evolved into *HAN.* The character remains a *keiseimoji.* Compounds with 斑 tend to be charming descriptions of nature: 斑犬 *(madara inu:* spotted dog), 斑馬 *(madara uma:* piebald horse or zebra), 斑猫 *(buchi neko:* tabby cat), and 斑雪 *(madara yuki:* snow remaining in spots), as well as two descriptions of phenomena related to human bodies: 雀斑 *(sobakasu:* freckle) and 母斑 *(bohan:* birthmark). Perhaps the two kings' text decrees that certain creatures should receive spots and marks!

What do these kanji sandwiches have in common? All are from China. The first depicts adult torture (the battle of the sexes), whereas the second situates that torture in classrooms, back when boys dipped girls' braids in inkwells. And if the kings' text is about taxing the people, that, too, indicates a type of torture. On the brighter side, all these kanji combine things with neat yin-yang relationships: men with women, needles with thread, and governing officials with paperwork.

Kanji Word Find

Reading from left to right or from top to bottom (but not diagonally), circle all the viable two-kanji compound words. Each circle will overlap with another, as shown below, where the top pair forms *igai,* "except," and the bottom pair says *gaishutsu,* "going out."

Work through the grid in this way, forming multiple chains of kanji. Each linear chain represents part of one large kanji. The shape of that big kanji should emerge when you find all the words. If the image isn't clear, lightly shade in boxes containing kanji chains. Now, what kanji do you see? How do you read it? What does it mean?

Answers appear in the Answer Key. *Ganbatte kudasai!*

短	縮	小	説	明	白	鳥	肉	屋
目	森	間	名	日	町	雪	通	同
以	寝	南	北	光	速	力	山	和
外	前	米	形	年	面	点	由	風
出	痛	国	連	中	分	数	仕	船
発	味	内	涼	古	返	学	月	便
音	女	部	首	都	人	生	六	利
読	酒	流	十	門	決	牛	若	用
書	道	具	眼	科	長	所	得	意

#66 JUST THE FACTS

Genkōyōshi

In Japanese schools, students write essays on grid paper called *genkōyōshi* (原稿用紙: original + manuscript + use + paper). This resembles graph paper, but it stops looking that way as soon as the squares (typically four hundred per page) fill with vertical writing. You read the text from top to bottom and right to left. A sample is below, with a detailed view at right.

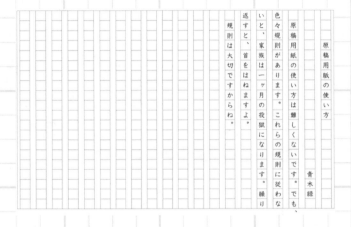

The Japanese follow strict guidelines when using *genkōyōshi*:

- One character goes in each box. That's also true for small kana such as っ and ょ.
- Punctuation marks (periods, commas, quotation marks) all go in individual boxes. But rather than being centered within those boxes, they lie to the right, possibly in a corner. However, you never want to isolate a punctuation mark at the top of a column; either squeeze it into the bottom box or let it hang below that box.

- The dash representing a long vowel in katakana gets its own box.
- The title goes in the first column, three boxes down.
- Your name goes in the second column, lower than the title. Count backward so there's room for a blank box at the end of your name.
- Indent paragraphs by skipping a box at the top of a column.

So far, so good (if a bit finicky). But there's one catch. What if you're six hundred characters into an essay and you spot a mistake at the beginning? You wrote a word in kana with a short vowel, and it should have been a long vowel. Making space for that one character will push the end of the paragraph into the next column. That means you'll have to erase back to that point (assuming you've written in pencil) and rewrite everything that follows! Essentially, you're

S
C
R
E
W
E
D
!

原稿用紙の使い方

青木緑

原稿用紙の使い方は難しくないです。でも、色々規則があります。これらの規則に従わないと、家族は一ヶ月の投獄になります。繰り返すと、首をはねますよ。

規則は大切ですからね。

Here is the text at left in rōmaji:

Genkōyōshi no Tsukaikata
     Aoki Midori
Genkōyōshi no tsukaikata wa muzukashikunai desu. Demo iroiro kisoku ga arimasu. Korera no kisoku ni shitagawanai to, kazoku wa ikkagetsu no tōgoku ni narimasu. Kurikaesu to, kubi o hanemasuyo.
     Kisoku wa taisetsu desu kara ne.

Here is the translation:

How to Use *Genkōyōshi*
     By Midori Aoki
Genkōyōshi are not difficult to use. But there are some rules. If you don't follow these rules, your family will be imprisoned for a month. Repeat offenders will have their heads chopped off.
     Rules are important, right?

Don't Use These Kanji!

After going to all the trouble of learning kanji, the Japanese must learn which ones *not* to use. Even though the words in the following chart have kanji, the Japanese tend not to write them that way, opting instead for hiragana.

It's unclear why they do this, but I have a few ideas. People use these words so often that perhaps ordinary hiragana seems more fitting. And maybe there's been resistance to writing such old and quintessentially Japanese expressions with Chinese characters. Moreover, the Japanese tend to say, rather than write, the words in the Gratitude and Greetings columns below, so perhaps that factors into the hiragana usage; kanji is meant, after all, for the written word. Finally, hiragana must come as a relief to someone facing the stroke-intensive 御座居ます, *gozaimasu* (a polite form of "to be" or "to have").

You can use kanji for the words categorized below as Possible to Write, but it's best not to use kanji for the expressions under Almost Never Written.

GRATITUDE	GREETINGS	MISCELLANEOUS
Possible to Write	**Possible to Write**	**Possible to Write**
有り難う *arigatō* Thank you (casual)	お早う *ohayō* Good morning! (casual)	出来る *dekiru* to be capable of
	今日は *konnichiwa* Good afternoon! (casual or formal)	居る *iru* to be, exist
	今晩は *konbanwa* Good evening! (casual or formal)	有る *aru* to be, have
Almost Never Written	**Almost Never Written**	**Almost Never Written**
有り難う御座居ます *arigatō gozaimasu* Thank you very much (polite)	お早う御座居ます *ohayō gozaimasu* Good morning! (formal)	沢山 *takusan* many
頂きます *itadakimasu* expression of gratitude before meals	左様なら, 然様なら *sayōnara* Goodbye	何方 1. *donata* who 2. *dochira* where, what place, which
御馳走様でした *gochisōsama deshita* expression of gratitude after meals		如何 *ikaga* how
		只 *tada* free, merely

Typing Kanji

People often lament that with the increasing use of computers in Japan, the younger generation is forgetting how to read kanji and especially how to write it. I believe that's only half the story. The other half involves the history of the technology used to type Japanese. Before computers came into widespread use in Japan, people drew kanji all the time, because ordinary folks had no access to typewriters. This inaccessibility must have been quite frustrating, but it did keep people's kanji in tip-top form. If the Japanese typewriter had ever taken off, people would have forgotten how to write kanji long ago.

In the United States, the prototype for the first typewriter appeared in 1867. But Japan didn't ride the same technological wave for nearly fifty years, as it faced much greater technological challenges, thanks to multiple scripts and nearly 50,000 characters. Kyōta Sugimoto saved the day by isolating the most frequently used kanji and then, in 1915, creating a keyboard featuring these 2,400 characters. The keyboard covered one square meter! Five thousand more characters stayed in a box until a typist needed them. In 1917 the Nippon Typewriter Company began producing typewriters based on Sugimoto's model. Over the next seventy years, Japanese typewriters had anywhere from 2,400 to 3,000 keys and as many as seven "shift states." (Hitting the Shift key on an English-language keyboard allows you to toggle between lowercase and uppercase letters, or between two "states." Japanese typewriters had seven such states.)

These machines barely caught on in Japan, because they were exceedingly difficult to use. They required specially trained typists, who still couldn't go very fast. In *Asia's Orthographic Dilemma,* William C. Hannas notes that these machines took 160 to 200 times longer to master than Western typewriters. At most, a person could type ten pages a day, because it took forever to locate each key. This technology gave "hunt and peck" a new meaning! Hannas says that because typing required full concentration, an individual couldn't possibly write original, creative text on such a machine.

Rather than making extensive use of these unwieldy, expensive typewriters, most companies relied on clerks to handwrite a multitude of documents. If something needed to be typed, the company could send out for that service. Authors wrote books by hand—on *genkōyōshi!* In a 1965 article, *New York Times* writer Robert Trumbull noted, "Japanese authors write on large sheets of paper ruled into 400 small squares, each square for one character, which they buy at stationery shops. The writer is paid by the page, and many have been known to stretch out their prose for this reason." Referring to writer Yukio Mishima, Trumbull said, "Mr. Mishima often uses a Kanji that his publisher's printer happens not to have in stock, in which case a type foundry has to cast it specially."

In 1978, Japan arrived at a partial solution when Toshiba produced the first Japanese-language word processor. Like the typewriter, though, this new machine was still enormous and expensive, so it didn't come into common use. In the mid-1980s, smaller models finally appeared and found an enthusiastic market. As one writer has observed, the Japanese jumped from longhand to the word processor, skipping an evolutionary phase.

Character recognition has made it easy for a computer to produce upward of 6,700 kanji. Keyboards either display fifty kana keys or twenty-six of the QWERTY variety. With both set-ups, you type a word phonetically. For *ageru,* you hit three kana keys *(a-ge-ru)* or five alphabetic ones. The computer then produces a list of kanji and ateji that say *ageru:* 上げる, 挙げる, 揚げる, and 擧げる, prompting you to choose the one you desire. When you type with a romanized keyboard, the computer goes through two steps to arrive at this point, first converting rōmaji into kana. You can therefore skip a step by using a kana keyboard. However, kana keyboards are twice as big, so that slows things in terms of locating what you want. And if you've used a QWERTY keyboard for years, you'll probably never be as quick with a kana layout.

To type kanji on your computer, you need to activate the Japanese part of your word-processing software by following its instructions. Those directions will also explain how you can toggle back and forth between Japanese and English. For instance, on a Mac you do this by holding down the Command key (with a cloverleaf symbol) and tapping the space bar. Once you've figured this out, you're set to go, but it helps to know a few inputting tricks.

When a Japanese friend used to send me email in rōmaji, her spelling often mystified me. *"Hennji wo matte imasu,"* she would say. "I'm waiting for your reply." (This sounds kind of pushy in English, but it goes over fine in Japanese.) Ordinarily one would write this as *"Henji o matte imasu."* Now I realize that even though the email was in rōmaji, she typed it as though the letters would turn into kanji. To produce ん, you need to hit *n* twice. Otherwise, the computer thinks you want something like *ni* or a contraction such as *nya*. For *onna* (woman), you need to hit *n* three times. Whenever I forget this and type *o-n-n-a*, the computer gives me おんあ. Typing it correctly yields おんな, which is the only way to convert the word to 女. Similarly, you need to type *wo* for an object *o* (を) or else the computer will give you お.

Other such oddities include the following (the last five of which are small vowels):

To get this:	Type this:
づ	du
ぢ	di
っ	xtu
カ	xka
ケ	xke
あ	xa
い	xi
う	xu
え	xe
お	xo

Furthermore, whenever you want は *(ha)* to represent a subject marker pronounced *wa*, you need to type *ha*. It can be difficult to reprogram the brain to do this, especially

with words such as *konbanwa* (Good evening!), which should be typed *konbanha*. But typing does prove helpful in revealing spelling misconceptions. I often get strange results by typing おお *(oo)* instead of おう *(ou)* to lengthen the *o* in words.

To produce katakana, hold down the Shift key. Once, when typing a Japanese person's name, I instinctively capitalized it, which gave me katakana for the first character. Bewildered, I deleted the mistake and repeated it, going through this process perhaps ten times before concluding that the guy's name had something weird about it that made my computer misbehave!

If you ever need to type part of a kanji compound (say, in a discussion about that particular kanji), you may run into a problem. Most likely you will input an on-yomi shared by dozens of other characters. The computer might offer scads of choices before arriving at the one you want. To save time, think of a compound containing the desired kanji. Type the whole compound, then erase the part you don't need. It's a weird way to type, but then, in typing Japanese, you've entered a whole other realm. And erasing half your work is nothing compared with what Japanese typists endured before word processors came along.

This old typewriter gives new meaning to the "hunt" of "hunt and peck." It also gives new meaning to the word "tedious."

DOUBLE HAPPINESS

"Where you been? Haven't seen you for long time!" May said, smiling warmly.

It had been fifteen days since my last visit to the dry cleaners. Is that such a long time? Maybe not for most people, but May seems to enjoy seeing me. I feel the same way about her, though our communication is hit-or-miss.

"I've been busy working on my kanji book," I said.

"Oh, I love to read! Love it!" she said. "But now with three kids, no time!" She said she used to read romance novels, then laughed hard at the follies of her youth . . . or the unbridled passion she used to feel . . . or . . . Actually, I rarely know why she's laughing. "Now I like to read . . ." She stopped, unable to produce the right word. She patted her chest. "It's about things deep in the heart."

"Beliefs?" I suggested, but she didn't understand my English. "Write it in Chinese," I said.

So she did: 心理, the same shapes as in Japanese. I still wanted to see "beliefs," so initially that's what I saw. But a moment later, I puzzled out the on-yomi: *SHIN RI.* Of course! *Shinri*—"psyche," or "state of mind," as in *shinrigaku,* "psychology." To be sure we were talking about the same thing, I added 学 (*GAKU:* study) and said, "Like that?"

"Yes!" she said, and we were all smiles, both of us stunned that we had actually communicated. Moreover, she had hit on one of my favorite topics. I can't convince half the Americans I know about the merits of therapy, but my Chinese dry cleaner seems inclined to agree! She explained how, now that she has kids, she wants to understand why they do what they do. She particularly likes reading the advice of one doctor.

"Not Dr. Phil?!" I said in horror.

She smiled. "Not Dr. Phil." Oh, thank goodness. Another point of agreement.

I was buoyant for the rest of the day, finally having had the kind of experience I've dreamed of having with kanji. I've long wanted my knowledge of Japanese to serve as a bridge to China.

But the bridge is usually quite a bit creakier. Take, for instance, the first time I told May I was writing about kanji.

"What?" she said, grasping nothing.

"Chinese characters," I said.

"Calendars?"

"No," I said, flipping over my dry-cleaning receipt and drawing 漢字. "Kanji," I said as clearly as possible.

She looked at me askance. "That's hanzi," she said, affronted that I had "mispronounced" the word. She knows I study Japanese, not Chinese, so I couldn't think how else to explain the discrepancy. I simply nodded.

With a strange expression on her face, she said, "But that's hard!"

And that was as much agreement as we could muster up that day.

Searching for a Point of Entry

I don't think it's unusual for students of Japanese to feel curious about Chinese. The more you research Japan, the more you find signs pointing to China, the source of so much in Japanese culture. This is particularly true with kanji research; when you investigate the etymology of a character or compound, you often touch on its history in ancient China. But if you don't know Chinese, you may not find satisfying answers.

Say I want to know how 心 came to mean "heart" in China. Using Jim Breen's online Japanese dictionary, I stare at a bewildering assortment of codes. I gather that "Yxin1 Wsim" are related to hanzi. But what on earth do these notations mean? Hoping to find out, I follow links to Chinese dictionaries, and . . . they're largely in Chinese! I can't grasp much at all. I also confront a potpourri of codes. Here's the listing for 心 on Timothy Huang's Big5 database:

CCCII code: **213D78**
Radical: **2C61**
Stroke Count (without Radical): **00**
Total Stroke Count: **04**
Three Corner Input Code (Huang): **930000**
Four Corner code: **3300**
Lin's frequency number: **0098**
Dar-Zen Liu's phonetic code: **1216**
Taiwan Telephone and Telegraph Telex code: **001800**
Very Old CNS code: **35A9**
Old CNS code: **4540**
CNS code (around 1988): **004540**
Big5: **A4DF**
Dragon Code (TsangJie 2nd gen. input code): **.N>**
Dragon Input (TsangJie 4/5th gen. input code): **P**
internal code used by CDC: **BC-**
internal code used by Syscom: **90B9**
First/Last Stroke Input Code: **MCC**
Huang Card Number: **567**
Glyph Pattern (needs Big5 fonts): み
JuYin Phonetic: **VUP**
Radical number: **61**

Do I need to study Chinese or programming to make sense of this? I don't even understand the name of the database—Big5. Is it half a football conference? At such moments, Chinese seems impenetrable, as if someone has hung a Keep Out sign.

But more than a billion people speak Chinese. If it's not incomprehensible to them, maybe kanji students can suss out at least a little. All we need is some background information. And then, even if kanji doesn't provide the hoped-for bridge, maybe we'll understand why the bridge collapses so often!

If you want a reality check about how far apart Chinese and Japanese tend to be, see Exhibit 69, "Just the Facts: Mind the Gap." For definitions of terms such as "Mandarin," "Cantonese," and "pinyin," see Exhibit 70, "Just the Facts: A Crash Course in Chinese Terminology." To ease your way into Chinese, see Exhibit 71, "Thematic Explorations: Chinese Words You've Heard." One noticeable difference between Chinese and Japanese has to do with tones. To learn about tones, see Exhibit 72, "Just the Facts: The Tones of Hanzi." That discussion might bring on-yomi to mind, so it's a good time to try your hand at Exhibit 73, "Game: On-Yomi Tongue Twister."

As it turns out, Big5 is an official character set standard in Taiwan. The name refers to the five companies that collaborated in its development. Big5 includes 13,494 characters, "including 13,053 Hanzi and 441 non-Hanzi," according to one website. A collection of hanzi that includes non-hanzi? I tell you, this research can suck you into a warren of tunnels!

Communication Breakdowns

In addition to Mandarin and Cantonese, major Chinese languages include Min, Wu, Xiang, Gan, and Hakka. And each has several dialects! According to William C. Hannas in *Asia's Orthographic Dilemma,* there may be hundreds of mutually unintelligible languages in China. Of course, these statements hold true only if you subscribe to the many-separate-languages theory of Chinese, which is complicated, political, and way beyond our purposes here.

But whatever ideology people embrace about these issues, everyone agrees on the lack of uniformity in spoken Chinese. Owing to differences in accents, vocabulary, and syntax, speech varies so much across China that people who travel outside a native region are lucky if they can communicate at all, as far as I can tell. It's as if they become strangers in a strange land. Tian Tang, the blogger introduced in Exhibit 69, explains some of the ensuing problems: "One of my parents' friends from Wuxi didn't speak Mandarin very well. When he was in Beijing on a business trip, he couldn't find a public restroom because he forgot the Mandarin term for that." Tang also offers this word of caution: "If you're in Shanghai, and you don't speak the local dialect, expect to pay more. No one will give you a good price when you haggle." Mandarin speakers face the same difficulties in Canton, he says. Even traveling minuscule distances can create communication difficulties; May told me that she can't talk to her in-laws, who come from a Canton village as close to her own village as San Francisco is to Oakland.

So . . . hanzi to the rescue? Well, yes and no. Hanzi certainly allows for more common ground than spoken words. It largely bridges the Mandarin-Cantonese divide. And for fifty years the Chinese government has worked to make all Chinese citizens use hanzi (rather than native scripts, such as the ones Mongolians, Manchurians, and Tibetans have used for their distinct, non-Mandarin languages).

But the various languages and dialects of China create vocabulary differences, so people sometimes express identical concepts with different characters. Then, too, because Taiwan has stuck with the traditional shapes of characters, "Materials published on one side of the Taiwan Strait are largely unintelligible on the other," says Hannas (p. 22). Finally, about 91 percent of Chinese people are considered literate (by UNICEF's count in 2004), but that means as many as 9 percent aren't. (According to a 2005 region-by-region study cited on Wikipedia, the province of Jilin boasts the lowest illiteracy rate at 3.85 percent, and apart from Tibet with its 44 percent rate, the province of Qinghai is the most illiterate area at 22 percent. Taiwan, incidentally, has 3.9 percent illiteracy, which is particularly impressive when one considers the more complex characters used there.)

Well, then, perhaps romanization can help with communication. Unfortunately, that's not the case. Many people don't know pinyin, especially those with poor educations and the elderly. (China officially adopted this romanization system in 1958.) Unlike rōmaji, pinyin has diacritical marks (as in the word *pǔ tōng huà*), which reflect tones. Changing a tone alters the meaning of a word. So when people from different regions use different tones, their pinyin follows suit, becoming equally unintelligible to Chinese "foreigners." And although certain words may come across in pinyin, syntax varies with dialect, so the meaning of the sentence also comes into question.

Pinyin in Taiwan

In Taiwan, pinyin might not get you too far. This has to do with politics and history in China and Taiwan. Attempts to romanize Chinese date back to the sixteenth century. More recently, at the 1913 government-sponsored Conference on Unification of Pronunciation, delegates voted to create a phonetic system for all the provinces. *Zhù yīn zì mǔ,* or "phonetic alphabet," was later renamed *gúo yīn zì mǔ,* "national phonetic alphabet," and in 1930 it acquired yet another name, *zhù yīn fú hào,* which still exists today. This system is not in fact a romanization; rather, it contains symbols derived from hanzi. To see samples and to learn more, check out Exhibit 74, "Just the Facts: Phonetic Markers Used in Taiwan."

Why do I refer to markers "used in Taiwan" when they've also been used in China? Well, that came to a halt when the Communists took power in China. Along with many other simplifications of the language, Mao Zedong ordered his subjects to stop using *zhù yīn fú hào* and to substitute pinyin instead. With the Communists in charge of mainland China, Taiwan went its separate way under the government of the Republic of China. People in Taiwan didn't make the switch to pinyin, and today they are the only Chinese speakers to use *zhù yīn fú hào.* They tend not to know pinyin, but that's changing. In a 2004 comment on the blog Language Hat (www.languagehat.com), "xiaolongnu" wrote, "Pinyin is catching on in Taiwan, quietly, piecemeal, and without fanfare; I think purely for practical reasons, since people just weren't lining up to use Wade-Giles or zhuyin fuhao (bopomofo), despite the political angle. Both systems are certainly still used, though, and each has its partisans."

Making Hanzi Meet Chinese Needs

The Japanese and Koreans have molded Chinese to complement their indigenous languages. (To learn about the use of Chinese characters in Korea, see Exhibit 75, "Just the Facts: Hanja in Korea.") But could this work in the opposite direction? In some ways, that has in fact happened. Check out Exhibit 76, "Just the Facts: Kanji Compounds That China Imported from Japan," for a few examples of borrowed or even "repatriated" characters. But the phenomenon explored in this exhibit is small potatoes compared to a much larger one. The Chinese have adapted hanzi to represent foreign words.

The Japanese use katakana for this purpose, and Koreans write loanwords in hangeul, English, or both. Phonetic representation isn't an option for the Chinese, of course. But they *have* made use of another maneuver known well to the Japanese—ateji, which we explored in Exhibit 36, "Just the Facts: Doesn't Sound the Way It's Spelled." To represent foreign words with hanzi, the Chinese disregard the meanings of certain characters and use them solely for their phonetic value. This comes in handy with personal names, country names, and foreign terms. For some reason, 達 *(dá)* seems particularly handy for representing loanwords. We see this in *léi dá* (radar), written as 雷達 in traditional hanzi and as 雷达 in simplified characters. Another example is Darfur, the Sudanese province. The pinyin is *dá ěr fú ěr,* and the characters are 達爾福爾 (traditional) and 达尔福尔 (simplified). Finally, here's the way to write "Dalai Lama": *dá lài lǎ ma,* represented as 達賴喇嘛 (traditional) and 达赖喇嘛 (simplified).

Grafting foreign sounds onto Chinese characters is no small job. I already knew that from my exposure to Japanese ateji. But my understanding of this deepened when I read on Tian Tang's blog that whereas 迈克尔 is the Chinese way of writing "Michael," the characters change to 米盖尔 for "Miguel," the same name in Spanish!

Phonetic representations of foreign words are also inconsistent across the vast Chinese-speaking world. Different versions of the same word pop up in mainland China, Taiwan, Hong Kong, Singapore, and Malaysia.

To avoid confusion, modern Chinese newspapers and official documents often include a phrase from a foreign language, as well as a Chinese translation, rather than taking a stab at phoneticization.

So much for representing foreign words. What about using hanzi to reflect grammar? To learn about that, see Exhibit 77, "Just the Facts: Representing Grammar with Hanzi." And for yet another type of representation with Chinese characters, see Exhibit 78, "Thematic Explorations: Animal Signs in the Zodiac."

How Many Hanzi Does It Take?

If you've been reading the exhibits in this chapter, you have Chinese grammar and characters all sewn up, tones and everything! The next question is how many hanzi you'll need for complete literacy.

In some ways, this question brings us right back to grammar. As the Chinese represent all their grammar with hanzi, it makes sense that they would use more characters than the Japanese. In fact, Chinese people use twice as many! And whereas high school graduates in Japan must know 2,136 characters, their Chinese peers need to know about 5,000!

The word "about" in that sentence reveals one interesting difference between the two cultures. The Japanese obsessively count the number of kanji they know or need to know, and the Chinese speak of such issues much more loosely. Because of his blog, Tian Tang is deeply involved with hanzi, but when I asked how many characters he knows, he said, "I never really counted."

Compared with kanji, it's much harder to calculate the number of hanzi one needs in China. Hannas spends ten pages citing reasons for this. He notes that a Chinese literature professor, a pharmacologist, and a mathematician will need different sets of characters. If you want to read texts predating the hanzi simplification of the 1950s, that adds characters to your must-learn list. And if you aim to read classical Chinese texts, you'll need old versions of characters. As we've seen, character usage varies according to regional vocabulary differences. Finally, there's the issue of whether knowing 5,000 hanzi just means passively identifying them or also includes drawing them correctly from memory.

Hannas figures that 6,900 characters are now commonly used in China versus 3,120 in Japan. However, he says, "Getting by in Japanese seems to require mastering a higher proportion of that inventory. I find 4,500, or two-thirds, of the characters in use in Chinese adequate for most reading in that language but I need most of the 3,100 characters 'in use' for comparable reading in Japanese. . . . Proportionately more use is made of the characters that are used in Japanese" (p. 135). He explains this by surmising that the Japanese represent rare indigenous vocabulary with hiragana.

He then makes a point that I've never heard elsewhere. If Japanese people need more than 3,000 kanji, he says, then their schools don't prepare them well for daily life, sending them out into the world with only a minimum requirement of 1,945. Hannas neglects to say that most high school students take electives, which teach them far more kanji by the time they finish high school. But if there is indeed any kind of gap in graduates' kanji knowledge, it's hard for me to imagine how Japanese society could remedy the situation. Should kids head for cram school when kindergarten lets out for the day?

The Rigors of a Chinese Education

From what I hear, that's pretty much what happens in China! But there the "cram school" is in the home and in the parents' attempts to make the world seem like one big classroom. When Tang was quite young, his mother brought him on shopping trips and forced him to read every sign. From the butcher shop to the fish market, he needed to call off the names of the shops, the products for sale, and the costs, all while learning about money, weights, and calculations of price per gram.

Even though both his parents worked full-time, more drilling occurred at home. "My mother taught me about five thousand characters before I entered first grade when I was five and half," says Tang. Five thousand?!?! Was he a wunderkind? No, he says, "I did not think I was a special case. It wasn't hard at all," he says. His mom taught him radicals, components, and commonly used characters, exploring how they built on each other "like Lego." He found it particularly helpful to study a grid resembling a multiplication table. In place of numbers, it displayed hanzi categorized by radicals and components. Although he grew up on the mainland in Jiangsu Province, his parents didn't want him to settle for learning simplified forms. With his parents' encouragement, he also learned the traditional, more complicated versions of many characters.

Meanwhile, over in Jinan (the capital of Shandong Province in northern China), Yaling Zhu mastered about fifteen hundred to two thousand characters by age seven, when her formal schooling began. This was far more than most of her classmates knew. The pressure didn't end there, though. Her parents insisted that she learn English in third grade, four years before schools would teach her this subject. She always had plenty of homework and excelled academically. But her parents wanted her to keep that competitive edge, so they loaded on more assignments, including essays, reading, and arithmetic problems. They also required her to play the violin.

Like Tang, Zhu doesn't consider her childhood unusual. She explains that because of stiff academic competition in China, "Most parents teach their kids hanzi and math before they go to school. Chinese kids have a miserable life, forced to study, study all the time, with endless homework every day. On weekends, they are forced to learn drawing, play the piano, dance, study English, etc.," all so they can cultivate a "special talent" and stand out from the crowd.

Born in 1970, Zhu now lives in California but has heard about changes in Chinese education since her childhood. These days, she says, kids start preschool at age three. And it's typical nowadays for kids to learn a thousand characters before first grade, though two thousand will help them read children's books more easily.

In China, attending school is like holding down a job, one that goes from 8 a.m. to 6 p.m., Monday through Saturday, at least in Tang's experience of elementary and middle school. Vacation wasn't really a vacation; during winter and summer breaks, he had assignments in all subjects. While at school, kids face a barrage of quizzes and tests.

Chinese youngsters also gear up for major entrance exams. These enable them to enter middle school, high school, college, and then graduate school. And there's no "try, try again" mentality. As Tang puts it, the college entrance exam "determines a person's fate." If you fail, "You better pray that you can go to a trade school and learn a skill."

Why So Much Pressure?

As Tang and Zhu told me about the rigors of Chinese schools, I figured that it had to be that way so kids could learn five thousand hanzi. But it turns out that the world doesn't entirely revolve around Chinese characters, even in China! That is, there's a strong cultural context for all this academic pressure.

In a country four times as populous as the United

States, hordes of people compete for very few slots. Tang notes that, "Starting at a very young age, all kids realize the meaning of competition. Uneducated people were made an example of. The teacher would ask the kids, 'Do you want to grow up to be a successful (insert occupation), or would you rather be an uneducated peasant who hauls shit buckets everyday?'"

Humiliation and punishment also serve as motivators. Tang observes that whereas smart kids are ridiculed in American schools (such as the high school he attended in Tempe, Arizona), the opposite happens in China. He recalls, "Whoever got the lowest grade on a test had to stand up for one period and be humiliated in front of everyone."

Chinese families cannot advance economically unless their children attend good schools, which later translates into good job opportunities. Public schools in China aren't free, and the costs of tuition, textbooks, and supplies are beyond the poorest families. It's considered a privilege and a luxury to attend school in China, says Tang. Therefore, everyone supports children in their scholastic pursuits.

Parents may provide their kids with material incentives for success. Tang notes, "If one kid in a class got the highest score on an exam, and his parents bought him a Gameboy as a reward, other kids would want the same thing from their parents. If that means their children would get higher grades, parents would be willing to spend money to buy a Gameboy. The business of education is taught at a very early age."

How to Learn Five Thousand Hanzi

In this juiced-up environment, do kids have a magical way of learning hanzi quickly? That doesn't appear to be the case. As in Japan, Chinese schools teach a set number of characters every year. Working from textbooks, teachers instruct the students about certain strokes, showing how they appear in simple characters.

From there the lesson progresses to more complex ones. The children learn about radicals and components. They also learn which hanzi represent particular ideas and which ones serve as connective tissue in sentences. After studying singletons, kids learn how to combine them into compounds. In other words, although hanzi differ in several ways from kanji, both require an intensive learning process, day after day, year after year.

And that's how you get to five thousand! (Or if you master five thousand before school ever starts, you just dispense with the whole education thing!)

Double Happiness

So where does that leave those of us who limp along with far fewer than five thousand characters? How do we stop feeling inferior to first graders?! And how would we fare in a hanzi environment?

Well, you can test this out by glancing at a hanzi newspaper or visiting a nearby Chinatown. And if you venture further afield, say to China, you can achieve functional communication by writing notes in kanji. From what I hear, people will be both confused and amused that you can write characters but can't speak the language. When it comes to reading signs, you'll definitely recognize similarities to Japanese displays of that sort, but you'll want to be aware of where they differ. To see how kanji and hanzi signs compare, check out Exhibit 79, "Just the Facts: Signs for the Traveler."

For my part, whenever I understand hanzi, I feel excited and lucky. Knowing something about Chinese via Japanese is a bonus that I never expected when I took up Japanese. It's a gift that I savor because it comes without any extra work. I felt that sense of good fortune while watching the Chinese movie *Saving Face*. When I glimpsed the character for "double happiness" behind a wedding altar, I knew what it meant! (See what this character looks like in Exhibit 80, "Spectacular Shapes: Double Happiness.") Although the "double" refers to a marrying couple, I choose to interpret it another way. For me, it represents the thrill of recognizing Chinese characters in two languages.

Mind the Gap

As a train in London's Tube pulls to a stop, the operator tells disembarking passengers to "mind the gap" between the train and the platform. Those who study kanji and hanzi would similarly do well to mind the gap between the two, as meanings of singletons and compounds can differ significantly. Sometimes the discrepancies are as simple as this: 走 means "to run" in Japanese but "to walk" or "to leave" in Chinese. At other times, one can make quite a gaffe, as people have found out through Hanzi Smatter (www.hanzis-matter.com), a blog exposing unfortunate choices that Westerners have made with kanji/hanzi tattoos. Tian Tang, the blog's creator, has displayed scads of tattoos by people (and by tattooists) who clearly don't know Japanese or Chinese. The tattoos tend to contain ill-formed characters that amount to gibberish. Occasionally, the results are passable in Japanese but unwittingly funny in Chinese. Take a look at these:

	Japanese	Chinese
我慢	patience	I'm slow
油断大敵	unpreparedness is one's greatest enemy	oil crisis
妖	charming	female goblin
恋痛い	love hurts	loves the pain

To read this last concoction, Japanese people would need to overlook the unnatural syntax, and Chinese people would have to disregard the hiragana.

In other cases, the tattoo works well enough in Chinese (even if it's a puzzling choice) but is downright laughable in Japanese. Some cases in point:

	Chinese	Japanese
腕白	white wrist	naughtiness
魚精	fishlike, fish essence	fish semen
巨根	giant root	large penis

Two of Tang's favorites make no sense in either language. They're strange in Japanese but uproarious in Chinese. NBA player Shawn Marion sports a tattoo saying 魔鳥樟. As near as anyone can figure out, this was intended to be read as マトリクサ (matorikusa), a phonetic rendering of *The Matrix* using the on-yomi (MA) of 魔 and the kun-yomi (tori and kusa) of 鳥樟. (Incidentally, most Japanese refer to that movie as マトリックス, matorikkusu.) But in Chinese, the compound means "demon bird mothballs." As for a woman with 狂瀉 tattooed on her lower back, Japanese people might scratch their heads over "mania decanting," but Chinese people would have a belly laugh upon reading it as "crazy diarrhea."

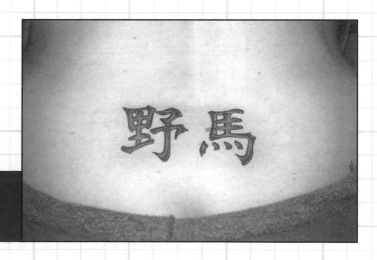

This tattoo, on a woman's lower back, says 野馬. The first character means "wild," and the second means "horse." Although 野馬 isn't a compound in Japanese, it is a real Chinese word, pronounced as yěmǎ and meaning "wild horse."

A Crash Course in Chinese Terminology

If you want a crash course in Chinese terminology, see the table on the opposite page for different representations of basic terms. Just for the sake of comparison, it shows the same words in Japanese. Many of the terms in the table require further explanation, starting with the column heads!

- **Pinyin:** This is the most widely accepted and used romanization of Chinese. Actually, it's the romanization of Mandarin speech; Cantonese has other romanization systems. But we'll only concern ourselves with Mandarin in this chapter, so just think of pinyin as romanized Chinese. Pinyin appears in road signs, maps, brand names, computer input, Chinese Braille, telegrams, and books for Chinese children and foreign learners.

- **Traditional and Simplified Chinese:** Taiwan uses traditional shapes for hanzi. Mainland China uses simplified forms. Hong Kong and Macao mostly use traditional forms but have also adopted some simplified ones. Of course, the shapes of nearly all characters have evolved over the millennia, even the "traditional" Chinese characters used in Taiwan. But the Taiwanese government has never ordered people to eliminate great quantities of strokes, as happened in mainland China in the 1950s. Instead of writing the thirteen-stroke 漢, mainlanders and Singaporeans write the five-stroke 汉. Aren't they lucky? Except for one thing. According to Tian Tang, who writes the blog *Hanzi Smatter,* traditional characters contain etymological history that disappears with simplification. Tang was born in 1977 and grew up in mainland China, but he prefers traditional forms, scoffing that simplified hanzi are the "poor man's Chinese." He explains that when the Communists came to power on the mainland, the majority of them were rumored to be illiterate peasants. "They had to be educated," Tang says, as it would be "very embarrassing" for such powerful people to be exposed as illiterate. The idea behind simplified characters was to educate the masses, including government officials.

So much for the column heads. Here's a guide to the terms in the first column of the table.

> Although Chinese has a term for "written language," there is no general term for "spoken language."

- **Written Chinese:** You may wonder how written Chinese *(zhōng wén)* differs from hanzi. Hanzi are the tools with which people produce *zhōng wén,* or Chinese text. But that's not the real distinction to draw here. Instead, *zhōng wén* contrasts sharply with spoken Chinese. Natives recognize important differences between the two.

- **Mandarin:** Some say that Chinese isn't one language but many separate ones. To linguists who hold this position, Mandarin isn't the main Chinese dialect but rather the main language. Many Chinese speakers in Singapore, Malaysia, and Vietnam also use Mandarin. Around the world, about 870 million people speak it as a first language. Written Chinese is based on spoken Mandarin and is essentially a uniform script throughout China. Therefore, people who speak a non-Mandarin type of Chinese must learn Mandarin grammar and vocabulary if they want to read and write. The Chinese government uses Mandarin and wants all its citizens to do the same.

- **Cantonese:** Fewer people speak Cantonese, but they still constitute a large crowd. I've seen estimates of the number of Cantonese speakers ranging from 66 million to 100 million. You'll find these people in southeast China, especially in the province of Canton, as well as in Hong Kong. Cantonese is the primary language in Macao, though Mandarin is also an official language there. Cantonese speakers have modified Mandarin characters and have created their own characters. According to www.omniglot.com/writing/cantonese, Cantonese includes "over a thousand extra characters invented specifically for Cantonese"!

English Term	Pinyin	Traditional Chinese	Simplified Chinese	Japanese
Chinese characters	*hàn zì*	漢字 Han people + letter	汉字	漢字 *(kanji)*
China	*zhōng guó*	中國 middle + country	中国	中国 *(Chūgoku)* middle + country
written Chinese	*zhōng wén*	中文 Chinese + writing	中文	中文 *(chūbun)* Chinese + writing
pinyin	*pīnyīn*	拼音 to combine + sound	拼音	ピンイン, 併音 *(pin'in)* to combine + sound
Mandarin	*pǔ tōng huà*	普通話 common + language	普通话	北京語 *(Pekingo)* north + capital + language
Cantonese	*guǎng dōng yǔ*	廣東語 wide + east + language	广东语	広東語 *(Kantongo)* wide + east + language

China has produced coins since as far back as 770 BCE. The hole in the middle of such coins enabled people to carry them on strings, rather than in purses.

To read such a coin, think of it as a clock and then read the characters in the 12:00 and 6:00 positions as one compound. This vertical pair represents the name of either a dynasty or an era, indicating when the coin was in use. Then read the other pair from right to left; that is, start with the 3:00 hanzi and then finish with the 9:00 character. This twosome indicates the type of currency. On the reverse side (not shown here), you would find how much that particular coin was worth.

The following characters appear on this coin, which now serves as an earring:

- top: 光 (*guāng*: light)
- bottom: 緒 (*xù*: beginnings; clues; mental state; thread)
- right: 通 (*tōng*: to go through, connect, flow freely)
- left: 寶 (*bǎo*: treasure)

The vertical pair gives us Guāngxù, the name of an emperor in the Qing dynasty who ruled from 1875 to 1908. The hanzi at 3:00, 通, tells us that the coin circulated universally. The 9:00 hanzi, 寶, is the traditional form of 宝, which mainlander Chinese and Japanese use for "treasure."

Chinese Words You've Heard

I've been amazed to discover how many English words came from Chinese, including three dog names:

shar-pei
shih tzu
chow chow
chow (the food)
chow mein
chopstick
chop suey
chop chop (to hurry)
gung ho
wonton
kumquat
loquat
wok
pekoe
ketchup

Nowadays, these words don't sound anything like their corollaries in Mandarin. That's partly because some of the above words came from Cantonese (and therefore never sounded like Mandarin), including

"chow mein," which was *chaumin,* and "chop suey," which was *tzapseui,* meaning "mixed pieces." Another reason is that if English speakers weren't the ones to romanize these words, they may have acquired sounds that matched neither Chinese nor English. Also, methods of romanizing Chinese have changed since those words came into English; through pinyin, we now pronounce Mandarin words differently.

At any rate, the Mandarin and the English still sound reasonably close when it comes to several other terms that appear in the table below. The kanji is often a carbon copy of the hanzi. In the cases of "typhoon," "mah-jongg," and "lychee," the Japanese used ateji; they adopted the characters and their sounds, disregarding certain meanings. With "oolong tea," the Japanese ignored the meaning of 烏 and the usual reading of 龍 so they could match the Chinese compound and its reading.

In the table, when Chinese and Japanese compounds share a breakdown, only one breakdown appears. But when they differ, you'll see separate analyses (as for "tai chi chuan").

Familiar Word	Traditional Chinese	Simplified Chinese	Pinyin	Japanese
yin	陰	阴	*yīn*	陰 (*IN, kage:* shade, yin, negative)
yang	陽	阳	*yáng*	陽 (*YŌ, hi:* sunshine, yang, positive)
feng shui	風水 wind + water	风水	*fēng shuǐ*	風水 (*fūsui*)
tai chi chuan	太極拳 greatest + utmost + fist	太极拳	*tài jí quán*	太極拳 (*taikyokuken*) plump + utmost + fist
kung fu	功夫 achievement + man, combining to mean "efforts" in Chinese	功夫	*gōng fu*	カンフー, 功夫 (*kanfū*)
mah-jongg	麻將 hemp + a general	麻将	*má jiàng*	麻雀 (*mājan*) hemp + sparrow

Familiar Word	Traditional Chinese	Simplified Chinese	Pinyin	Japanese
ping-pong	乒乓球 bing + bang + ball (the 1st two hanzi are onomatopoeia)	乒乓球	*pīng pāng qiú*	ピンポン
ping-pong (alternate)	桌球 table + ball	桌球	*zhuō qiú*	卓球 (*takkyū*)
qigong	氣)功 vital breath + achievement	气功	*qì gōng*	気功 (*kikō*) spirit + achievement
yen (craving)	癮 addiction, esp. to opium	瘾	*yǐn*	憧れ (*akogare*)
kowtow	叩頭 to knock + head	叩头	*kòu tóu*	叩頭 (*kōtō*)
gong	鑼	锣	*luó*	銅鑼 (*dora*) copper + gong
typhoon	颱風 typhoon + wind	台风	*tái fēng*	台風 (*taifū*) table + wind
dim sum	點心 dot + heart, maybe to mean a "touch of heart"	点心	*diǎn xīn*	點心, 点心 (*tenshin*)
lychee	荔枝 lychee + branch	荔枝	*lì zhī*	荔枝 (*reishi*) scallion + branch
hoisin	海鮮 sea + fresh, meaning "seafood" sauce	海鲜	*hǎi xian*	—
bok choy	白菜 white + vegetables	白菜	*bái cài*	白菜 (*hakusai*)
oolong tea	烏龍茶 black + dragon + tea	乌龙茶	*wū lóng chá*	烏龍茶 (*ūroncha*) crow + dragon + tea
ramen	拉面 to pull + noodles	拉面	*lā miàn*	ラーメン, 拉麺 (*rāmen*) to kidnap + noodles

The Tones of Hanzi

Each Chinese syllable can have five tones (or as many as nine, depending on the language, dialect, and method of counting tones). There are four basic tones:

1st	high
2nd	rising
3rd	falling rising
4th	falling

These descriptions have nothing to do with the volume of speech. Instead, they refer to ways of modulating the voice, as in singing (Tone 1 comes closest to this), expressing surprise with "What?!" (Tone 2), or giving the curt command "Stop!" (Tone 4 approximates this). There's also a fifth tone, a neutral one. As tone changes, so does meaning. Let's see how this works with the syllable *da:*

Trad'l Hanzi	Pinyin	Alt. Pinyin	Tone #	Meaning
搭	dā	da1	1	to place upon, climb aboard
答	dá	da2	2	to answer
打	dǎ	da3	3	to beat, strike
大	dà	da4	4	big

You see here the four basic Chinese tone markers: *ā* (Tone 1), *á* (Tone 2), *ǎ* (Tone 3), and *à* (Tone 4). It's all neat and logical! Because it can be difficult to type these diacritics, you can also represent them in pinyin by adding a tone number, as in the Alt. (Alternate) Pinyin column. (Or go to http://pinyin.info/unicode/marks3.html, which converts entries such as *da*3 into *dǎ* for you!)

The fifth tone marker, the neutral one, comes with no accent: *da.* However, I can't show you a meaning for any given *da* because a neutral tone never stands on its own. Rather, it exists only in connection with a preceding tone.

When it comes to the meanings I *did* display above, these represent only a small selection of the characters and meanings associated with each syllable. For instance, *dá* also corresponds to the following hanzi and meanings:

> This may remind you of voicing in Japanese, the way syllables have a phonetic alchemy (e.g., *hito* + *hito* turns into *hitobito,* "people").

Trad'l Hanzi	Meaning
打	dozen
妲	concubine of last Shang emperor
怛	distressed, alarmed, shocked, grieved
瘩	sore, boil, scab
笪	(surname), rough bamboo mat
達	to attain, to pass through, to inform
靼	(phonetic), dressed leather
韃	Tartar

You may have noticed that 打 has appeared twice thus far, representing both *dá* (dozen) and *dǎ* (to beat). Just as with kanji singletons, a hanzi character can have multiple readings and meanings. However, whereas a kanji may have up to three distinct on-yomi (as discussed in Chapter 1 with the example of 行 as *GYŌ, KŌ,* and *AN*), hanzi tend to be more consistent; 打 has *only* the two *da* readings.

You can imagine that, with so many readings and meanings for *dá,* there could be a big homonym problem in Chinese. When singleton hanzi serve as words, this does in fact create confusion. For example, *zài* translates in these various ways:

再	again
在	in, at
載	to carry, also, simultaneously

Fortunately, most hanzi tend to appear in compounds. In fact, this is such a strong tendency that Tian Tang finds it "meaningless" to discuss characters as singletons. Compounds create a context within which characters acquire new meanings. Consider three compounds containing the hanzi you've just seen:

> By the way, compounds can be just as fun in China as in Japan. "Penguin" is 企鵝 (qǐ é): "to stand on tiptoe" + "goose"!

再保證	*zài bǎo zhèng:*	to reassure
在車	*zài chē:*	aboard
載重	*zài zhòng:*	load, carrying capacity

Compounds and tones largely solve the homonym problem in Chinese. It may be easier to understand this by looking at the converse situation in atonal Japan, where a plethora of words sound exactly alike. According to Hannas, the Japanese syllable *kō* corresponds to 180 characters! This, in turn, has led to twenty-four versions of *kōkō,* twenty-three types of *kōshō,* eighteen kinds of *kōtō,* and fourteen species of *kōchō.* If Japanese phonetics had been able to accommodate tones when Japan borrowed hanzi, then these words wouldn't sound identical. But every four Chinese syllables funneled down into one Japanese sound, creating four times as many homophonous syllables in Japan (at least in theory, as this may not work out numerically).

By contrast in Chinese, only 1 percent of commonly used words are homonyms, according to a study cited by Hannas. For example, Mandarin doesn't contain two words called *er shi.* Instead, there's *èr shí* and *ěr shǐ,* respectively "twenty" and "ear wax." And of course hanzi makes the distinction even clearer. Just as in Japanese, "twenty" is 二十. And just as in Japanese, "earwax" is 耳屎, which breaks down as "ear" + "excrement"!

In Japanese and Korean, the homonym problem creates a major rationale for continuing to use Chinese characters (despite the educational burden they impose). It seems to me that if these cultures really wanted to jettison the hanzi they borrowed, they could clarify homonyms by developing tones for their languages!

At first glance, it may be difficult to tell whether the characters on this calligraphy practice sheet are Japanese or Chinese. After all, one can spot quite a few characters here that have the following meanings in both Japanese and Chinese: 下 (under, below), 花 (flower), 前 (before), 上 (above), 三 (three), 加 (addition), 永 (eternity), and 字 (character).

Closer examination may leave you scratching your head about two more characters. One is 竿 (at the bottom of the image). This character turns out to mean "pole" in both languages, but 竿 is not in general use in Japan. Mandarin speakers pronounce this character as *gān.*

And then there's the character to the left of 下. This puzzler seems to have 日 on the bottom, but the rest looks quite weird . . . until you realize that the page is upside-down! This character is 是, which hanzi readers know as *shì,* "to be," and which Japanese people know as *SHI* or *koko,* "just so; justice; right; this."

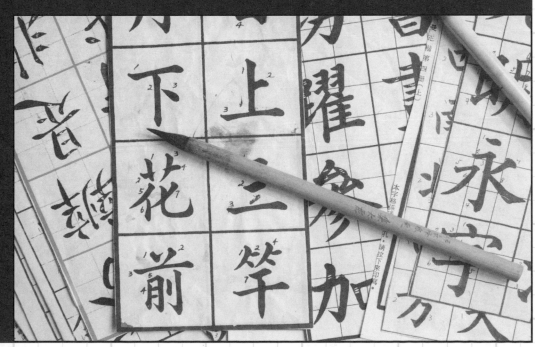

#73 GAME! GAME! GAME! GAME!

Kana Needed: N / Kanji Level: 3 / Difficulty Level: 3

On-Yomi Tongue Twister

This game has several steps:

1. Go down the list, checking off the one correct on-yomi for each kanji. For example, consider this:

   心 ❑ *KO* ❑ *SHIN* ❑ *MEI*

   The on-yomi of 心 is *SHIN,* so you would check off the second choice.
2. Read down the list through all the on-yomi you have marked. The correct on-yomi form a sentence, a tongue twister of sorts. Write the sentence in hiragana or rōmaji.
3. What does the sentence mean? Punctuate as needed to make sense of it.
4. Write the English translation of the sentence.
5. Extra credit: Rewrite the sentence with the correct kanji! They have little or no connection to the kanji displayed below.

Answers appear in the Answer Key. *Ganbatte kudasai!*

古 ❑ *KO* ❑ *KU* ❑ *SHŌ*

小 ❑ *KI* ❑ *CHI* ❑ *SHŌ*

正 ❑ *JI* ❑ *SHI* ❑ *SHŌ*

消 ❑ *JI* ❑ *KETSU* ❑ *SHŌ*

私 ❑ *JI* ❑ *SHI* ❑ *SHŌ*

汚 ❑ *HO* ❑ *O* ❑ *SHŌ*

少 ❑ *KO* ❑ *SU* ❑ *SHŌ*

章 ❑ *KO* ❑ *SŌ* ❑ *SHŌ*

商 ❑ *TEKI* ❑ *RITSU* ❑ *SHŌ*

由 ❑ *YU* ❑ *SHIN* ❑ *SHŌ*

相 ❑ *MOKU* ❑ *SHU* ❑ *SHŌ*

焼 ❑ *KA* ❑ *YA* ❑ *SHŌ*

The sentence in hiragana or rōmaji:

____

____

The sentence in English:

____

____

The sentence in kanji:

____

____

Phonetic Markers Used in Taiwan

When I heard Taiwan had a phonetic system for annotating hanzi, I poked around for information. I wanted to know if it was like Japanese furigana (small hiragana written under or above kanji to indicate their pronunciations). And what was the name of the system? I amassed a dizzying array of responses:

1. 注音符號
2. *zhù yīn fú hào*
3. *zhùyīn*
4. *bopomofo*
5. *BPMF*

So many names for a simple mechanism?! Well, as it turns out, these terms aren't so far apart. The first line represents the idea in hanzi, the characters breaking down as "to annotate" (注) + "sound" (音) + "symbol" (符號). Line 3 is an abbreviation of line 2, which is the way to romanize this expression.

So far so good. But what about *bopomofo,* which sounds like an obscene threat involving someone's mother? This term is actually quite innocent; much as "ABCs" is shorthand for "alphabet," *bopomofo* refers to the first four symbols of the phonetic system. It's a popular term—so popular that it has spawned its own abbreviation, BPMF.

And just as we associate "ABCs" with children, Taiwanese kids primarily use *bopomofo* as an aid in reading hanzi. (The same is true of furigana in Japan. But one slight difference is that furigana also appears for the benefit of Japanese adults in the case of unusual or complicated words.) In Taiwan, children's books include *bopomofo,* as do dictionaries, textbooks for foreign students, and some magazines and newspapers. Adults use this system to type hanzi. Furthermore, the phonetic symbols enable people in Taiwan to represent words for which no hanzi exist.

As angular as katakana, the symbols are simple and crude, resembling ancient cave etchings. The *bopomofo* below says 標準外國語 (*biāo zhǔn wài guó yǔ:* correct foreign pronunciation or language).

ㄅ　ㄓ　ㄨ　ㄍ　ㄩˇ
ㄧ　ㄨˇ　ㄞˋ　ㄨˊ
ㄠ　ㄣ　　　ㄛ

When written alongside vertical hanzi to indicate their pronunciations, the symbols go to the right of each character. *Bopomofo* contains thirty-seven symbols and reflects hanzi tones.

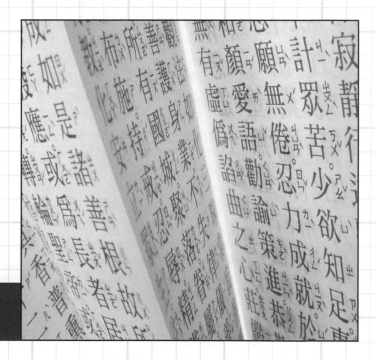

This image, from a Buddhist manuscript, shows columns of hanzi. To the right of each character, *bopomofo* provides a guide to pronunciation.

Hanja in Korea

Imagine a country where the government has abolished the use of Chinese characters but requires students to learn them. Welcome to North Korea, where the characters known as hanja (漢字) pose any number of paradoxes.

North and South Korea split in 1945. Four years later, North Korean president Kim Il-Sung decreed that his communist country would no longer use hanja, only the alphabetic script called *hangeul*. (Up till then, the two had been used together, much as Japanese texts interweave kanji and kana.) Considerably easier to learn than hanja, hangeul presented a way to stamp out illiteracy and bourgeois educational elitism in one fell swoop. Moreover, Kim associated hanja with the Japanese, who had occupied Korea from 1910 through 1945. In 1933, the Japanese forbade the use of hangeul, allowing only hanja. And in 1938, they even forbade Koreans to speak their native language. Not surprisingly, when the occupation ended, people in both Koreas wanted to reclaim their national identity and language. After 1949, hanja quickly disappeared from written materials in North Korea.

But in 1966, Kim ordered schools to resume teaching Chinese characters as "foreign orthographic symbols." As he explained, people needed hanja so they could translate classic Korean literature and understand the characters used in South Korea, China, and Japan. Nevertheless, it was still illegal to publish works containing hanja!

Using data from 1994, William C. Hannas compared educational curricula in the Koreas and Japan. He noted that by the time they finished high school, South Koreans could have chosen to study 1,800 hanja, Japanese had no choice but to acquire 1,945 kanji, and North Koreans had had to learn the most of all—a whopping 2,000 characters! I'm not sure Hannas's last figure is accurate anymore. A Wikipedia article places the number at 600. Scratching my head over this gross discrepancy, I consulted Professor Rodney Tyson, who taught in South Korea for fifteen years and who has published translations of Korean texts. He said, "I doubt if there's any reliable source to find out for sure" about the accurate number required in North Korea.

Hanja usage is just slightly less complicated in South Korea. However, the question of when to use hanja versus hangeul is clear-cut. People need to write all indigenous Korean vocabulary in hangeul; no Chinese characters represent those words. If they so desire, South Koreans can use hanja to write words of Chinese origin (referred to as *kango* in Japanese), but hangeul works equally well for that purpose.

As neat as this system seems to be, hanja are fading fast in South Korea. Tyson told me, "The use of Chinese characters has decreased in South Korea much more quickly than I would have predicted. Although the basic characters are still taught in middle and high schools, and still used quite a bit in academic and technical publications, they've become relatively rare in more popular publications." This vanishing act is undeniable and may be inevitable in light of historical, cultural, and linguistic forces.

Hanja over the Millennia

It's not as if Chinese characters are new to Korea. They arrived on the Korean peninsula even before China colonized it in 108 BCE, an occupation that lasted until 313 CE. As was true in Japan, the characters gave Koreans their first script, allowed them to study Buddhism, and enabled Chinese vocabulary to flow into the national language.

In 1446, things changed when King Sejong the Great invented (or took credit for inventing) hangeul, which one might call "Korean for dummies." The idea was that even stupid people could learn this very logical system in ten days. Sharper folks could master it in several hours. Nationalistic in intent, hangeul supposedly allowed people to express uniquely Korean meanings. However, the *han* in *hangeul* refers to the same thing as the *han* in *hanja*: China. Scholars continued to write solely in hanja, viewing hangeul as the realm of the uneducated and the lowly. Not much changed in this sense until the twentieth century.

Then, during the Japanese occupation of Korea, thousands of hanja compounds streamed into Korean via Japanese. Therefore, many hanja and kanji compounds look the same (e.g., 高速道路, "expressway," read as *kōsokudōro* in Japanese and *gosokdoro* in Korean). Aside from using hanzi and kanji compounds, Koreans have also coined their own, ones that Chinese people can't begin to recognize.

In current times, with an upswelling of nationalism, South Koreans use hanja only in limited contexts. Newspaper headlines might include hanja to highlight key words, even if the article is entirely in hangeul. In one mid-1990s headline about an impending inspection of North Korean nuclear facilities, the newspaper used hanja for "North Korea" and for "nuclear," rendering all other words in hangeul. South Koreans also use hanja to emphasize important words in ads, product packaging, and street signs.

As in Japanese, hanja serve to clarify words that look and sound exactly alike in hangeul. Hanja often appear parenthetically after such homonyms. Dictionaries also provide Chinese characters. As Wikipedia explains, these provide a "shorthand etymology, since the meaning of the Hanja and the fact that the word is composed of Hanja often help to illustrate the word's origin."

Atlases, academic literature, technical works, and university textbooks also include hanja. Signs at railway stations appear simultaneously in hangeul, hanja, and romanized Korean. And, as noted in *A Window on Korea* by the Korean Overseas Information Service, "Koreans have a flair for decorating things with Chinese ideographs, the most common being su, meaning long life, and pok, bliss."

Form and Function

South Koreans place hanja alongside hangeul in their horizontal texts, which are read from left to right. Hangeul contains many circles, but because each hangeul block combines at least two alphabetic symbols, hangeul and hanja have similar, rectangular proportions. Visually, the two scripts therefore combine well in sentences, though until the advent of word processing, it required much more effort to type them together. (Now typing hanja on a computer is much like typing kanji.) Notably, each word fills the same amount of space in hangeul and hanja. Unlike the Japanese (who save space with kanji, e.g., 大切 versus たいせつ for *taisetsu*, "important"), Korean printers have no economic incentive to use hanja.

Many hanja closely resemble modern traditional

hanzi. But because the languages have radically different syntaxes, the order of characters in compounds often differs. Korean and Chinese pronunciations of the characters have also diverged over the millennia, particularly because Koreans altered sounds to fit their native phonetic system. Korean has many more syllables than Japanese does, so Koreans had a harder time mapping the spoken language onto hanja. This partly accounts for the current phasing out of hanja; linguistically speaking, it wasn't as good a fit in Korea as in Japan.

Much as Japanese has kun-yomi (訓) and on-yomi (音), Korean has *hun* (訓) and *eum* (音). But these serve a different function in Korean than in Japanese. *Eum* is the sound—the actual pronunciation—of an individual character. *Hun* is the meaning of the hanja, the definition. Some characters have multiple *eum,* and some have multiple *hun*.

Personal names and place names mostly have hanja representations, though not the word for "Seoul." According to Tyson in an unpublished paper, "The great majority of Korean words written in Chinese characters are nouns. These nouns can then be changed into other parts of speech by adding Korean inflections written in *hangeul*." He provides this example:

靜肅 　　　*jeongsuk:* silence (noun)
靜肅하다　*jeongsuk-hada:* to be silent (verb)
靜肅한　　*jeongsuk-han:* silent (adjective)
靜肅히　　*jeongsuk-hi:* silently (adverb)

South Koreans sometimes use hanja to represent grammatical particles, too. In that context, characters function in an ateji-like way, acknowledged for their sounds, not their meanings.

However, South Koreans usually choose to write all words in hangeul. According to Hannas, South Koreans figure that if they can understand a term in hangeul, then they should render it that way. By contrast, he says, the Japanese expect people to use kanji for words consisting solely of Jōyō characters.

Hannas notes great "performance differences" between Japanese and Koreans in drawing Chinese characters, as well as vastly different inclinations to do so: "A Japanese person, like a Chinese, will draw a character (not the *kana*) when asked to write a word, if he or she can remember it, or be embarrassed if he or she cannot. . . . Koreans usually find some way to parry the request or end up writing it mechanically, without the grace and style of long habit" (p. 53).

He attributes this contrast to differing "psychological dispositions toward the characters" (p. 53). In his view, most South Koreans "feel no attachment to the characters and would just as soon be rid of them entirely" (p. 48). Strangely, even though the characters entered both countries in similar ways, the Japanese see them as an integral part of their language, and Koreans don't. Representing only borrowed words, hanja scream out "alien." As Hannas notes, "Koreans have to be persuaded by linguists that Chinese characters . . . are historically as much a part of Korean writing as *hangul*. Koreans just do not accept this on a gut level" (p. 53).

Hannas pins this Japanese-Korean difference on

This brings to mind Kindaichi's comment about writing "foreign words in stiff *katakana* . . . as if they were objects of our enmity. . . ." (p. 154).

people's feelings about kana versus hangeul. Derived from kanji, hiragana and katakana can't arouse much national pride. Hangeul, by contrast, are logical, elegant, home-grown phonetic symbols, inspiring so much nationalistic fervor that South Korea has a holiday (October 9) to commemorate them. Until recently, workers even had the day off on October 9! Korea stands apart as the only country to honor a script in this way.

Given this passion for a system that's immeasurably easier to learn and write than Chinese characters, and considering Korea's anger about Japan's repressive occupation, it's no wonder that hanja are fast disappearing in South Korea.

This Korean banner is dedicated to the memory of Korean president Park Chung-hee, assassinated in 1979. At the top it says 追慕 (*tsuibo:* cherishing the memory of). After that comes *hangeul,* roughly translating as "The more time passes, the more beloved you become." The banner went up for Memorial Day, June 6, which is when Koreans picnic in cemeteries to commemorate those who have died in the service of their country. Seoul National Cemetery is visible in the background of the photograph. Reserved for Korean veterans, it is the equivalent of Arlington National Cemetery, just outside Washington, D.C. Park, a veteran, lies in this cemetery.

Kanji Compounds That China Imported from Japan

Although most kanji originated in China and were later disseminated to Japan, the tide has sometimes flowed in the other direction. The Chinese have imported a few kanji compounds made in Japan, such as those in the table below.

According to Victor Mair, author of "East-Asian Round-Trip Words" in the journal *Sino-Platonic Papers,* the Chinese have also borrowed back at least sixty-five compounds that originated in ancient or archaic Chinese and that were then absorbed into Japanese. His list of "repatriated" or "round-trip" words includes many common Japanese terms, such as the following:

文学　*bungaku:* literature
文化　*bunka:* culture
文明　*bunmei:* civilization
物理　*butsuri:* physics
保険　*hoken:* insurance
法律　*hōritsu:* law
意味　*imi:* meaning
自由　*jiyū:* freedom
住所　*jūsho:* residence

計画　*keikaku:* plan
経済　*keizai:* economics
機械　*kikai:* machine
規則　*kisoku:* rule, regulation
社会　*shakai:* society

Informally speaking, the Chinese have adopted the repetition kanji 々, too. Whereas the Japanese typically indicate a plural with 々, as we saw in Exhibit 53, "Thematic Explorations: You Can Say That Again!" the Chinese use 々 to mean "etcetera" or to add emphasis, though this symbol never appears in printed materials. For instance, 謝 (simplified: 谢), *xiè,* suffices for "thank you," but doubling the character by writing it again or by adding 々 heightens the sense of gratitude. Doubling the character also makes the Chinese more comfortable, because they prefer compounds. For "wait a little while," the Chinese double 等 (*děng:* to wait), writing it as 等等 or 等々 (*děng děng*). Words containing 々 are known as 疊音字 (simplified: 叠音字), *dié yīn zì,* which breaks down as "to repeat" + "sound" + "character."

MADE IN JAPAN, IMPORTED BY CHINA

Meaning	Traditional Chinese	Simplified Chinese	Pinyin	Japanese
loyalty, sincerity	忠誠	忠诚	*zhōng chéng*	忠誠 *(chūsei)*
loyalty, devotion	忠義	忠义	*zhōng yì*	忠義 *(chūgi)*
justice, righteousness	正義	正义	*zhèng yì*	正義 *(seigi)*
science	科學	科学	*kē xué*	科学 *(kagaku)*

Representing Grammar with Hanzi

Whenever I gaze at Chinese newspapers, trying to see what I can understand, the following question dominates my thoughts: If the Japanese use hiragana to inflect verbs and adjectives and to show how words relate to each other, what do the Chinese do?

Let's consider a sample sentence in each language. Here it is in Japanese:

机の上に花瓶があります。
The vase is on the desk.
Tsukue no ue ni kabin ga arimasu.
Desk + 's + top + on/in + vase + (subject marker) + is.

Without the hiragana particles, this Japanese sentence would be sorely lacking in meaning. Here's the Chinese version of the same sentence:

花瓶 在 桌 上。
The vase is on the desk.
huā píng zài zhuō shàng
vase + placed + desk + on

What remarkable economy! The Chinese dispense entirely with the small directional words that abound in Japanese. And the meaning comes through clearly.

Here's a nice surprise—Chinese and English have similar word order, both being subject-verb-object (SVO) languages. That is, in English, we represent key concepts in this order: "vase-is-desk." (In this sentence, "desk" serves as the object of the preposition "on," which is why this equation sounds a bit odd.) In Chinese, the schematic turns out to be "vase-placed-desk." By contrast, Japanese verbs go at the end of sentences.

Speaking of verbs, the Chinese make some small additions to express verb tense:

花瓶 放 在 桌 上 。
(I am) Placing the vase on the desk.
huā píng fàng zài zhuō shàng
vase + am doing + to place + desk + on

放 (*fàng*) means "the action of doing."

花瓶 已經放 在 桌 上 。
The vase has been placed on the desk.
huā píng yǐ jīng fàng zài zhuō shàng
vase + have done + to place + desk + on

放 (*fàng*) again means "the action of doing," and 已經 (*yǐ jīng*) expresses "already," functioning as a kind of "-ed."

This sign welcomes travelers to Shanghai. The pinyin of 欢迎您 is *huānyíng nín*. The first character means "happy, pleased." The second means "to receive, welcome, greet." Together, these mean "welcome." The third hanzi is a respectful form of "you," often used when addressing elders or anyone to whom you want to show respect.

Animal Signs in the Zodiac

In 2000 (the Year of the Dragon, or 龙年, *lóng nián*), I gave some Chinese-speaking friends a red clock as a wedding present. The twelve Chinese zodiac signs appear on its face in place of numbers. I love that clock, and whenever I visit the couple, I always hope to decipher more characters than before. Unfortunately, I never seem to progress. Next time, I think I'll bring the cheat sheet shown below.

The Japanese column appears here just for comparison purposes. This last column also introduces some confusion! In the context of the zodiac, characters for animals tend to be quite different from characters used in nonzodiacal contexts. That is, the Japanese usually represent "monkey," "rooster," "dog," and "pig" this way:

monkey	猿	(*saru*)
rooster	雄鶏	(*ondori*)
dog	犬	(*inu*)
pig	豚	(*buta*)

But that's not true in zodiacal contexts, as you can see below in the last four rows of the Japanese column.

Meanwhile, in nonzodiacal contexts, the Japanese represent the other eight animals (i.e., "rat," "ox," "tiger," "rabbit," "dragon," "snake," "horse," and "sheep") with the corresponding characters in the Traditional Chinese column. For instance, the nonzodiacal kanji for "rat" is 鼠, which you'll also see in the Traditional Chinese column. Although eight Japanese zodiacal animals have atypical kanji, the yomi of all the zodiacal characters (e.g., *ushi* for "cow" and *inu* for "dog") correspond to the usual Japanese vocabulary for animals.

Here's another surprise: In the Japanese column, some characters represent partial words. That is, 卯, *u*, stands for *usagi*, "rabbit," and 亥, *i*, represents *inoshishi*, "wild boar." Even further removed from yomi logic, 巳 is read as *mi* but represents *hebi*, "snake." The rest of the kanji seem to function in an ateji-like way, too, in that they have readings or meanings other than the ones with which we usually associate the characters. For example, 子 usually means child. But in the context of the zodiac, with the yomi of *ne*, 子 officially represents the rat and is not considered ateji. All the other kanji here have also officially been assigned certain readings and meanings in this one context.

Why are there so many irregularities in the Japanese column? I asked a native speaker, who said it's quite complicated, having to do with several religions and an ancient Chinese system of clocks and compass directions. Well, what's a zodiac without complication and mystery?!

Animal	Traditional Chinese	Simplified Chinese	Pinyin	Japanese Zodiac Sign
rat	鼠	鼠	*shǔ*	子 (*ne*: rat)
ox	牛	牛	*niú*	丑 (*ushi*: cow, ox)
tiger	虎	虎	*hǔ*	寅 (*tora*: tiger)
rabbit	兔	兔	*tù*	卯 (*u*, representing *usagi*: rabbit)
dragon	龍	龙	*lóng*	辰 (*tatsu*: dragon)
snake	蛇	蛇	*shé*	巳 (*mi*, representing *hebi*: snake)
horse	馬	马	*mǎ*	午 (*uma*: horse)
sheep	羊	羊	*yáng*	未 (*hitsuji*: sheep)
monkey	猴	猴	*hóu*	申 (*saru*: monkey)
rooster	雞	鸡	*jī*	酉 (*tori*: rooster)
dog	狗	狗	*gǒu*	戌 (*inu*: dog)
pig	豬	猪	*zhū*	亥 (*i*, representing *inoshishi*: wild boar)

Signs for the Traveler

Japanese signs may stop Chinese speakers in their tracks when the characters have different meanings. In Japanese, 引 *(hi·ku)* means "to pull." But in Chinese, it means "to lead, guide, divert water."

In light of that issue, you may wonder how far your knowledge of kanji will take you in Chinese-speaking countries, particularly when it comes to reading signs and catching trains. To gauge the differences, I showed some Japanese signs to a Taiwanese man who has lived in Japan. He explained various discrepancies, then laughed and said that Taiwan doesn't have nearly as many restrictive signs as Japan.

STRIKINGLY DIFFERENT CHARACTERS FOR TRANSPORTATION

Although both Chinese and Japanese represent "car" in the same way (with 車), that's as much as they seem to share when it comes to characters for transportation.

Meaning	Japanese	Traditional Chinese	Simplified Chinese
station	駅 *eki*	站 *zhàn*	站
train	電車 *densha* electricity + car	火車 *huǒ chē* fire + car	火车
subway	地下鉄 *chikatetsu* ground + below + iron	地鐵 *dì tiě* ground + iron	地铁
bus	バス *basu*	公共汽車 *gōng gòng qì chē* public (1st 2 chars.) + car (last 2 chars.)	公共汽车
taxi	タクシー *takushī*	出租車 *chū zū chē* to rent (1st 2 chars.) + car	出租车

IDENTICAL CHARACTERS

Fortunately, when it comes to signs alerting people to important items, the two writing systems agree in many ways. Only the pronunciations differ in the following signs:

Characters Used	Meaning	Japanese	Chinese
入口	Entrance	*iriguchi*	*rù kǒu*
出口	Exit	*deguchi*	*chū kǒu*
注意	Caution	*chūi*	*zhù yì*
故障	Out of Order	*koshō*	*gù zhàng*
禁煙 (*Simp.*: 禁烟)	No Smoking	*kin'en*	*jìn yān*

SLIGHT MODIFICATIONS

In several terms, the order of characters changes from one language to the other. Also, the characters may not be identical, but the gist is the same.

Meaning	Japanese	Traditional Chinese	Simplified Chinese
Parking Lot	駐車場 *chūshajō*	停車場 *tíng chē chǎng*	停车场
No Parking	駐車禁止 *chūsha kinshi*	禁止停車 *jìn zhǐ tíng chē*	禁止停车
No Photographs	撮影禁止 *satsuei kinshi*	禁止攝影 *jìn zhǐ shè yǐng*	禁止摄影
Do Not Use	使用禁止 *shiyō kinshi*	禁止使用 *jìn zhǐ shǐ yòng*	
Under Construction	工事中 *kōjichū*	施工中 *shī gōng zhōng*	
Danger	危険 *kiken*	危險 *wēi xiǎn*	危险
Open for Business	営業中 *eigyōchū*	營業 *yíng yè*	营业
a.m., p.m.	午前, 午後 *gozen, gogo* noon + before, noon + after	上午, 下午 *shàng wǔ, xià wǔ* previous + noon, latter + noon	

ONLY IN JAPAN

Signs containing hiragana tip you off that they're exclusively Japanese. So it is that お手洗い (*otearai:* toilet), 切符売り場 (*kippu uriba:* ticket counter), and 売切 (*uriki•re:* sold out) exist only in Japan. That's obviously because of the linguistic differences between Japanese and Chinese. But what about cultural differences? Although the following signs contain only kanji, they too exist only in Japan. It's interesting to consider whether some of these only-in-Japan signs reflect anything about Japanese culture.

Kanji	Yomi	Meaning
土足厳禁	*dosoku genkin*	Remove Shoes
年中無休	*nenjū mukyū*	Open Every Day of the Year
案内	*annai*	Information
両替機	*ryōgaeki*	Change Maker
改札口	*kaisatsuguchi*	Ticket Gate
非常口	*hijōguchi*	Emergency Exit
立入禁止	*tachiiri kinshi*	Keep Out
火気厳禁	*kaki genkin*	Caution: Flammable

Double Happiness

This is how the Chinese write "double happiness," pronounced *xĭ*. At Chinese weddings, a large red version of this character hangs where the bride and groom will be sure to see it. In Japanese, 喜 means "to be glad, rejoice" (*KI, yoroko•bu*).

Marit & Tai
August 5, 2000

The large character on the front of this wedding invitation is the double-happiness hanzi, drawn with a calligraphic swooshiness. Along the bottom, the same character appears 17 more times in a more rigid typeface. So what we have here is no longer double happiness but rather happiness x 36.

TEN TIPS FOR STUDYING KANJI

Have you caught kanji fever yet? In off moments, do you find yourself tracing kanji in the air? When someone speaks in English, do you flash on how the equivalent Japanese word would look in kanji?

Or do you find kanji to be such a struggle that you can never force yourself to study? When kanji feels torturous, it's hard to find that motivation. A few pointers can smooth the path and let kanji-joy flood in. Except where indicated, all these tips come from my personal experience. You will probably find other methods that suit you better.

Tip 1: Avoid Mindless Drilling

When I first started learning kanji, I asked my teacher how to memorize the characters. A kind native speaker with little imagination, she shrugged and said, "I guess you just write them over and over." Several of my classmates came from China, and they agreed that they had learned by copying each character a hundred times. That sounds like repeatedly writing on the board, "I will not chew gum in class." What a joyless way to learn!

I was therefore thrilled to find this observation from James Heisig in *Remembering the Kanji: A Complete Course on How Not to Forget the Meaning and Writing of Japanese Characters:* "You have probably gotten into the habit of writing the character several times when memorizing it, whether you need to or not; and then writing it *MORE* times for kanji that you have trouble remembering. There is really no need to write the kanji more than once, unless you have trouble with the stroke-order and want to get a better 'feel' for it" (p. 45). He recommends instead spending time on the imagery of difficult characters. How liberating this is!

And how sensible, as it's fallacious to think that knowing how to write a character means knowing how to read it. I can write a character fifteen times in one sitting, only to blank out when I see it the next day. Reading and writing kanji seem to draw on different parts of the brain. (That's not a scientific assessment, just an experiential one.)

In other linguistic endeavors, such as studying Japanese vocabulary, production and recognition of a word go hand in hand. That is, if my flash card says *hakubutsukan*, I should think "museum." And if my card says "museum," I should think *hakubutsukan*. I'll need both types of knowledge in conversation, so it's helpful to practice translating in each direction.

But I don't think the same holds true for kanji. When I started learning characters, I worked on 地下鉄 (*chikatetsu:* subway) until I could write it fairly easily. In reading sentences, though, I always failed to recognize this word, largely because my eye didn't go to all three characters at once, seeing them as a unit. That leap requires lots of reading practice, something emphasized far too little in the push to draw kanji.

I also believe that because certain characters will always prove elusive, it makes little sense to draw them repeatedly. I'll never be able to memorize the stroke order and configuration of particular kanji, but I can recognize them in a snap. And that's my whole goal with kanji—deciphering signs and other text. I can readily understand 営業中 (*eigyōchū:* open for business) and 非常口 (*hijōguchi:* emergency exit), and I don't feel compelled to practice writing them. Occasionally, I forget their readings, and even that's OK with me. I care most about knowing what they mean. Will there ever come a time when I need to draw 博物館 (the famous *hakubutsukan*) and don't have a dictionary at hand? I doubt it. It's more realistic to conserve one's energy with certain kanji and to focus on simply recognizing them. Fortunately, that's easy with characters that reveal their meaning through their shapes and sounds. You'll find a smattering of those in Exhibit 81, "Thematic Explorations: Inadvertently Appropriate Kanji."

Tip 2: Engage Fully with Each Character

Don't get me wrong; I do think it's essential to practice writing characters. I was shocked when a student in my

intermediate Japanese class said he tried to memorize kanji by looking at them for awhile. Out of everyone in the class, he had the worst grasp of kanji, but I had figured that was just because he never did homework; I'd never imagined that he studied in such a passive way.

Writing kanji is crucial because it makes you an active participant in a process. But the writing needs to happen in a meaningful context, I believe. Rather than drilling on paper that soon gets discarded, I like to feel that I'm building something. For each kanji I study, I create a flash card containing everything I know about that character.

For example, I jot down kanji compounds containing the character, especially any compound in which I already know the accompanying character. In this way, I build on a foundation, rather than always feeling that I'm starting from scratch. This method also helps me maintain and practice what I've learned before.

As I record the translations of words containing a particular character, I sometimes spot trends. In presenting 色 (*SHOKU, SHIKI, iro:* color), my textbook supplied only two compounds, 原色 (*genshoku:* primary colors) and 特色 (*tokushoku:* a characteristic), so I searched Spahn for more. He painted a very different picture with this "color." His word list included "lust" (色好み, *irogonomi*), "mistress" (色女, *iroonna*), "love letter" (色文, *irobumi*), "amorous glance" (色目, *irome*), and "sexual passion" (色道, *shikidō*). Through these words, I learned about a side of 色 that I never would have known otherwise.

Breaking kanji apart feels even more informative. Taking my cue from Rowley and Henshall, I dissolve characters down to their smallest components. I record this information on the flash card, too, usually creating a mnemonic sentence. See Exhibit 82, "Just the Facts: Flash Card Layout," for an idea of how a card might display all this information.

I then take this analysis a step further, creating flash cards for each component, such as the movement radical (辶) or the grass radical (⺾), and listing all the kanji I know that contain this shape. I even go so far as to create cards for shapes that have no meaning as individual elements but that recur in kanji nonetheless. One card shows all characters containing a cross (e.g., 真, 準, and 苦). Gathering kanji with shared shapes allows me to make unexpected connections and to notice *on*-echoes.

When doing this close-up study of components, I find it helpful to give them names. Because 辶 looks like a 3 when written by hand and because I first learned 辶 in the context of 近 (*chika•i:* near), I call 辶 "*chika* 3" (which distinguishes it from "*san* 3," 三). The particular names you assign don't matter; it's just important to have them. The brain works better with symbols than with vagueness. To find out more about my component classification system, see Exhibit 83, "Just the Facts: Sample Landmark Cards," and Exhibit 84, "Just the Facts: Landmark Categories."

Truth be told, I don't remember a fraction of what goes on my cards after I record information there, but that's not the point. When I emerge from this kind of analysis, I feel I've investigated every nook and cranny of a character, making it seem 3-D, alive, and very much mine. Think about how different it feels to pass a dog on the street and to live with him for two months; the latter is comparable to the in-depth knowledge one can attain by analyzing characters. And with both canine cohabitation and kanji analysis, this intimacy can make you fall in love.

Or familiarity can breed contempt! I despise certain characters. They've betrayed me again and again, their on-yomi flipping in all directions, their strokes refusing to stick in my brain, the meanings vanishing as soon as I need them. I particularly hate characters that strike me as ugly. There's nothing quite like drawing a shape that looks too creepy for words, such as anything with the humpbacked, hairy "beast" radical, 犭!

Visceral responses to kanji sometimes develop without reason. I feel excited whenever I see 農 (*NŌ:* farming, agriculture), and I can't begin to explain why, especially as it's so tough to draw. But whatever the reason and however positive or negative the feelings are, it's good to let them find full expression. Passion of any kind makes you more likely to remember a character.

Tip 3: Think Holistically About Patterns

Kanji can seem overwhelming unless one draws back from all the strokes and finds patterns. The adage about seeing the forest and not the trees really kicks in here. When I first encountered 暴 (*BŌ, aba•reru:* to be violent), I had trouble locating it in a dictionary list of compounds because I couldn't count the strokes. (I could barely even see any.) Finally, I teased the character apart, realizing that it contained 日 (sun) + a structure resembling 寒 (cold) + 水 (water) at the bottom. In terms of reading, it helps immeasurably when you recognize such shapes, rather than losing yourself in minutiae. For more on patterns within characters and compounds, see Exhibit 85, "Thematic Explorations:

Parallel Features." And to explore patterns among kanji with a certain sort of radical, look at Exhibit 86, "Spectacular Shapes: Swooping and Cradling Characters."

Spotting patterns will prove helpful when you glimpse unknown characters out in the world and need to remember them until you reunite with your dictionary. Let's say you see 美術 and have no idea how to interpret these nineteen strokes. Try searching for familiar forms. There's a sheep (羊) on top of 美. What remains when you remove the sheep? Hey, it's 大 (*ō•kii:* big)! And how about 術? Well, that has a lot going on, but when you look at it closely, you can identify the two parts of 行 (*i•ku:* to go), sandwiching a katakana *ho* (ホ) with an extra stroke on the upper right. Forget about that stroke for now. Just remember a big inverted sheep going toward a hoe (or going "ho ho ho"). By conceiving of four or five things, rather than nineteen, you'll remember 美術 until you can look it up, finding that it's *bijutsu* (fine arts).

Viewing sentences holistically is also quite handy. When you read, it's ideal to take in a whole string of kanji at a time, up to the next kana or even the *maru* (the hollow period used in Japanese). That's the goal, anyway—skipping over characters you don't know and hoping that more familiar kanji will help you fill in the blanks. (I'm terrible at this; I just know it's the goal!) It's rather like what a friend told me when I was learning to drive and felt nervous on a winding road: "Don't respond to all the curves so much. Focus farther ahead."

Tip 4: Memorize Words with Each Yomi

Rather than trying to memorize particular yomi for a character (which is extremely difficult), memorize a word that uses each yomi. When I think of 資, I associate it with 投資 (*tōshi:* investment). Similarly, 料 makes my mind go to 料理 (*ryōri:* cooking, cuisine). So when I encounter 資料, I can build on associations with *tōshi* and *ryōri,* thereby deducing the reading (*shiryō:* materials). It's easier to think about whole words than about yomi that scads of other characters share (e.g., SHI and RYŌ). Similarly, it's more natural to think about the meanings of whole words versus the meanings of characters that rarely, if ever, appear alone (e.g., 料, "fee, materials" and 資, "capital, funds").

Tip 5: Break the Furigana Addiction

When we learned hiragana, the teacher discouraged us from annotating them with romanized readings. We were incredulous. "You mean, we're actually going to have to read these characters?!" But before long, it felt fairly comfortable to do so. That wouldn't have happened if we'd used the crutch of romanization. In terms of kanji, furigana create a similar dependency. When I see a row of small hiragana written underneath kanji, my eye fixates on the lower line and avoids the kanji at all costs. If you're working on a passage that you intend to read repeatedly for practice, it's best not to annotate the kanji with furigana. You can make notes on the bottom of the page or in the margins instead. Breaking the furigana dependency will help train your mind to recognize kanji.

Tip 6: Don't Let Stroke Rules Strangle You

Here's my unorthodox take on stroke order rules: Only adhere to them insofar as they help you draw characters more fluidly or help you count strokes. If you can't see that the rules make a difference at a particular time, then don't worry about them! They're there to help you, not to strangulate you into writer's block. Many other aspects of kanji require you to be finicky; save your energy for those. Exhibit 87, "Thematic Explorations: Take Care," covers some of those situations.

Tip 7: Learn to Use a Dictionary Efficiently

If you become a kanji devotee, you'll want to own at least one specialized kanji dictionary, which could prove to be enormous and expensive (but worth it!). Excellent dictionaries certainly exist online, but printed dictionaries have certain benefits. Exhibit 88, "Just the Facts: Kanji Dictionaries," examines your options and presents basic methods for navigating kanji tomes, as well as tips on doing so efficiently.

Tip 8: Assume There Are Other Readings

You've seen 何 loads of times, always reading it as *nan* or *nani* (what), so you figure that's all there is to that character. But a kanji dictionary also presents these less-common yomi: *KA,* "what," and *izu•re* or *do•re,* "which." Surprisingly, 何故 (*naze:* why) contains 何.

Here's a bigger shock. The ultra-ordinary 食 (*SHOKU, ta•beru:* to eat) has another side to its personality with these readings:

JIKI: food, eating
ha•mu: to eat, feed on, receive (an allowance)

ku•enai: unable to eat, shrewd, cunning
ku•eru: to be able to eat
ku•rau, ku•u: to eat, drink, receive a blow
ku•rawasu: to feed, make (someone) eat, give (someone a punch), trick (someone)

Of course, we've already talked about how kanji have many yomi, some uncommon. But I mention this now because it's relevant to dictionary usage. When you've looked up scads of surrounding kanji, the last thing you feel like doing is researching 何 or 食. Until you do, though, you may not have the information you need.

Tip 9: Make Time to Study Kanji Regularly

Make room in your life for kanji. Create a regular time to study it, rather than hoping you'll absorb characters on the fly. Teachers of Japanese conversation and grammar often make kanji a sideline, a mandatory part of the curriculum that they treat as a nuisance. But you can't take that approach if you hope to get anywhere with kanji. Your mastery of kanji won't happen on its own.

Unlike conversational practice, kanji is a solitary pursuit. It can feel weird to spend hours alone, engrossed in something esoteric (by Western standards anyway). But this is also the joy of studying such complex symbols. You can delve into them as deeply and as idiosyncratically as you like, making them yours, all yours.

A little bit of kanji every day helps keep it fresh in the brain. You don't need a lengthy session. If I spend ten minutes looking up characters I spotted somewhere, that satisfies something inside. But quick visits to the vast world of kanji won't make me proficient. If I want great clarity about the characters, I need to study three-plus hours a day for at least a week. Then my associations go from being fuzzy to crisply precise, and I can reason my way through what I see, rather than panicking or drawing a blank. But spending three-plus hours on kanji is unsustainable in daily life. It's a great experience to have once in awhile, like an arduous hike. On regular days, though, walking around the block may have to suffice, metaphorically speaking.

Tip 10: Find Ways of Testing Yourself

Life can seem like one big, ongoing test. That's a sour way to look at the world, but when it comes to kanji, this is a positive outlook to have. There are opportunities all around to test your knowledge of kanji.

It appears that people develop electronic kanji-study aids every week. Most include the full range of Jōyō kanji, and some programs are geared toward those studying for the annual Japanese Language Proficiency Tests (JLPT). Nowadays, many self-quizzing programs have progress-tracking systems; the software can remember which characters you've gotten wrong before and will quiz you on those tough ones more often. Electronic flash cards are common, and they're good because they don't let you cheat! That is, you can't tell yourself that you know certain kanji when your score indicates otherwise. Many kanji-study aids also include stroke-order animations, yomi and definitions, lists of compounds featuring the kanji in question, and sample sentences for a given character.

As so many study aids have similar features, your choice may well depend on what kind of computer you use. For instance, Mac users can take advantage of iKanji from ThinkMac Software. They can download at least two programs—one simply called Kanji, and another called Kanji Flip—from iTunes.

Nintendo produces quite a few study aids that require you to own a handheld Nintendo DS console, which features a touchscreen and comes with a stylus. For Nintendo products, the instructions and the software itself may be entirely in Japanese.

That's true of Perfect Kanji: Kakitori Kun. With this learning tool, you can try writing any of the 1,006 characters that Japanese sixth graders know. A digital teacher inside the game judges how well you drew them. Similarly, Nintendo's DS Bimoji Training comes with a special stylus designed to feel like a calligraphy pen. You can practice drawing nearly 3,100 characters with proper calligraphy, making your strokes curve and slant just so. With My Japanese Coach from Ubisoft Nintendo, you practice your strokes by tracing over the characters you see on the screen.

Advanced students might like Nintendo's なぞっておぼえる大人の漢字練習~完全版 (Nazotte Oboeru Otona no Kanji Renshū: Kanzenhan), as well as 意味までわかる大人の熟語練習~角川類語新辞典から5万問 (Imi made Wakaru Otona no Jukugo Renshū: Kadokawa Ruigo Shinjiten Kara 5-Man Mon), which Now Productions has recently released.

For much more information on electronic offerings, you can read users' opinions at http://forum.koohii.com (enter "Kanji Games for the Nintendo DS" as your search term) or check out the product list at www.whiterabbitpress.com.

Free online resources abound, as well, such as Kantango (www.kantango.com), which once helped me prepare for a big kanji exam. The Mnemosyne Project (www.mnemosyne-proj.org) also features kanji flash cards and a progress-tracking system. If you go to Mary Sisk Noguchi's Kanji Clinic website (www.kanjiclinic.com) and hit "Links," you'll see several other possibilities for online self-evaluation. Finally, with a paid membership at the Japanese-language-learning site JapanesePod101.com, you'll find kanji flash cards with an audio component, JLPT practice tests, and more.

The variety of programs available in electronic form and on the Internet is constantly changing. If you can't find any of the projects I've mentioned here, use a search engine or other online resources to find programs with similar and ever-improving features.

Charts in reference books provide low-tech ways of testing yourself. Spahn contains grids of the most frequently used kanji and of the characters that Japanese kids memorize at each grade level. The yomi and meanings don't appear; there's nothing but naked kanji to let you see what you've acquired and what remains fuzzy. In Spahn you'll also find displays of kanji with a common radical (say 3e, 女). How many do you know?

The options for quizzing yourself are endless, once you become creative about doing so. If you pass Japanese or Chinese shops, read all the signs you can. On TV stations broadcasting in Japanese and Chinese, subtitles often appear in kanji (or hanzi). Have a go at it and see how well you do. You may even stumble upon kanji in unexpected places such as Wales! To find out about that, see Exhibit 89, "Just the Facts: Kanji Wood."

And We're Off (in Several Senses!)

In anything, success has a great deal to do with attitude. That's especially true of kanji. Whenever I feel more confident about my kanji ability, I find that I can do more. If a teacher hands me a paper containing kanji, I assume that the characters have come from our textbook and that I therefore know them. That keeps me focused on figuring out what they say. By contrast, when I see Japanese signs, I often presume that they contain kanji I've never encountered before. Not surprisingly, I can't read those signs. Later, when I realize that I did in fact know those kanji, I kick myself for having assumed otherwise.

Kicking oneself is a popular part of the sport of kanji, but of course self-abuse doesn't help. In the all-too-likely event of errors, you need to accept yourself. If you find kanji tough, you're not stupid, and you're not alone. It's just that kanji can be, as a classmate said to me one day, a "strucking fuggle." Kanji makes everyone feel dumb at times, even Japanese people. Kanji is bigger than you are. Don't fight it any more than you would fight a panther. You won't win. Accept that you're small and less-than-fanged, and just admire the panther for all that it is. This will save you considerable mental energy and prevent you from spiraling downward with self-loathing.

There's something peculiar about the way kanji has little staying power in the mind. Titles of several resource books reflect this aspect, especially the title and subtitle of James W. Heisig's *Remembering the Kanji: A Complete Course on How Not to Forget the Meaning and Writing of Japanese Characters*. I believe kanji affords an early glimpse of Alzheimer's. How many times have I realized that the radical 月 can mean not only "moon" but also "flesh"? Whenever this insight used to hit me as if for the first time, I would flip over my flash card for 脱 (*nu•gu:* to undress) to record this information, only to see it there already. And then I would remember that the same scenario had played out many times before with that very card.

These kinds of demoralizing experiences prompt many students to give up on kanji. But I've arrived at a different place with this issue. I now find it comforting that I can have the same wonderful insights again and again, always with a fresh, intense feeling! Those of us afflicted with Kanji-Induced Dementia (from which one can derive the acronym KID) are eternally young at heart. By giving ourselves permission not to know, we create room to grow, to learn, and to feel the thrill of discovery.

When we put a great deal of emphasis on the knowledge we've acquired in life, we forget the joy of *not* knowing, of feeling a little lost. But that's precisely the appeal of puzzles and mazes. Easy ones aren't as fun. Most of us like to tease our brains by cracking the codes of vanity plates. We may figure out the cryptic letters, and we may not, but it's essentially OK with us not to know. We like to be outwitted at times. Feeling stumped makes us eager for the next challenge.

Kanji is an ongoing discovery, an endless game. You'll certainly find that to be the case in Exhibit 90, "Game: Kanji Crossword." In this puzzle and in all your kanji pursuits, I wish you every possible success. I hope that you, too, become "crazy for kanji."

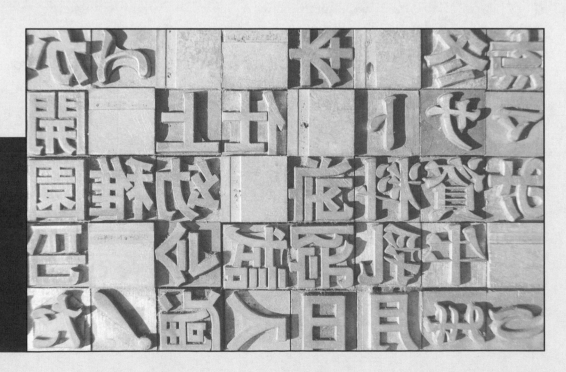

Here's a puzzle for you. Try reading kanji when they're inverted and oriented in random ways, as in the photo. A Yokohama bookstore sold this printer's tray of metal type, which includes the mirror images of kanji, hiragana, punctuation, and numbers. Of course, in the cases of 本 (*hon:* book, origin) and 日 (*NICHI, hi:* day, sun), inversion doesn't make a difference.

Inadvertently Appropriate Kanji

Some characters provide visual clues to the meanings of singletons and compounds, even when the kanji aren't pictographs. In the following examples, the comments indicate what the kanji look like.

Kanji That Look Like What They Mean

高 (*KŌ, taka•i:* tall, expensive)
Tall, expensive real estate.

固 (*KO, kata•i:* hard, stiff)
"Old" (古) in a box, which corresponds to our idea of a "stiff"!

費 (*SHI, tsui•yasu:* expense, cost)
A backward dollar sign atop a component associated with money (貝).

脳 (*NŌ:* brain, memory)
Three hairs on a head, with **X** marking the location of the brain.

殺 (*SATSU, koro•su:* to kill)
Here, the **X,** along with all the other spiky lines, looks violent.

難 (*NAN, muzuka•shii:* difficult)
A difficult character to remember how to draw!

複雑 (*fukuzatsu:* complicated)
A complicated mess!

均等 (*kintō:* equal)
Equal signs in both characters. The second kanji (*hito•shii:* equal) seems to be all about equality and balance, with two pieces of bamboo perched symmetrically on top.

渋滞 (*jūtai:* [traffic] congestion)
The first character means "not going smoothly." In its bottom part I see vehicles converging at a jammed intersection. As the 止 on top indicates, they've completely stopped. The busy second character, 滞 (to stagnate), enhances the sense of chaos. I spot something like a city (市) in its bottom part.

明日 (*ashita:* tomorrow)
You'll find a wonderful bit of logic if you treat the components as autonomous kanji: 日 月 日. Today's sun + tonight's moon + tomorrow's sun will get you to tomorrow!

Kanji That Sound Like What They Mean

Other Japanese words sound like their meanings. Without being loanwords, they happen to sound like English words for the same concepts:

買	**BAI**, *ka•u:* to **buy**, purchase
彼	**HI**, *kare:* **he,** that
背骨	*se***bone:** back**bone**
軍	*gun:* military
乱暴	*ranbō:* violence
名前	*nam**ae:* name
移民	*imin:* immigrant
子孫	*shi***son:** descendant
起	*o•koru:* to occur
懊悩	*ōnō:* anguish

Two more such words require brief explanations:

渦中 (*kachū:* vortex, maelstrom)
Kachū brings to mind a sneeze, and isn't that a maelstrom in the respiratory system?

強引 (*gōin:* forced, coercive)
You can easily hear a captor's commanding a captive, "Go in!"

Flash Card Layout

Here are two sample flash cards, first the front, then the reverse. The layouts of these cards work well for me, but another approach may work better for you.

I. Singleton

A. Front

The information on this card comes from *Basic Kanji Book* (BKB) by Chieko Kano and others. The number 241 means that 治 (the character in question) is kanji #241 in that series, and "L22" means that 治 comes from Lesson 22.

The left-hand column contains vocabulary formed with the kun-yomi of 治. Meanwhile, the right-hand column displays words containing the on-yomi. To test yourself, say the yomi of all four words. Also list as many yomi as you can associate with this kanji.

B. Reverse

The meaning of the character appears in the center of the card.

The upper corners display the various yomi, *kun* to the left (in hiragana), *on* to the right (in katakana). As indicated, this kanji has two intransitive-transitive verb pairs: *osamaru-osameru* and *naoru-naosu*. The on-yomi are *JI* and *CHI*.

The readings for the words appear halfway down on the left (again in hiragana) and on the right (again in katakana). The left-hand ones say *osameru* and *naosu*, whereas the right-hand ones say *seijika* and

Singleton Front

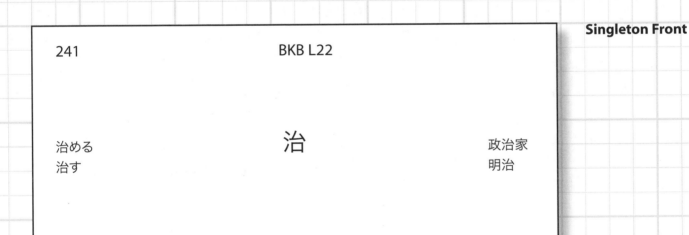

241	BKB L22

治める
治す

治

政治家
明治

Singleton Reverse

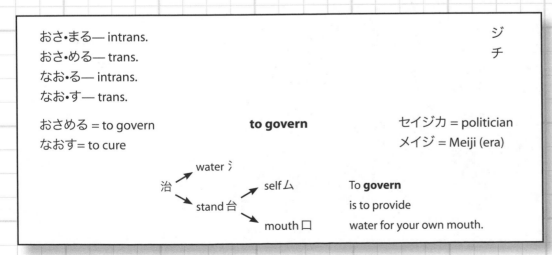

おさ・まる— intrans.
おさ・める— trans.
なお・る— intrans.
なお・す— trans.

ジ
チ

おさめる = to govern
なおす= to cure

to govern

セイジカ = politician
メイジ = Meiji (era)

治 → water 氵
治 → stand 台 → self ム
stand 台 → mouth 口

To **govern**
is to provide
water for your own mouth.

Meiji. Visualizing words on the left versus right and in hiragana versus katakana may help you remember whether certain yomi are *kun* or *on*.

The bottom lines contain a breakdown of the components in the kanji, inspired by Rowley's analyses in *Kanji Pict-o-Graphix*. To the right of the breakdown lies a mnemonic sentence containing as many key words as I could lasso at once.

II. Compound

A. Front

Pretty simple! This word comes from the *Situational Functional Japanese* (SFJ) series, Lesson 17, as shown. The compound in question is 都合. This type of self-quizzing is hard because there's no other information on the front to tip you off about the yomi and meaning. If you don't know those, think of other words containing these characters. Does that help?

B. Reverse

The answer lies in the center. The word is *tsugō,* "circumstances" or "convenience" (written in hiragana no matter what kind of yomi it contains). Analyses of each character appear on either side of the card, including breakdowns, on-yomi, and kun-yomi. You might want to circle or underline the yomi that's pertinent to this card. Finally, a mnemonic sentence lies at the bottom. The underlined portion is the best English approximation I could make of the word's yomi.

Compound Front

SFJ L17

都合

Compound Reverse

都 = capital, metropolis → person 者
→ village ß

合 = to suit, combine

ト (as in 京都, Kyōto)
ツ
みやこ

つごう
circumstances, convenience

ゴウ
ガッ
あ(う)

<u>Sue, go</u> to Kyoto if it's suitable and convenient.

Sample Landmark Cards

When I learned enough kanji to start mixing them up, I decided to create order out of chaos. I gathered all kanji with a common component and listed them on a single flash card. I suppose you could say it's a reference card, rather than a flash card, because I don't use the front and back to quiz myself. But I can still create test situations by covering all but one column and seeing if I know how the rest of the row goes.

Below you'll find some samples. Note that the names of components are my own (or have come from Rowley's or Henshall's often fanciful suggestions). Sometimes I create cards for shapes that dictionaries and other reference sources would probably never call "components" (e.g., 牛, "deformed cow," as in 先, 生, and 告). I realize that the second horizontal stroke in 生 is shorter than the top one, whereas that's not the case in 牛. But I take liberties with my landmarks. Rather than calling these unorthodox shapes "components," I call them "landmarks," as they orient me in the landscape of kanji.

In addition to putting 続 on my card for 宀 ("Carport"), I also include 続 on cards with the landmarks 糸 ("Thread"), 土 and 士 ("Soil and Samurai"), and 儿 ("Legs"). Therefore, it's not as if "Carport" is an exclusive categorization for 続. Such exclusivity could limit my ability to locate this character in my system, Instead, I can find it any number of ways. I've learned that this is one case in which repeating myself proves incredibly useful. By adding a character such as 続 to my flash card file, I end up writing it on four cards (jotting down its yomi and meaning each time). And that imprints something on the brain—not only the readings and translation but also a sense that four discrete parts occupy certain positions in this kanji. If you can visualize the layout of characters, you've won half the battle. Whenever I need to write *kekkon* (marriage), I gear up to draw two kanji with identical structures—one component on the left and two stacked ones on the right. On a good day, I can fill in the blanks and produce 結婚. Most days I can't!

Landmark: 广, "Building Frame"

Kanji	Kun-Yomi	On-Yomi	Meaning
広	ひろ•い	コウ	wide, spacious
店	みせ	テン	shop
度	たび	ド	degree, frequency
府	–––	フ	administrative prefecture
座	すわ•る	ザ	to sit
席	–––	セキ	seat

Landmark: 厂, "Lean-to"

Kanji	Kun-Yomi	On-Yomi	Meaning
歴	—	レキ	career
返	かえ•る, かえ•す	ヘン	to return (an item)
農	—	ノウ	farming, agriculture
備	そな•える, そな•わる	ビ	to provide
原	はら	ゲン	field, origin
願	ねが•う	ガン	to request
産	う•む	サン	to produce
感	—	カン	to feel, sense
顔	かお	ガン	face
反	—	ハン	opposite

Landmark: 宀, "Carport"

Kanji	Kun-Yomi	On-Yomi	Meaning
写	うつ•る, うつ•す	シャ	to copy, to project
運	はこ•ぶ	ウン	to carry, fate
深	ふか•い	シン	deep
続	つづ•く	ゾク	to continue
受	う•ける, う•かる	ジュ	to receive
寝	ね•る	シン	to sleep

(The last three kanji here have the landmark tucked midway down their structures.)

Landmark Categories

In Exhibit 83 we focused on 广 ("Building Frame"), 厂 ("Lean-to"), and 冖 ("Carport"). All three landmarks come from the same landmark category, "Buildings and Roofs." That is to say, I file landmark flash cards by category. This is crucial because they do accumulate, and if you can't find them efficiently, they won't serve you well. Below you'll find a personal, idiosyncratic list of the categories with which I organize landmarks, along with just a few of the many kanji in each category. Each group represents one flash card, which would resemble the ones displayed in Exhibit 83.

I present this as a way to get you started on your own similar system, should you so choose. If you want something more "official," *Basic Kanji Book,* Vol. 2, and *Intermediate Kanji Book* have pattern indexes that group kanji by radicals. However, that approach excludes some of the oddball shapes I've collected. Also, those indexes present radicals only in a certain position within kanji (e.g., on top, on the bottom, on the left, on the right, etc.). I find it helpful to think more broadly about the issue. That allows me to collect 白 and 階 on the same card, "Acute Accent," filed under "Rays and Legs," as you'll see below.

Buildings and Roofs

(including anything vaguely architectural)

Building Frame (广)	広	店	度
Lean-to (厂)	歴	返	農
Carport (冖)	写	運	深
House Roof (宀)	安	宅	家
Takai Roof (亠)	高	京	文
Steps (彳)	待	行	彼
Gate (門)	間	聞	問
Hill, Village (阝)	都	階	院

Diagonal Lines

Deformed Cow (牛)	先	生	告
Strike (攵)	政	教	数
Handle (𠂉)	毎	海	族
Money (金)	鉄	銀	鈞
Weird **T** (𠂇)	石	面	残
Big (大)	太	犬	笑

Cut-through (丿)	史	者	必
Kana *He* (へ)	会	合	今

Numbers

2 (二)	天	賛	暖
Chika 3 (⻍)	近	遊	返
San 3 (彡)	形	残	実
5 (与, 丂)	写	号	考
9 (九)	究	雑	熱
10 (十)	真	準	苦

Katakana

E (工)	式	試	空
Chi (チ)	午	話	活
Ha (ハ)	公	港	器
Hi (ヒ)	指	階	老
Ho (ホ)	術	述	
Ka (カ)	勉	効	加
Segmented *Ka* (方)	放	族	遊
Stunted *Ka* (勹)	場	物	約
Weird *Ke* (仾)	旅	遠	園
Ku (ク)	色	急	魚
Ma (マ)	予	払	野
Mu (ム)	私	有	強
Na (ナ)	友	社	右
Ne (ネ)	礼	裕	神
Complex *Ne* (ネ)	初	経	複
Nu (ヌ)	友	割	寝
Ri (リ)	帰	多	別
Ta (夕)	夕	夏	移
Long *Ta* (夂)	冬	流	落
Takai-Mu (亠)	育		
(combining *Takai* Roof [亠] and *Mu* [ム])			
Yo (ヨ, E, 王)	帰	住	紙

Tools and Weapons

Sword (刀)	分	切	留
Fishhook (冂)	服	報	印
Rake (尹)	書	静	事
Dart (矢)	短	知	医
Needle's Eye (立)	音	商	接

> The handwritten version of this contains マ.

Grill (开)	研	形	
Ladder (爿)	面	済	期
Ax (斤)	所	折	質
Thread (糸)	練	終	結
Halberd (戈)	成	感	議
Partial Halberd (弋)	貸	式	代

Body Parts

Head (頁)	頭	願	類
Heart (心)	急	思	悪
Arrow Through Heart (忄)	性	情	快
Ear (耳)	聞	取	恥
Mouth (口)	味	同	合
Tongue (舌)	辞	活	
Hand (扌)	持	押	打
Dirty Arm (至)	室	屋	到

(Heisig [kanji #753] sees 至 as an elbow hanging from the ceiling [厶] with soil [土] below. I abbreviate this as "Dirty Arm.")

People

Person (亻)	化	仕	借
Hito (人)	次	以	座
Onna (女)	好	始	妻
Child (子)	学	教	遊

Nature

Fire (灬,⺌,火)	黒	赤	談
Cloud (云)	会	転	伝
Rain (雨)	電	雲	雪
Water (氵)	治	涼	洗
Ice, Ice Chips (冫,⺀)	冬	寒	次
Sheep (羊)	美	着	議
Bird (鳥)	鳥	島	
Horse (馬)	駅	験	驚
Snake (己,弓)	記	引	起
Soil and Samurai (土,士)	地	場	経
Grass (艹)	茶	荷	薬
Bamboo (竹)	答	笑	簡
Tree (木)	村	様	業
Beans (豆)	頭	短	喜
Watashi Grain (禾)	私	科	秋

Rice Star (米)	数	料	歯
Plant (龶)	情	割	表
Blue (青)	静	情	晴

(In "Nature" because 青 has a plant on top.)

Rays and Legs

Equally Spaced Rays (⺍)	業	当	消
Gaku Rays (⺍)	学	覚	単
Sickness (疒)	病	疲	痛
Horns (丷)	説	並	洋
4 Side Rays (⿰㇒⿰)	楽	様	求
6 Side Rays (非)	非	悲	料
Rice Measure (斗)	科	料	
Acute Accent (ˊ)	白	向	階
Grave Accent (ˋ)	約	太	主
Words (言)	記	誌	訪
Table Legs (⺶)	真	寒	選
Pi Legs (儿)	院	売	見

Hooks

Moon (月)	朝	前	有
Moon Frame (冂)	週	市	橋
Inch (寸)	対	得	府
Temple (寺)	時	待	持
Little (小)	原	願	涼
Horizontal Hook (一)	予	務	欠
Left Hook (丿)	水	静	呼
Right Hook (乚)	以	良	風

Quadrangles

Sun (日)	百	明	晩
Eye (目)	県	組	真
Shell (貝)	質	題	員
Net (罒)	買	置	
Rice Field (田)	町	番	留
Dirty Rice Field (里)	理	黒	野
Incomplete Grid (隹,用,冊)	離	備	論
"P" (尸)	所	民	眠
Rectangle (冖)	中	号	史
Basket (襾)	価	悪	要
Dish (皿)	温	盗	盆
Car (車)	運	連	軽

Easily Confused

(my personal challenges, with mnemonics presented for some)

Exchange (交)   効   校   較

Tomo Grid (共)   共   港   選   横

Stop (止)   歴   歩   歯
vs. *Tada·shii* (正)   正   政
vs. Roofless *Tei* (疋) 定   足   走   起   題

Halberd Shack (戊)

成 (*SEI, na·ru:* to form)
An <u>ear</u> <u>form</u>s, they <u>sei.</u> (I see an ear inside the "shack.")

減 (*GEN, he·ru:* to decrease)
The <u>water</u> (氵) level <u>gen</u>(erally) <u>decreases.</u>

感 (*KAN:* to feel, sense)
The <u>heart</u> (心) <u>kan</u> feel.

Characters including "to seize" (㕁), "happiness" (幸), and spicy (辛, which I think of as *takai* yen, because it contains 亠 + ¥)

報 (*HŌ, muku·iru:* to report)
<u>Dirty yen</u> (土 + ¥)—<u>seize</u> and <u>report</u> to me, <u>hō.</u>

服 (*FUKU:* clothes)
My <u>flesh</u> (月) <u>seizes</u> up on me with these <u>clothes.</u>

辞 (*JI, ya·meru:* to resign, term)
<u>Resign,</u> and you'll be <u>licking</u> (舌) <u>spices</u> (辛).

Sun and Eye

質 (*SHITSU:* question, quality)
<u>Ax</u> (斤) a question and you <u>shell</u> (貝) receive <u>shitsu.</u>

宿 (*SHUKU, yado:* lodging)
The <u>Shuku</u> lodge holds <u>100</u> (百) <u>people</u> (亻).

題 (*DAI:* title, theme)
<u>Son</u> (日: sun), if you get <u>kicked</u> (疋 resembles 足, foot) in the <u>head</u>, you'll <u>dai.</u>

Dover Publications printed a small book of temporary kanji tattoos. You peel back the protective plastic on top, press the image face-down on the skin, moisten the back of the paper (to activate the ink), and then lift up, leaving behind a "tattoo" that should last three to five days. The kanji here are all mirror images of the characters you would produce with this method. From left to right, they are: 平 (*HEI:* peace), 幸 (*KŌ:* good fortune), 美 (*BI:* beauty), 愛 (*ai:* love), 安 (*AN:* tranquility), 福 (*FUKU:* happiness), 英 (*EI:* excellence), and 健 (*KEN:* health). You may know 英 as "England" in 英語 (*eigo:* English). But it also has other meanings. "Courage" doesn't seem to be one of them, even though that's what the tattoo book says.

Parallel Features

Here is a memory trick that I've found very useful. In a few kanji with right-hand and left-hand sides, the first strokes in each element look alike. Consider these:

作   *SAKU, tsuku•ru*: to make
物   *BUTSU, MOTSU, mono*: thing

Now visualize them as separate components:

亻   乍
牛   勿

The initial stroke for all four components is a diagonal line on the upper left.

We see this pattern again in a different way with this character:

持   *JI, mo•tsu*: to hold, have

It resolves into the following components:

扌   寺

Each starts with a + sign of sorts, though this may not be obvious until you draw them.

Now look at the next character:

硬   *KŌ, kata•i*: hard, stiff

This one doesn't fit the pattern in terms of stroke order; you start 石 by drawing a **T** shape, but you don't approach 更 that way. However, the finished product makes the left-hand and right-side look like **T**-twins, and it might help if you remember this kanji as such.

The pattern of parallel strokes applies to at least one compound:

先生   *sensei*: teacher

The first four strokes are alike in 先 and 生!

Finally, it may help to remember the following compounds if you focus on the identical components each contains:

健康   *kenkō*: health
全国   *zenkoku*: the entire nation

In 健康, you see two variations on a "writing brush" (聿), and then 全国 includes two instances of a "king" (王). We saw many more examples of repeating components in Exhibit 47, "Thematic Explorations: Look-Alikes in Compounds."

In Japan, people hang paper lanterns (提灯, *chōchin*) outside drinking establishments, shops selling *yakitori* (skewers of grilled chicken and vegetables), and the like to attract business. If there is kanji on the paper, the typeface style is usually *chōchinmoji*. The lanterns here are from China, where shop owners similarly use lanterns to attract attention. The middle one says 福 (*FUKU*: good fortune), whereas the one to the right says 春 (*haru*: spring).

Swooping and Cradling Characters

The component 辶 means "movement," and it certainly creates that feeling as it swoops beneath other shapes, extending to the right. That happens in these common kanji:

近	KIN, chika•i: near
返	HEN, kae•su: to return, answer
遊	YŪ, aso•bu: to play
適	TEKI, kana•u: suitable
過	KA, su•giru: to exceed
連	REN, tsu•reru: to take along, connect
退	TAI, shirizo•ku: to retreat

Another swooping form, 廴, also means "movement." The following characters contain 廴:

建	KEN, ta•tsu, ta•teru: to build
健	KEN, suko•yaka: healthy
延	EN, no•biru: to prolong

All these bottom liners provide the finishing touches on characters. That is, if you follow the stroke order, you start by drawing the items to the right, then end with 辶 or 廴. But in another type of kanji construction, you draw the swooper in preparation for a component that will go on top. In the following examples, it looks as if the bottom line is cradling the soon-to-be-drawn component:

起	KI, o•kiru: to rise, rouse, happen
勉	BEN: exertion, endeavor
題	DAI: title, theme
趣	SHU, omomuki: gist, to tend
越	ETSU, ko•su: to surpass, cross over, Vietnam
超	CHŌ, ko•eru: to transcend, super-, ultra-

Finally, here's an oddball with the swooper in the middle of the character:

導	DŌ, michibi•ku: to guide, lead

We saw this one at the tail-end of Exhibit 24 in "Game: Radicals."

STRANGE THINGS ON THE MOVE

	What's Apparently Moving	Yomi and Meaning of Whole Kanji
逐	pig	CHIKU: to accomplish
運	army	UN, hako•bu: to advance
週	perimeter	SHŪ: week
道	neck, head	DŌ, michi: road, way
迫	white	HAKU, sema•ru: to draw near
進	bird	SHIN, susu•mu: to advance
透	excellence	TŌ, su•kasu: to penetrate
迭	to lose	TETSU: to transfer, alternation
迷	rice	MEI, mayo•u: to lose one's way
逝	to fold	SEI, yu•ku: departed, to die
速	bundle	SOKU, haya•i: fast
違	tanned leather	I, chiga•i: difference
遠	long kimono	EN, tō•i: far

Take Care

Kanji reminds me of calculus, particularly integration by parts. (Remember that?!) Both involve fussy details that require considerable concentration. If you make the slightest mistake, you can alter the results significantly. For that reason, be sure to double-check the kanji you write by hand. Here are a few potential trouble spots that particularly come into play when you take tests.

1. When using hiragana or rōmaji to write the yomi of a kanji, don't shorten long vowels. It's easy to forget the long *o* when indicating the reading for, say, 投資 (*tōshi*: investment) or when typing that compound. But a short *o* gives you *toshi*, which means "year" (年) or "city" (都市).

2. Conversely, don't lengthen a vowel when a word doesn't call for that. It's hard to remember which *o*'s are long and which are short in a word such as 歩道橋 (*hodōkyō*: footbridge). It helps to think about other contexts in which these syllables appear. For instance, 道 lends the *DŌ* sound to many of the words we saw in Exhibit 62, "Thematic Explorations: The Way of Culture and the Arts."

3. If it tires you out to write a complicated bit of kanji, you may forget the rest of the compound or its okurigana. This often happens to me with 難しい (*muzukashii*: difficult).

4. When you need okurigana, it's easy to write too little or too much. That is, when you write *tsukuru* (to make), it's hard to remember whether 作 represents *tsu* or *tsuku*. (It's the latter.) Make sure your choice of okurigana reflects the yomi precisely. I've long searched for memory tricks or patterns to help me with this issue but have unfortunately come up empty. Exhibit 86 contains several toughies: 過 (*su•giru*); 連 (*tsu•reru*); 延 (*no•biru*); 起 (*o•kiru*); and 超 (*ko•eru*). Whew, that's a lot of exceptions to remember!

5. It's easy to combine two similar shapes while drawing. I've added horse hair to a bird, making a hybrid creature that doesn't exist. (Then again, "horsefeathers" means "nonsense," so perhaps it's appropriate after all!) That is, to draw 集 (*atsu•meru*: to collect), I started with 隹 (bird) and finished the character just as one would finish 馬 (horse). It all feels logical enough to the hand, so make sure to keep the mind on the job, too.

6. When two kanji have similar components but different arrangements, it's easy to forget the order of things. I can never remember where to put the 阝 in 障 (*SHŌ* of *koshō*, "broken") versus 部 (*BU* of *zenbu*, "all"). And I confuse the layout of 部 with that of 暗 (*AN*, *kura•i*: darkness) and 音 (*ON*, *oto*: sound).

Perhaps when it comes to kanji, we should feel happy if we can remember anything at all!

Careful attention to kanji study will help you reach the pinnacle of literacy and fluency! Tomohiro Matsuzaki has already reached the mountaintop. After climbing Mount Iwasuge (岩菅) in Nagano Prefecture, he reached the 2,295-meter summit (山頂, *sanchō*). For those of us who don't think in meters, that's more than 7,500 feet. お疲れさまでした！(*Otsukaresamadeshita*: Well done!)

Kanji Dictionaries

Buying a kanji dictionary is tricky and somewhat paradoxical. You need to buy one and spend a lot of time learning its ways before deciding whether you really want to own it. By then, you've probably exceeded the store's time limit for returning books. Also, if you want to know how that dictionary stacks up against others, you'll need to buy those, too! Or maybe you want a portable, electronic dictionary (電子辞書: *denshi jisho*), which everyone in my advanced Japanese classes considered indispensable. If you often need a dictionary when you're away from your desk (e.g., while traveling through Japan), an electronic gadget may indeed suit you best. Deskbound sorts often find that online resources such as Jim Breen's site (www.csse.monash.edu.au/~jwb/cgi-bin/wwwjdic.cgi?1C) entirely meet their needs. I use that site constantly and can't imagine how I lived without it.

I won't make a recommendation about print versus electronic, but I can share my experience. When I bought a *denshi jisho,* I figured I was an intermediate user and selected one advertised for that level. Lo and behold, the thick user's manual was entirely in Japanese. So was the interface, until by some stroke of luck I figured out how to change it to English. I could never figure out how to use the machine in any meaningful or efficient way, so I returned it (proceeding to get burned by the company's return policy, but that's another story). My new rule of thumb: If you're so unmechanical that you struggle to check cell phone messages, you'll likely be none too adept at a *denshi jisho.* Save yourself a few hundred dollars.

Print dictionaries will run you more in the range of $40 to $70. I own three popular ones:

- *The Kanji Dictionary* by Mark Spahn and Wolfgang Hadamitzky
- *The New Nelson Japanese-English Character Dictionary*, originally by Andrew N. Nelson and revised by John H. Haig
- *The Kodansha Kanji Learner's Dictionary* by Jack Halpern

Each has a different look-up method, and all have pluses and minuses. I've used Spahn for years, so I'm biased toward that. I'll tell you what I know about the

Over 47,000 Japanese Character Compounds

The Kanji Dictionary

Find Any Compound Using Any of Its Component Characters

漢英熟語字典

**Mark Spahn
Wolfgang Hadamitzky**

With Handy Kanji Lists, Charts, and Maps

others, then share detailed information about Spahn.

The revised Nelson has disappointed many who adored the classic version. Based on a new "Universal Radical Index" (URI), the book now allows you to look up characters based on virtually any component you spot in the kanji. As the revised Nelson says, "Attention to detail and a forgiving attitude toward inexperienced users has resulted in an index in excess of 30,000 individual listings, or roughly four to five for any given character." This built-in redundancy means that the book weighs four pounds. And as one disgruntled user wrote on Amazon.com, the redundancy of the URI "is analogous to equipping a car with 5 extra gas tanks and 4 extra engines—in case you run out of gas or have some sort of engine problem." Some say it's hard to get the hang of the URI. I confess

that the only part of Nelson I've ever used is the yomi index. Although assorted people praise Nelson for its completeness, others point to a major flaw. It provides only compounds that include a given kanji in the first position. Take 純. The one word with which I associate this kanji is 単純 (*tanjun:* simplicity), but Nelson doesn't include it, because 純 occupies the second position in this compound.

Halpern is by far the most portable and affordable of the three. Geared toward beginners, Halpern helps you learn as you look up kanji. In the case of 活, you'll find two meanings, "active" and "live." Halpern first presents compounds influenced by the meaning "active" (e.g., 活動, *katsudō:* activity), then lists those informed by "live" (e.g., 生活, *seikatsu:* life, existence, livelihood). This arrangement thereby conveys etymological information in a clear, concise way. The compact dictionary lists only eighteen compounds for 活, whereas Spahn and Nelson each provide more than sixty. But multiple Amazon reviews have said

that Halpern presents the compounds you're likely to need. Halpern has invented a SKIP (System of Kanji Indexing by Patterns) method, involving the layout of each character (e.g., whether you can divide it into left and right parts). One Amazon user found SKIP easy to use but would rather have acquired practice in using radicals, as that skill is transferable to other dictionaries.

And that brings us to Spahn. After buying this 1,766-pager, I gazed at it fearfully for weeks, having no idea how to use it. But once I took a few tentative stabs at it, I fell deeply in love, for all the wonderful words it allowed me to find serendipitously. Spahn is incredibly thorough, providing almost every compound you could hope to find. The book also contains fascinating, information-packed appendixes. But this thoroughness does add up to 4.5 pounds.

As much as I adore Spahn, I never bothered to read the "user's manual" until recently. How much time I've wasted, not knowing how to use the book properly!

And yet . . . the brain can take in information only when it's ready to do so. There's no way I could have absorbed all the tricks of the trade when I first started looking up kanji. Gradually, one is ready to become more sophisticated, as with any tool.

You can search Spahn by radical or by yomi. Let's start with a sample radical search. If you want to find out what 酒 means (and don't know the yomi), consult the radical chart. Your choices will be 3a, 氵 (the water radical), and 7e, 酉. For some reason, whenever water is present, that trumps all other radicals, so the answer is 3a. You can turn to the 3a section of the book and find the kanji there (by scanning one and a half pages of small 3a characters, as I unthinkably used to do!). Or you can count the number of residual strokes in 酒. That is, take the total stroke count of the character (10) and subtract the number of strokes in the radical (3). Your residual stroke count is 7. Now you have 3a7._, nearly the whole Spahn code for 酒. (The underline represents the digit that's still unknown to us.) You can flip to the few pages of 3a7 listings to find 酒, conveniently the first kanji presented in this category.

Spahn has consolidated the typical set of 214 radicals into 79. I think this makes life simpler, though others disagree. A huge weakness of his approach is that he considers nearly three hundred characters to have no radical. As a result, they're lumped together in 143 pages, and you can't find them via a radical search. This unclassified group includes many common kanji, such as 気 (KI: spirit), 北 (HOKU, kita: north), and 出 (SHUTSU, de•ru: to go out).

One thing I wish I'd done earlier is study Spahn's chart of radical variants in the front. It isn't beach reading, but it *is* essential if you don't want to waste a half hour trying to locate 忄 in the dictionary, only to realize later that this radical is a variant of 心.

Fortunately, a yomi index is a convenient fallback with any kanji dictionary. If you know at least one reading of a character, you can locate it in the book. The main yomi for 酒 are SHU and *sake,* and you can look up either word in the yomi index, arranged in Spahn according to a Western alphabet (not a kana syllabary). Somewhat annoyingly, Spahn's yomi index differentiates between *kun* and *on* readings, providing

separate categories for AI and *ai,* to take one example. If you're looking for *ai,* you'll need to know whether you're working with a kun- or on-yomi (or else you can scan both groups of listings). In any case, both SHU and *sake* will lead you to listings for 3a7.1 fairly quickly.

Even so, there are ways to speed up a Spahn yomi search. Here are some tips:

- Let's say you want to look up 離 in the yomi index so you can find compounds containing this kanji. And let's say you know both the kun-yomi *(hana•reru)* and the on-yomi (RI). Work with *hana•reru,* because you'll find only three listings for that word, rather than thirty-four for RI. That's typically true of kun- versus on-yomi, because as we saw in Exhibit 46, "Thematic Explorations: Syllabic Similarity," on-yomi are limited and repetitive.

- Now you want to know what 式典 says. Let's say you know the first yomi, SHIKI, but not the second. Rather than looking up the latter kanji (as instinct would tell you to do), look up 式. You already know its yomi, so it won't take long for you to locate that reading in the yomi index. (It's much more confusing to isolate the radical, which is 弋, oddly enough.) Once you arrive at the page containing 式 compounds, scan the ones with eight-stroke characters (e.g., 典) in the second position. You'll find that 式典 is *shikiten,* "ceremony." Although you still won't know that 典 means "code" or "ceremony," you'll know its reading, which enables you to find it in the yomi index. I think that's faster than figuring out that its radical is ハ. I never would have guessed that!

- Say you already know the radical and yomi of 典 but want to see words formed with this kanji. Look up ハ to see its radical code—2o. Now locate TEN in the yomi index. There are about sixty such listings. But when you look at the index, you can head right for the 2o section under TEN. You don't need to read over all the entries, as I used to do.

Using a printed kanji dictionary is never a quick affair, so efficient methods such as these are critical.

Kanji Wood

If you're thinking of traveling to countries rich in kanji, consider Wales! The characters are a central attraction in one part of Afan Forest Park, near the South Wales town of Neath.

In some senses, the park dates back to the World War II era, when the British government bought large tracts of sheep-grazing land from farmers and planted conifers high in the hills. These contrasted beautifully with the original ancient oak woodlands on the lower slopes. With the lovely Afan River snaking along the valley floor, all was paradisial, except for one thing. A robust coal-mining industry had blighted the valley, polluting waterways and depositing slag heaps. When the last mines closed in the 1970s, this only made matters worse, leaving many people unemployed and the region depressed.

Things turned around in the late 1970s when Sony and Panasonic (as well as Ford Motor Company) opened factories in the Bridgend-Swansea area, restoring jobs. Land restoration also began, primarily in the park, which was formally established in 1972 as Afan Argoed Country Park and renamed in 1993. The clean-up effort brought back trees and streams, which encouraged wildlife to return.

In 1984, this effort inspired a former Neath resident to do something similar in Japan's Nagano Prefecture, where he lives. Impressed by a visit to the Welsh park, C. W. Nicol—a well-known naturalist, author, and longtime Japanese citizen—bought parcels of neglected woodland in Nagano and nursed them back to health. Nicol donated the land to a prefectural trust, with which Afan Forest Park now has a close relationship, too.

Nicol's actions inspired a sense of a Welsh-Japanese link. Moreover, 2002 marked the hundredth anniversary of an alliance between the United Kingdom and Japan. On top of that, the Welsh community wanted to solidify their ties with the Japanese who had moved to Wales to work for Sony and Panasonic. For all these reasons, the staff of the Forestry Commission of Wales planted Japanese trees and shrubs in a small section of the park. Later, the head gardener teamed up with the local Japanese community to create "Kanji Wood." This garden includes flowerbeds and picnic tables that, from a bird's-eye view, form the shapes for 人 (*hito:* person), 森 (*mori:* forest), and 生 (*i•kiru:* to live). Large wooden sculptures feature the same three kanji. One Japanese visitor wondered why the park had a kanji for "cow" (牛, *ushi*). As it turns out, the grass around it needed mowing. The tall grass had obscured the bottommost stroke in 生.

This is 生, which has scads of meanings, many of them related to "life." In Exhibit 20, "Just the Facts: The Empty Sky and Other Variable Meanings," we saw just how many yomi this character has.

Kana Needed: N / Kanji Level: 3 / Difficulty Level: 3

Kanji Crossword

Ganbatte kudasai!

ACROSS

3. Carpenter
5. Traffic, transportation
6. Air, atmosphere
8. Household chores
9. Doghouse (dog + little + house)
11. Focal point (center + heart + point)
13. Probably
15. Western-style food
16. Psychiatry (lit., the study of the divine spirit)
17. Operating room (surgery + room)
18. University student
22. Dwarf, midget, or child
23. Active
25. Overseas (sea + outside)
26. Volcano
28. One year
29. Work
30. Device for measuring wind speed (wind + speed + measuring instrument)
32. Prophet (in advance + word + person)
33. Region
34. To disembark from vehicles
35. Painter
36. Pastime shared by U.S. and Japan
37. Women's handwriting (i.e., old name for hiragana)
38. Journalist
39. __ __ __ go means "silence" (lit., "no words, no language")
41. Habit, way, peculiarity (to learn + character, nature)
42. Unfortunate, regrettable
44. Like learning swimming on dry land; i.e., useless book learning vs. life experience (cultivated field + water + training)
45. Business holiday (to rest + business + day)
46. Killing two birds with one stone

DOWN

1. Japanese dog (Hint: Not a breed but all Japanese dogs)
2. *yaoya* (vegetable store)
3. Landlord
4. Under construction
5. Intersection
7. Feeling, mood
10. Check used in banking (little + stamp)
12. Psychology (lit., studying the reasons of the heart and mind)
13. Polytheistic (many + gods + religion + -*ic*)
14. Department, section (division + subject of study)
15. Western-style room
18. Adult
19. Life
20. Minor (not yet + adulthood [to become + year] + person)
21. Major northern Japanese island
22. Hill
24. Animal
26. Fire
27. High-speed
28. A word or two (Hint: Be literal here!)
29. _____ *ga nai* means "It cannot be helped."
30. Windmill (wind + car)
31. Planner
33. Planet Earth
34. Unskillful
36. Vegetable garden (vegetable + cultivated field)
37. Female
38. Anniversary
40. Phoenix (the bird, not the city; lit., the bird that doesn't die)
41. Practice, training, drill
42. Overtime
43. One by one

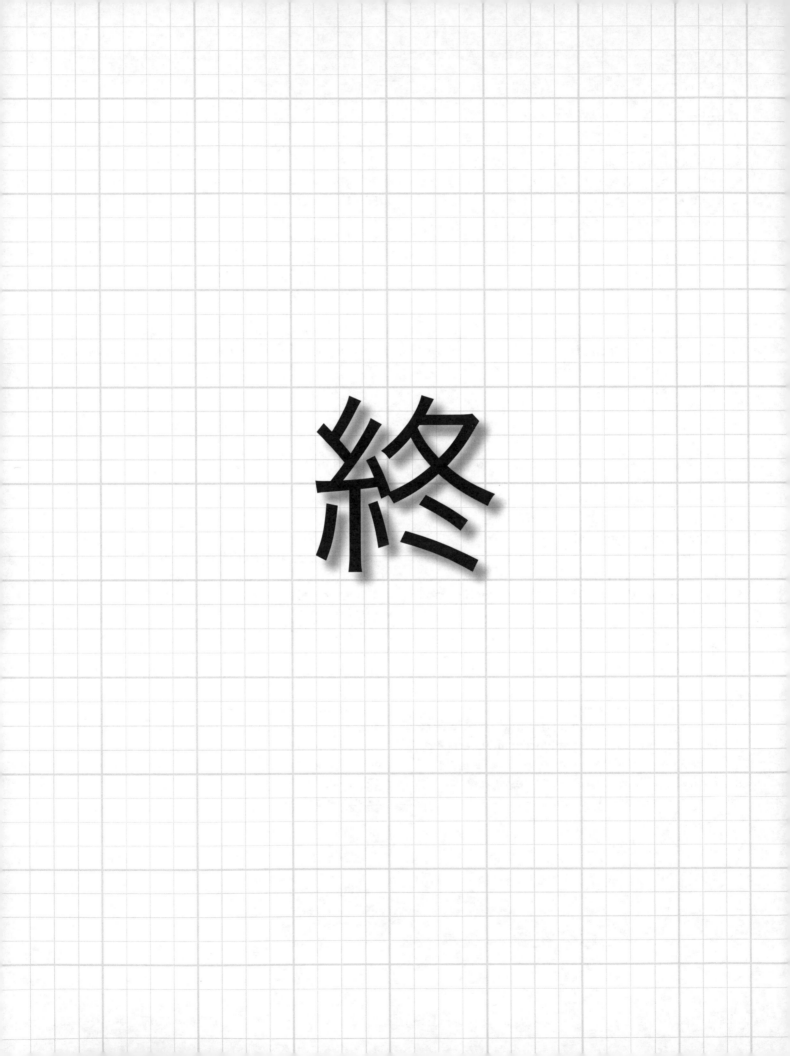

ANSWER KEY

Exhibit #4 "Game: What Do You Get?"

1. a. Beautiful: 美, *utsuku•shii*, is 羊 (sheep) on top of 大 (big).

2. d. Teaching: 教, *oshi•eru*, is 孝 (filial piety) + 攵 (to strike).

3. Both c and d are right. 親 means "intimate" when read as *shita•shii*, "parent" when read as *oya*, and either one when read as SHIN. The left side of 親 means "needle," and the right side (見) means "to see."

4. c. Yes, it's bizarre, but in terms of kanji, the answer is "special," 特, TOKU, which combines 牛 (cow) with 寺 (temple).

5. Both c and d are right. 忙, *isoga•shii*, means "busy" and combines 忄 (heart) with 亡 (to die), placing them side by side. 忘, *wasu•reru*, means "to forget" and combines 亡 with 心 (also "heart") but stacks one atop the other.

6. b. Public: 公, KŌ, combines 八 (to split) with ム (self).

7. a. Snow: 雪, *yuki*, stacks 雨 (rain) atop ヨ (a hand holding a brush).

8. d. Blowfish: 河豚, *fugu*, puts one rendering of "river" (河) alongside "pig" (豚).

9. c. Whale: 鯨, *kujira*, combines 魚 (fish) with 京 (capital). Years ago, filmmakers combined *kujira* with *gorira* (gorilla) to produce *Gojira* ("Godzilla" in Japanese).

10. d. Paradise: 楽園, *rakuen*, mixes 楽 (pleasure) with 園 (garden).

Exhibit #19 "Game: *Kun* or *On*?"

1. a. *yama (kun)*　　b. SAN *(on)*

2. a. *kuruma (kun)*　　b. SHA *(on)*

3. a. KŌ *(on)*　　　　b. *taka•i (kun)*

4. a. GETSU *(on)*　　b. GATSU *(on)*　　c. *tsuki (kun)*　　d. GETSU *(on)*

Exhibit #20 "Game: One Kanji, So Many Yomi"

1. なごやかな　おんな　の　ひと　は　わしょく　に　みそ
を　あえる　と、　きもち　が　やわらぎます。

   Nagoyakana onna no hito wa washoku ni miso o aeru to, kimochi ga yawaragimasu.

   When a congenial woman puts miso in Japanese food, it makes her feel calm.

2. かれ　は　ふく　を　ぬいで、　せかい　から　だっして、
だつぞく　に　なりました。

   Kare wa fuku o nuide, sekai kara dasshite, datsuzoku ni narimashita.

   He took off his clothes, escaped from the world, and became a hermit.

3. かれ　は　せいりょくてきに　こめ　の　せいせいほう　を
くわしく　せつめい　しました。

   Kare wa seiryokutekini kome no seiseihō o kuwashiku setsumei shimashita.

   With great energy, he gave a detailed, precise description of how he refines rice.

4. かれ　は、　じっさい　に、　まこと　の　こころ　で
ぜんぶ　の　き　に　くだもの　と　き　の　み　が　み
のる　と　いいました。

   Kare wa, jissai ni, makoto no kokoro de zenbu no ki ni kudamono to ki no mi ga minoru to iimashita.

   He actually said with real sincerity that all trees bear fruits and nuts.

5. はな　の　のはら　で　うまれて、あの　がくせい　は、
いけばな　を　する　の　と　みしょう　を　はやす　の
が　すき　です。

   Hana no nohara de umarete, ano gakusei wa, ikebana o suru no to mishō o hayasu no ga suki desu.

   Born in a field of flowers, the student likes arranging flowers and growing seedlings.

6. じてんしゃ　が　なおせない　と　こまって　いた
こども　が　いました。　せいねん　が　きて
「すぐ　なおるよ」　と、　じめん　に　じかに
すわって　ただち　に　さぎょう　に　かかり、
「じきに　いえ　に　かえれる　から　ね」　と　やさしく
いいました。

   Jitensha ga naosenai to komatte ita kodomo ga imashita. Seinen ga kite, "Sugu naoru yo," to, jimen ni jikani suwatte tadachi ni sagyō ni kakari, "Jikini ie ni kaereru kara ne," to yasashiku iimashita.

   A child was in trouble, unable to fix his bicycle. A young man came and said, "It'll be fixed right away," and he immediately sat down right on the ground and got to work fixing the bike. He said kindly, "You can go home right away."

Exhibit #24 "Game: Radicals"

1. The answer is three: *hen* (偏), *kanmuri* (冠), and *nyō* (遶).

2. The kanji 導 is (DŌ, *michibi•ku, shirabe:* to guide, lead). Spahn says the radical is 目. (It's hard to see how he figured it this way.) Nelson, Halpern, and Breen have the radical as 寸.

Exhibit #28 "Game: Which Is Which?"

1. おおきくて　ふとった　いぬ　です　ね。

   Ōkikute futotta inu desu ne.

   That's a big, fat dog, isn't it?

2. とくべつな　もの　を　もって、　おてら　で　まって
   います。

   Tokubetsuna mono o motte, otera de matte imasu.

   Holding something special, I'm waiting at the temple.

3. セミナー　で　わたし　は　ちゃくせき　しました　が、
   ともだち　は　けっせき　した　ので、　とうとう　そと　に
   でて、　もう　いち　ど　どうろ　を　わたりました。

   *Seminā de watashi wa chakuseki shimashita ga, tomodachi
   wa kesseki shita node, tōtō soto ni dete, mō ichi do dōro o
   watarimashita.*

   I took a seat at the seminar, but my friend was absent, so I
   finally left and once again crossed the street.

4. この　しゅうまつ、　まだ、　おっと　が　みつかって
   いません。

   Kono shūmatsu, mada, otto ga mitsukatte imasen.

   This weekend I haven't yet found a/my husband.

5. からだ　を　やすめたい　ので、　この　き　の　した　で
   きゅうけい　して、　ほん　を　よみます。

   *Karada o yasumetai node, kono ki no shita de kyūkei shite, hon o
   yomimasu.*

   I want to rest my body, so I take a break under this tree,
   reading a book.

6. ぼうどう　の　げんいん　は　あの　しゅうじん　でした。
   いま　みんな　こまって　います。

   *Bōdō no gen'in wa ano shūjin deshita. Ima minna komatte
   imasu.*

   That prisoner was the cause of the riot. Now everybody will
   suffer for it.

7. ちから　を　もって　それ　を　する　ため　に　は、
   かたな　を　もって　いる　ひと　を　いちまんにん
   あつめる　こと　です。

   *Chikara o motte sore o suru tame ni wa, katana o motte iru hito
   o ichiman-nin atsumeru koto desu.*

   The way to do it powerfully is to assemble ten thousand
   people with swords.

8. かこ、　かい　は　どうぐ　でも　きんいん　でも
   ありました。　かい　で、　もの　を　かえました。

   *Kako, kai wa dōgu demo kin'in demo arimashita. Kai de, mono o
   kaemashita.*

   In the past, shells were both tools and money. One could buy
   things with shells.

Exhibit #34 "Game: The Missing Link"

1. 少　2. 京　3. 自　4. 楽　5. 間　6. 欠　7. 谷　8. 古
9. 右　10. 各　11. 雷　12. 東　13. 歯　14. 取　15. 音

Exhibit #35 "Game: Create a Kanji"

Kanji	Formation	Yomi	Meaning
1. 歩	(止 + 少)	HO, aru•ku	to walk
2. 京	(亠 + 口 + 小)	KYŌ, KEI	capital
3. 間	(門 + 日)	KAN, aida	between
4. 簡	(竹 + 門 + 日)	KAN	simple
5. 古	(十 + 口)	KO, furu•i	old
6. 右	(一 + ノ + 口)	U, YŪ, migi	right (i.e., not left)
7. 各	(夂 + 口)	KAKU, ono•ono	each
8. 竜	(立 + 日 + し)	RYŪ, tatsu	dragon

Exhibit #44 "Game: Will the Real Compound Please Stand Up?"

None of the following words are real, so they should have
been marked "False." You might have fun showing them to a
native speaker of Japanese and watching his or her reaction.

1. Compounds with 幸

   言幸　(to say + good fortune)　*genkō:* fortune teller

   幸日　(good fortune + day)　*kōbi:* lucky day

   幸当たる　(good fortune + to win a lottery)　*kōataru:* to win
   at gambling

2. Compounds with 激

   激血　(violent + blood)　*gekiketsu:* violent crime

   激運動　(severe + to move + to move)　*gekiundō:* extreme
   sports

   激心　(severe + heart)　*gekishin:* change of heart

3. Compounds with 能

   喜劇無能　(comedy [1st 2 chars.] + no + ability)　*kigeki
   munō:* comedy of errors

   欠能体　(lack + ability + body)　*ketsunōtai:* physical
   disability

   生能　(birth + ability)　*seinō:* innate

4. Compounds with 軽

   軽点　(light + focus)　*keiten:* to relax, unwind

   軽人　(light + person)　*keijin:* thin person

   軽心　(light + heart)　*keishin:* to unburden oneself
   emotionally

5. Compounds with 力

   過力　(to pass by + power)　*kariki:* power of past events
   over an individual or society

   報道力　(public news [1st 2 chars.] + power)　*hōdōryoku:*
   power of the press

感力する (to feel deeply + power) *kanryoku suru:* to be overcome with emotion

Note that 人力車, *jinrikisha,* is correct. We derived our word "rickshaw" from *jinrikisha!*

Exhibit #45 "Game: Homonym Match-Up"

A.1.b.; 2.a.　B1.b.; 2.a.; 3.c.　C.1.c. *shindo;* 2.d. *shindo;* 3.b. *shindo;* 4.a. *shindō*　D.1.a.; 2.b.　E.1.b.; 2.a.　F.1.c.; 2.b.; 3.a.　G.1.a. *shingo;* 2.b. *shingō*　H.1.b.; 2.a.　I.1.a. *shinju;* 2.b. *shinjū*　J.1.c.; 2.d.; 3.b.; 4.a.　K.1.b.; 2.a.　L.1.b.; 2.c.; 3.a.　M.1.a.; 2.b.

Exhibit #50 "Thematic Explorations: Metals"

1.b., 2.a., 3.d., 4.c., 5.a., 6.a.

Exhibit #51 "Game: What's the Meaning of This?!"

Part I 1.c. NAN, *yawa•rakai*　2.a. KO, *mizuumi*　3.b. KAN, *wazura•u*　4.a. EN, *kemuri, kemu•i*　5.c. SHŪ, *sode*　6.b and c. MYŌ　7.a. YŪ

Part II 1.b. *hijōguchi*　2.c. *kaifuku*　3.c. *kōza*　4.a. *kaisatsuguchi*　6.c. *gyūho*　7.b. *kasei*　8.b. *shussho*　9.c. *omimai*

Exhibit #52 "Game: International Intrigue"

1. Malaysia, Portugal, Belgium, Holland
2. France, Vatican, Mongolia, Sweden or Switzerland
3. Brazil, Great Britain, Germany, Malaysia, Greece
4. Denmark, Spain, Turkey, Egypt
5. Australia, Norway, India, Mexico

Chapter 5 Main text, quiz at beginning

1. d. *marugoshikkutai,* 丸ゴシック体, or "rounded Gothic typeface" (round + Gothic + style)
2. e. *poppushotai,* ポップ書体, or "POPshotai" (pop + calligraphy + style)
3. a. *sumōmoji,* 相撲文字 (sumo + characters)
4. c. *reisho,* 隷書 (civil servant + to write)
5. b. *minchō kaisho,* 明朝楷書 (Ming-cho typeface + noncursive or printed style)

Exhibit #59 "Game: Weekday *Sūdoku*"

土	火	月	水	木	日	金
火	木	日	金	月	土	水
月	日	水	土	火	金	木
日	金	火	月	水	木	土
水	土	金	木	日	火	月
木	月	土	火	金	水	日
金	水	木	日	土	月	火

Exhibit #65 "Game: Kanji Word Find"

短	縮	小	説	明	白	鳥	肉	屋
目	森	間	名	日	町	雪	通	同
以	寝	南	北	光	速	力	山	和
外	前	米	形	年	面	点	由	風
出	痛	国	連	中	分	数	仕	船
発	味	内	涼	古	返	学	月	便
音	女	部	首	都	人	生	六	利
読	酒	流	十	門	決	牛	若	用
書	道	具	眼	科	長	所	得	意

The kanji is 画 (GA, KAKU: picture, kanji strokes). Here are the compounds in the chains:

Top row:

短縮 (*tanshuku*: shortening)   縮小 (*shukushō*: reduction) 小説 (*shōsetsu*: novel)   説明 (*setsumei*: explanation) 明白 (*meihaku*: clear, unmistakable)   白鳥 (*hakuchō*: swan) 鳥肉 (*toriniku*: poultry)   肉屋 (*nikuya*: butcher)

Central vertical line:

明日 (*ashita*: tomorrow)   日光 (*nikkō*: sunshine)   光年 (*kōnen*: light-year)   年中 (*nenjū*: throughout the year)   中古 (*chūko*: secondhand)   古都 (*koto*: old capital, esp. Kyoto)

Central box, first line across:

南北 (*nanboku*: north and south)   北光 (*hokkō*: northern lights)   光速 (*kōsoku*: speed of light)   速力 (*sokuryoku*: speed)

Central box, second line across:

国連 (*Kokuren*: United Nations, abbreviated)   連中 (*renchū*: companions, party, company, crowd)   中分 (*chūbun*: half) 分数 (*bunsū*: fraction)

Central box, third line across:

部首 (*bushu*: radical [in kanji])   首都 (*shuto*: capital)   都人 (*tojin* or *miyakobito*: people of the capital)   人生 (*jinsei*: life)

Central box, left-hand vertical line:

南米 (*Nanbei*: South America)   米国 (*Beikoku*: United States)   国内 (*kokunai*: domestic)   内部 (*naibu*: interior)

Central box, right-hand vertical line:

力点 (*rikiten*: emphasis)   点数 (*tensū*: points, score)   数学 (*sūgaku*: math)   学生 (*gakusei*: student)

Perimeter chain, left side:

以外 (*igai*: except, other than)   外出 (*gaishutsu*: going out)   出発 (*shuppatsu*: departure)   発音 (*hatsuon*: pronunciation)   音読 (*ondoku*: reading aloud)   読書 (*dokusho*: reading)

Perimeter chain, bottom row:

書道 (*shodō*: calligraphy)   道具 (*dōgu*: tool)   具眼 (*gugan*: discernment)   眼科 (*ganka*: ophthalmologist)   科長 (*kachō*: department head)   長所 (*chōsho*: strong point)   所得 (*shotoku*: income)   得意 (*tokui*: strong point)

Perimeter chain, right side:

和風 (*wafū*: Japanese-style)   風船 (*fūsen*: balloon)   船便 (*funabin*: sea mail)   便利 (*benri*: convenient)   利用 (*riyō*: use)   用意 (*yōi*: preparation)

Exhibit #73 "Game: On-Yomi Tongue Twister"

古 (*KO*: old); 小 (*SHŌ*: small); 正 (*SHŌ*: correct); 消 (*SHŌ*: to extinguish); 私 (*SHI*: private); 汚 (*O*: dirty); 少 (*SHŌ*: a little, few); 章 (*SHŌ*: chapter, badge, mark); 商 (*SHŌ*: trade, merchant); 由 (*YU*: to be based on, due to); 相 (*SHŌ*: government minister); 焼 (*SHŌ*: to burn, roast).

Koshō shōshō, shio shōshō, shōyu shōshō.

A little pepper, a little salt, a little soy sauce.

胡椒　少々、　塩　少々、　醤油　少々。

Exhibit #90 "Game: Kanji Crossword"

Across

3. *daiku*
5. *kōtsū*
6. *kūki*
8. *kaji*
9. *inugoya*
11. *chūshinten*
13. *tabun*
15. *yōshoku*
16. *seishinka*
17. *shujutsushitsu*
18. *daigakusei*
22. *kobito*
23. *katsudōteki*
25. *kaigai*
26. *kazan*
28. *ichinen* or *hitotoshi*
29. *shigoto*
30. *fūsokukei*
32. *yogensha*
33. *chihō*
34. *gesha*
35. *gaka*
36. *yakyū*
37. *onnade*
38. *kisha*
39. *fugen-fu•go* （不言不語）
41. *shūsei*
42. *zannen*
44. *hatake suiren*
45. *kyūgyōbi*
46. *isseki-nichō*

Down

1. *Nihonken*
2. *yaoya*
3. *ōya*
4. *kōjichū*
5. *kōsaten*
7. *kibun*
10. *kogitte*
12. *shinrigaku*
13. *tashinkyōteki*
14. *bunka*
15. *yōshitsu*
18. *otona* or *dainin*
19. *seikatsu*
20. *miseinensha*
21. *Hokkaidō*
22. *koyama*
24. *dōbutsu*
26. *kaji*
27. *kōsoku*
28. *hitokoto futakoto*
29. *Shikata*
30. *kazaguruma* or *fūsha*
31. *keikakusha*
33. *Chikyū*
34. *heta*
36. *yasaibatake*
37. *josei*
38. *kinenbi*
40. *fushichō*
41. *renshū*
42. *zangyō*
43. *ichi ichi* or *itsu itsu*

1 日	■	2 八	■	3 大	4 工	■	5 交	通	■	6 空	7 気
本	■	百	■	8 家	事	差	■	■	■	■	分
9 犬	10 小	屋	■	11 中	12 心	点	■	13 多	14 分	■	■
■	切	15 洋	食	■	理	■	16 精	神	科	■	■
■	17 手	術	室	■	18 大	19 学	生	■	教	■	20 未
21 北	■	■	22 小	人	■	23 活	24 動	的	■	28 一	成
25 海	外	26 火	山	■	27 高	■	物	■	■	■	年
道	■	29 仕	事	■	30 風	速	31 計	■	32 予	言	者
■	33 地	方	■	34 下	車	■	35 画	家	■	二	■
36 野	球	■	37 女	手	■	38 記	者	■	39 不	言	40 不
菜	■	41 習	性	■	42 残	念	■	43 一	■	■	死
44 畑	水	練	■	45 休	業	日	■	46 一	石	二	鳥

GLOSSARY

ateji (当て字): Kanji whose usual sounds or meanings do not apply in the context of a particular word. There are several types of ateji. In one type, the Japanese selected kanji for their meanings, with no regard for their sounds. *EXAMPLE:* 無花果 (*ichijiku:* fig). None of these kanji carries the sounds *i, chi, ji,* or *ku.* But the meaning (not + flower + fruit) matches the old Japanese perception of the fig, which had visible fruit but flowers that were not visible. In another type of ateji, the Japanese chose kanji based on their sounds, with no regard for their meanings. *EXAMPLE:* 寿司 *(sushi).* The characters mean "longevity" and "to govern."

bushu. *SEE* **radical.**

component: Indivisible unit of meaning inside a character. *EXAMPLE:* 照 (*SHŌ, te•ru:* to illuminate) contains four components: 日 (sun, day), 刀 (sword), 口 (opening), and ⺍ (fire). *ALSO CALLED:* element.

composite: Usage coined for this book to refer to the type of singleton known as *keiseimoji.* The official term for "composites" is "semantic-phonetic compounds," but in this book "compound" refers to a union of two or more kanji, so "semantic-phonetic compound" would have introduced confusion. *SEE ALSO: keiseimoji.*

compound: Word consisting of two or more kanji. Typically, compounds use on-yomi. *EXAMPLES:* 大学 (*daigaku:* university); 電車 (*densha:* train). *EXCEPTION:* 友達 (*tomodachi:* friend) combines two kun-yomi. *COMPARE:* **singleton.** *SEE ALSO: jukugo.*

furigana (振り仮名): Small hiragana written underneath, above, or beside kanji, indicating their pronunciations. *EXAMPLE:*

ふ　が　な
振り仮名

This shows the furigana for the word *furigana. ALSO CALLED: ruby, rubi, agate.*

hangeul: Alphabetic script used in Korean.

hanja (漢字): Chinese characters used in Korean. In other words, *hanja* is the Korean equivalent of *kanji.*

hanzi (漢字): Chinese word for Chinese characters. In other words, *hanzi* is the Chinese equivalent of *kanji.*

hiragana (平仮名): Loopy, cursive writing used mainly for grammar (e.g., okurigana and particles) but also for kanji that are too difficult to write. *EXAMPLE:* ひらがな, which says *hiragana. COMPARE:* **katakana, kanji.** *SEE ALSO:* **kana.**

ideogram (指事文字, *shijimoji*): Kanji representing abstract concepts, such as numbers and directions. *EXAMPLES:* 三 (*SAN, mi•ttsu:* three); 上 (*JŌ, ue:* above); 凸 (*TOTSU:* protrusion, bulge). *COMPARE:* **pictogram.**

Jōyō (常用): Characters that the Japanese Ministry of Education selected for regular use in 1981. The ministry determined that newspapers and magazines would limit their kanji to this pool of 1,945 kanji, which schools would require students to know. However, the list changed in fall 2010, resulting in a set of 2,136 characters.

jukugo (熟語): Kanji compound.

kaiimoji (会意文字): Kanji in which all components contribute to the meaning, never to the pronunciation. This is true for nearly a quarter of Jōyō kanji. *EXAMPLE:* 花 (*KA, KE, hana:* flower), since a flower is grass (艹) that changes (化). *COMPARE: keiseimoji.*

kana (仮名): Umbrella term for *hiragana* and *katakana.*

kango (漢語): Word imported whole from China. Typically compounds, *kango* are composed solely of on-yomi. *EXAMPLES:* 食事 (*shokuji:* meal); 学校 (*gakkō:* school); 先生 (*sensei:* teacher). *EXCEPTIONS:* Some imported singletons use on-yomi, including 茶 (*cha:* tea); 絵 (*e:* picture); and 服する (*fukusuru:* to obey). *COMPARE: wago. SEE ALSO:* **on-on combination.**

kanji (漢字): Most complicated of the three scripts used in Japanese writing. Almost all the characters in this script originated in China. *ALSO CALLED:* Chinese characters. *COMPARE:* **hiragana, katakana.**

katakana (片仮名): Angular writing used for words not of Japanese or Chinese origin. *EXAMPLE:* マクドナルド, which says *Makudonarudo,* meaning "McDonald's." *COMPARE:* **hiragana, kanji.** *SEE ALSO:* **kana.**

keiseimoji (形声文字): Kanji in which the radical or the "semantic component" relates to the meaning of the whole character, while the "phonetic component" relates to the on-yomi. This is true for 67 percent of Jōyō kanji. *EXAMPLES:* 時 (*JI, toki:* hour, time); 組 (*SO, kumi:* group, set). *ALSO CALLED:* phonetic compounds, semantic-phonetic compounds, phonetic composites, semantic-phonetic composites. *COMPARE: kaiimoji.*

kokugo (国語): Word invented in Japan. Almost always a combination of on-yomi, *kokugo* combinations never existed in China before someone invented them in Japan. This makes them different from other compounds. *EXAMPLES:* 会社 (*kaisha:* company); 銀行 (*ginkō:* bank); 笑止 (*shōshi:* absurd). *SEE ALSO:* **on-on combination.**

kokuji (国字): Kanji invented in Japan from preexisting components. *EXAMPLE:* 畑 (*hatake:* field of crops). *Kokuji* don't have on-yomi. *EXCEPTION:* 働 (*DŌ, hatara•ku:* to work).

kun-kun combination: Compound that one reads by using the kun-yomi of each kanji (as opposed to the on-yomi, with which one typically reads compounds). *EXAMPLES:* 建物 (*tatemono:* building); 名前 (*namae:* name). Most place names in Japan combine kun-yomi. *EXAMPLE:* 成田 (Narita). *EXCEPTIONS:* The names of the four major Japanese islands (such as 本州, *Honshū*) and some major cities (such as 東京, *Tōkyō,* and 京都, *Kyōto*) use on-yomi. *COMPARE:* **on-on combination.** *SEE ALSO: wago.*

kun-yomi (訓読み): "Japanese" way of reading kanji. There are two distinct ways of reading many characters: a "Japanese" way and a "Chinese" way. Kun-yomi are the readings corresponding to the language spoken in Japan before kanji arrived. *Kun* rhymes with "noon" and means "teachings." *ALSO CALLED: kun* readings, Japanese readings. *COMPARE:* **on-yomi.**

nigori. SEE **voicing.**

okurigana (送り仮名): Hiragana that trail after kanji, though they can also pop up between kanji, as in the very word *okurigana*, 送り仮名. Okurigana are necessary because back when the Japanese imported kanji, they found it awkward to represent their spoken language with the written symbols of the Chinese. The Japanese could write most nouns entirely with kanji. But they needed hiragana to indicate the inflections of verbs and adjectives, among other things. Singletons generally have okurigana, whereas compounds do not. *EXAMPLES:* 明るい、明かり、and 明ける all have okurigana. This helps you know to use their kun-yomi: *akarui* (bright), *akari* (light, clearness), and *akeru* (to become light). By contrast, the compound 明白 (*meihaku:* clear, unmistakable) has no okurigana and is an on-on combination.

on-echo: Term coined in this book for instances in which kanji have a common phonetic component and the same on-yomi. *EXAMPLE:* 安, 案, 按, and 鮟 share the component 安 and the on-yomi *AN.* The shared shape may have no bearing on meaning. One can find *on*-echoes in about 20 percent of Jōyō kanji.

on-on combination: Compound that one reads by using the on-yomi of each kanji. *EXAMPLE:* 住所 (*jūsho:* address). Most compounds follow this pattern. All *kango* are on-on combinations, but not all on-on combinations are *kango;* some on-on combinations are *kokugo. EXAMPLE:* 現象 (*genshō:* phenomenon) is *kokugo* and uses on-yomi. *COMPARE:* **kun-kun combination.** *SEE ALSO: kango, kokugo.*

on-yomi (音読み): Pronunciation of a character that roughly corresponds to the ancient Chinese pronunciation of that character. Some people call on-yomi "Chinese readings," but this is somewhat misleading. From the time they were imported, Chinese pronunciations changed in Japanese mouths. Plus, in both China and Japan, these sounds have evolved over the millennia. *On* roughly rhymes with "bone" and means "sound." *ALSO CALLED: on* readings, Chinese readings. *COMPARE:* **kun-yomi.**

phonetic component: Part of a character that tells us how that kanji sounds. Not all kanji contain phonetics, but at least two-thirds do. When you can split a kanji into left-hand and right-hand sides, the radical (or the semantic component) will typically be on the left, the phonetic on the right. The on-yomi of the phonetic often matches the on-yomi of the whole character. *EXAMPLE:* The left side of 時 is the radical 日. The phonetic 寺 is on the right side. Because 寺 has the on-yomi *JI,* the bigger kanji 時 does, too. *ALSO CALLED:* the phonetic. *COMPARE:* **radical.**

pictogram (象形文字, *shōkeimoji*): Character that is a good likeness of the object it represents. *EXAMPLE:* 門 (*MON, kado:* gate); 串 (*KAN:* to pierce; *kushi:* skewer). *COMPARE:* **ideogram.**

pinyin: Most widely accepted and used romanization of Mandarin speech. Pinyin appears in road signs, maps, brand names, computer input, Chinese Braille, telegrams, and books for Chinese children and foreign learners.

radical (部首, *bushu*): Part of a character that enables people to categorize kanji and therefore to look them up in dictionaries. The radical may be a component with a clear meaning. *EXAMPLES:* 艹 (grass), 宀 (roof), or 刂 (sword). And that meaning may relate directly to the meaning of the whole kanji. *EXAMPLE:* 艹 (grass) is the radical in 薬 (*kusuri:* medicine). Clearly, medicines often come from grasses or plants. In other characters, however, the radical appears irrelevant to the significance of the whole kanji. *EXAMPLE:* The 宀 (roof) in 字 (*JI:* character, letter) seems unrelated to the meaning of the character. *ALSO CALLED:* semantic component, classifier. *COMPARE:* **phonetic component.**

rōmaji (ローマ字): Romanized letters (the same ones used in the English alphabet) used to represent Japanese words. *EXAMPLE: rōmaji* (as opposed to ローマ字, which expresses the same word with a combination of katakana and kanji).

semantic component. *SEE* **radical.**

shōkeimoji. SEE **pictogram.**

singleton: Term coined in this book for a kanji standing alone, rather than being bonded to another kanji. A singleton might have okurigana or might not. *EXAMPLES:* 茶 (*cha:* tea) is a singleton. As part of 喫茶店 (*kissaten:* café), it ceases to be a singleton. Similarly, 行 (*i•ku:* to go) is a singleton, but that's no longer true when 行 is part of 旅行 (*ryokō:* travel). Typically, you need to use kun-yomi to read singletons. *EXCEPTION:* Use on-yomi to read the singleton 茶. *COMPARE:* **compound.**

single-unit character: Yaeko Habein's term for the simplest kanji. Single-unit characters are remnants of ancient pictures and are therefore "indivisible" into smaller kanji. *EXAMPLES:* 小 (*SHO, chii•sai, ko, o:* small); 用 (*YŌ, mochi•iru:* to use); 県 (*KEN:* prefecture). Accounting for 9 percent of the Jōyō kanji, single-unit kanji appear inside many complicated characters. *EXAMPLE:* 犬 (*KEN, inu:* dog) is part of 伏 (*FUKU, fu•seru:* to lie prostrate, hide).

stroke order: Predetermined sequence with which one should draw lines in each kanji. Your writing utensil should also travel in the "correct" direction (i.e., left to right or up to down) as you draw characters. It is thought that when you learn a character, you should learn its stroke order.

voicing (濁り, *nigori*): Slight spelling changes that yomi may undergo when they're not in the first position of a compound. Voicing patterns match those that occur when adding a *tenten,* ゛, to certain kana. For instance, *k* becomes *g; s* becomes *z; sh* becomes *j;* and *h* becomes *b. EXAMPLE:* When *SHI* and *SHŪ* combine in 始終 (*shijū:* always, all the time), the second yomi changes from *SHŪ* to *JŪ. H* can also become *p,* the equivalent of taking a yomi starting with *h* and adding a *maru,* ゜. Technically, a *p* sound is considered a "plosive," not a voiced consonant.

wago (和語): Native Japanese vocabulary. Most singleton words are *wago,* and many *wago* words are singletons. *EXAMPLES:* 春 (*haru:* spring); 女 (*onna:* woman); 出 (*de•ru:* to appear, leave). But there are also quite a few kun-kun combinations, and these tend to be *wago. EXAMPLE:* お手洗い (*otearai:* bathroom). *COMPARE: kango. SEE ALSO:* **kun-kun combination, singleton.**

yomi (読み): Pronunciation of a character. There are generally two ways of reading any character, though there may be many more or as few as one. *Yomi* rhymes with "foamy." *SEE ALSO:* **kun-yomi, on-yomi.**

WORKS CITED

Addiss, Stephen. *How to Look at Japanese Art.* New York: Abrams, 1996.

Benedict, Ruth. *The Chrysanthemum and the Sword: Patterns of Japanese Culture.* Boston: Houghton Mifflin, 1946.

Betros, Chris. "The Subtleties of Subtitles." *Japan Today.* Aug. 10, 2005.

Cherry, Kittredge. *Womansword: What Japanese Words Say About Women.* Tokyo: Kodansha International, 2002.

Chino, Naoko. *Japanese Verbs at a Glance.* Tokyo: Kodansha International, 1996.

Covington, Richard Glenn; Joyce Yumi Mitamura; and Yasuko Kosaka Mitamura. *Let's Learn More Kanji: Family Groups, Learning Strategies, and 300 Complex Kanji.* Tokyo: Kodansha International, 1999.

Davey, H. E. *Brush Meditation: A Japanese Way to Mind & Body Harmony.* Berkeley, CA: Stone Bridge Press, 1999.

Davey, H. E. *The Japanese Way of the Artist.* Berkeley, CA: Stone Bridge Press, 2007.

Davey, H. E. *Living the Japanese Arts & Ways: 45 Paths to Meditation & Beauty.* Berkeley, CA: Stone Bridge Press, 2003.

DeFrancis, John. *The Chinese Language: Fact and Fantasy.* Honolulu: University of Hawaii Press, 1984.

"Editorial: Sacrificial Cash Cows." *Sunstar.* Oct. 10, 2005. www.sunstar.com.ph/static/ceb/2005/10/10/oped/editorial.html.

Habein, Yaeko S. *Decoding Kanji: A Practical Approach to Learning Look-Alike Characters.* Tokyo: Kodansha International, 2000.

Habein, Yaeko S. *The History of the Japanese Written Language.* Tokyo: University of Tokyo Press, 1984.

Habein, Yaeko S., and Gerald B. Mathias. *The Complete Guide to Everyday Kanji.* Tokyo: Kodansha International, 1991.

Halpern, Jack, ed. *The Kodansha Kanji Learner's Dictionary.* Tokyo: Kodansha International, 1999.

Hannas, William C. *Asia's Orthographic Dilemma.* Honolulu: University of Hawaii Press, 1997.

Heisig, James W. *Remembering the Kanji: A Complete Course on How Not to Forget the Meaning and Writing of Japanese Characters.* Vol. 1. Tokyo: Japan Publications, 1977.

Henshall, Kenneth G. *A Guide to Remembering Japanese Characters.* Boston: Tuttle, 1998.

Horvat, Andrew. *Japanese Beyond Words: How to Walk and Talk Like a Native Speaker.* Berkeley, CA: Stone Bridge Press, 2000.

Kano, Chieko, and others. *Basic Kanji Book.* 2 vols. Tokyo: Bonjinsha, 1989.

Kano, Chieko, and others. *Intermediate Kanji Book.* Vol. 1. Tokyo: Bonjinsha, 1993.

Kindaichi, Haruhiko. *The Japanese Language.* Rutland, VT: Tuttle, 1978.

Korean Overseas Information Service. "Belief, Philosophy, and Religion." In *A Window on Korea.* Seoul, Korea: Seoul Systems, 1994. CD-ROM. http://asnic.utexas.edu/asnic/countries/korea/beliefsystem.html.

Mair, Victor H. "East Asian Round-Trip Words." *Sino-Platonic Papers,* no. 34 (Oct. 1992).

Nakao, Seigo. *Random House Japanese-English English-Japanese Dictionary.* New York: Random House, 1997.

Nelson, Andrew. Completely revised by John H. Haig. *The New Nelson Japanese-English Character Dictionary.* Boston: Tuttle, 1997.

Noguchi, Mary Sisk. "TV Shows Confront Decline of Japanese Language." *Japan Times.* Nov. 22, 2005. http://search.japantimes.co.jp/cgi-bin/ek20051122mn.html.

Ozaki, Robert. *The Japanese: A Cultural Portrait.* Rutland, VT: Tuttle, 1978.

Pye, Michael. *The Study of Kanji.* Tokyo: Hokuseido, 1971.

Richie, Donald. "Signs and Symbols." In *A Lateral View: Essays on Culture and Style in Contemporary Japan.* Berkeley, CA: Stone Bridge Press, 1992.

Rowley, Michael. *Kanji Pict-o-Graphix: Over 1,000 Japanese Kanji and Kana Mnemonics.* Berkeley, CA: Stone Bridge Press, 1992.

Spahn, Mark, and Wolfgang Hadamitzky, with Kumiko Fujie-Winter. *The Kanji Dictionary.* Boston: Tuttle, 1996.

Traganou, Jilly. "The Fireworks of Edo—or Japan's Early (Post?) Modern Past." *Architronic: The Electronic Journal of Architecture* 6, no. 1 (May 1997). http://corbu2.caed.kent.edu/architronic/v6n1/v6n1.04a.html.

Trumbull, Robert. "How to Write in Japanese." *New York Times.* Sept. 19, 1965. http://partners.nytimes.com/books/98/10/25/specials/mishima-japanese.html.

Tsuda, Sanae. "Contrasting Attitudes in Compliments: Humility in Japanese and Hyperbole in English." *Intercultural Communication Studies* 2, no. 1 (1992).

Tsukuba Language Group. *Situational Functional Japanese.* Tokyo: Bonjinsha, 1992.

Tyson, Rodney. "A Successful Mixture of Alphabetic and Non-Alphabetic Writing: Chinese Characters in Korean." Chapter in unpublished book.

Unger, J. Marshall. *The Fifth Generation Fallacy.* Oxford, England: Oxford University Press, 1987. www.pinyin.info/readings/fifth_generation.html.

Vance, Timothy J. *Building Word Power in Japanese: Using Kanji Prefixes and Suffixes.* Tokyo: Kodansha International, 1990.

Websites and Web Documents

Site from which I gleaned much of the information in Exhibit 23, "Thematic Explorations: Kanji of a Feather Flock Together," as well as some of the items in Exhibit 12, "Just the Facts: What Else 'Kanji' Can Be": www.d.umn.edu/~jbelote/japanwriting.html.

Kanji Haitani's proverb site (mentioned in Exhibit 55, "Thematic Explorations: Hyperbolic Humility"): http://home.earthlink.net/~4jword/index3.htm.

Site about kanji typefaces (mentioned in Exhibit 57, "Just the Facts: Typefaces"): www.sljfaq.org/afaq/shotai.html.

Matt Treyvaud's blog post about kanji used in advertising (mentioned in the main text of Chapter 5): http://no-sword.jp/blog/2005/04/explaining-jokes-makes-them-funnier.html.

Blog post about kanji-themed Kyoto bonfires (mentioned in Exhibit 58, "Just the Facts: Kanji Ablaze"): http://japundit.com/archives/category/matsuri/page/1. Go to the entry for Aug. 18, 2005, "Towering Infernos," posted by "Ampontan."

Rev. Kanto Tsukamoto's site about the Lotus Sutra (mentioned in Exhibit 60, "Just the Facts: Kanji Meditation"): www.nichiren-shu.org.

Nadja Van Ghelue's site about Heart Sutra calligraphy (mentioned in Exhibit 60, "Just the Facts: Kanji Meditation"): www.theartofcalligraphy.com.

Blog comment about the use of pinyin in Taiwan (mentioned in the main text of Chapter 6): www.languagehat.com/archives/001202.php, posted by "xiaolongnu" on Mar. 11, 2004.

Tian Tang's blog about the misuse of Chinese characters in Western culture (mentioned in the main text of Chapter 6 and in Exhibit 69, "Just the Facts: Mind the Gap"): www.hanzismatter.com.

Site with kanji flashcards (mentioned in the main text of Chapter 7): www.kantango.com.

Mary Sisk Noguchi's Kanji Clinic site (mentioned in the main text of Chapter 7): www.kanjiclinic.com.

Jim Breen's Japanese Page (mentioned in Exhibit 88, "Just the Facts: Kanji Dictionaries"): www.csse.monash.edu.au/~jwb/cgi-bin/wwwjdic.cgi?1C.

The Fushimi-Inari Taisha shrine near Kyoto features thousands of pumpkin-orange torii engraved with columns of kanji. This is a close-up of one such kanji—武 (BU, MU, takeshi), which means "warrior." If you've made it this far in the book, you are indeed a warrior of kanji. Fight on!

Other Titles of Interest from Stone Bridge Press

Designing with Kanji: Japanese Character Motifs for Surface, Skin & Spirit. Shogo Oketani and Leza Lowitz. 144 pp, 7 x 9", paper, 125 2-color illustrations, ISBN 978-1-880656-79-2, $14.95.

Kana Pict-o-Graphix: Mnemonics for Japanese Hiragana and Katakana. Michael Rowley. 72 pp, 3 x 5", paper, ISBN 978-1-880656-18-1, $6.00.

Kanji Pict-o-Graphix: Over 1,000 Japanese Kanji and Kana Mnemonics. Michael Rowley. 216 pp, 8 x 8", paper, ISBN 978-0-9628137-0-2, $19.95.

Kanji Starter 1. Daiki Kusuya. 200 pp, 4 1/8 x 5 3/4 ", paper, 200 b/w illustrations, ISBN 978-1-933330-14-3, $9.95.

Kanji Starter 2. Daiki Kusuya. 208 pp, 4 1/8 x 5 3/4 ", paper, 300 b/w illustrations, ISBN 978-1-933330-15-0, $9.95.

Japanese the Manga Way: An Illustrated Guide to Grammar and Structure. Wayne P. Lammers. 312 pp, 8 1/4 x 10 1/4 ", paper, 500+ b/w illustrations, ISBN 978-1-880656-90-7, $24.95.

70 Japanese Gestures: No Language Communication. Hamiru-Aqui. 160 pp, 4 3/4 x 7 1/4 ", paper, 70+ b/w photos, ISBN 978-1-933330-01-3, $9.95.

A Homestay in Japan: Nihon to no Deai. Caron Allen, with Natsumi Watanabe. 204 pp, 7 x 10", paper, ISBN 978-0-9628137-6-4, $19.95.

Japanese Beyond Words: How to Walk and Talk Like a Native Speaker. Andrew Horvat. 176 pp, 5 1/2 x 8 1/2 ", paper, ISBN 978-1-880656-42-6 $16.95.

Sacred Sanskrit Words: For Yoga, Chant, and Meditation. Leza Lowitz and Reema Datta. 240 pp, 5 1/4 x 7 1/4 ", paper, 6 b/w illustrations, ISBN 978-1-880656-87-7, $14.95.

The Japanese Way of the Artist: Living the Japanese Arts & Ways, Brush Meditation, The Japanese Way of the Flower. H. E. Davey. 512 pp, 6 x 7 3/4 ", paper, 135 b/w photos and illustrations, ISBN 978-1-933330-07-5, $19.95.

The Heart Sutra in Calligraphy. A Visual Appreciation of the Perfection of Wisdom. Nadja Van Ghelue. 128 pp, 7 x 11", paper, 55 b/w illustrations, ISBN 978-1-933330-79-2, $19.95.

門 立 相 月 話

巳 輪 大 馬 か

ろ ハ 龍 風

武 猫 口

水 海 山 ム ん

陽

戦 頭 鷹 三国

門 立 相 月 話 巴

大 馬 ハ か

輪 ろ

猫 武 龍 風

水 海 山 ム 口

戦 頭 陽 ん 鷹

三 国